Sam George Arcus
Good Reading!

JOURNEYS

Rhoda Lewin
Thank you Rhoda!

JOURNEYS

Sequel to "Deja Views
of an Aging Orphan"

SAM GEORGE ARCUS

Copyright © 2001 by Sam George Arcus.

Library of Congress Number: 2001117884
ISBN #:   1-59109-489-5

All rights reserved. No part of this book may be reproduced or transmitted in any form or by any means, electronic or mechanical, including photocopying, recording, or by any information storage and retrieval system, without permission in writing from the copyright owner.

This is a work of fiction. Names, characters, places and incidents either are the product of the author's imagination or are used fictitiously, and any resemblance to any actual persons, living or dead, events, or locales is entirely coincidental.

This book was printed in the United States of America.

> **Additional copies (including hardbacks)**
> **Can be obtained from:**
> Xlibris Corporation 1-888-795-4274
> 436 Walnut Street, Philadelphia, PA 19106
> www.Xlibris.com or from
> Amazon.com or Barnes & Nobles stores

DEDICATED TO AND IN LOVING MEMORY OF

Solomon Arcus	10 months in 1919
Mollie Srulowitz Arcus	1893-1929
Rose Leah Relkin Rosenthal	1893-1931
Nathan Louis Arcus	1884-1938
Isadore Rosenthal	1892-1945
Bessie (Bashya) Friedman Arcus	1893-1956
Blanche Elkin Arcus	1924-1984
Libby Rosenthal Wolf	1916-1988
Mary (Manya) Arcus Finkiel	1911-1989
Harry (Herschel) Arcus	1913-1992
Jean Hoberman Arcus	1920-1998
Fanny Rosenthal McCabe	1912-2000

CONTENTS

PREFACE 9

I. NOCHEM 11

II. UNCERTAIN JOURNEY 25

III. CHUTZPAH UNDER FIRE 56

IV. ONE SMALL STONE 67

V. MOLLIE'S PERSPECTIVE 83

VI. TANTE SONIA'S STORY 93

VII. NEW ARRIVALS (COMING TO THE HOME) 103

VIII. COMPLETED JOURNEY 109

IX. ABORTED JOURNEYS 122

X. PARACHUTE 135

XI. NORMAN'S FIRST JOURNEY 138

XII. THE SET-UP 145

XIII. THE JAYWALKER 162

XIV. FAILED JOURNEY 166

XV. ZWEITACK'S BOIL 193

XVI. "TURN OFF THE IGNITION!" 216

XVII. ANTIGUAN IDYLL 223

XVIII. SAN ANDRES SABBATH 230

XIX. SILENT CRITIC 239

XX. SWISS ARMY KNIFE 275

XXI. COLLECT CALL 283

XXII. TAZ'S TATOO 292

XXIII. ARIZONA JOURNEY 304

PREFACE

Although each of the stories contained in this volume are "free-standing" short stories, Stories I through VIII can be perceived as "sequels" to my previous work, *DEJA VIEWS OF AN AGING ORPHAN* since they pick up on characters, themes and "plots" first introduced in that book. The central plot and theme involving Nochem, Bashya and her children, Sonia, Mollie and her children is told from various perspectives and points of view—not unlike the famous Japanese story of *Rashoman*. And while all of the stories in this book are based on actual happenings and real people, some fiction was required to fill gaps and round out the stories. In any event, each story can be perceived as a "Journey"—actual or figurative.

Another carry over from *DEJA VIEWS* are the two quotations from Scotland's two greatest poets/writers; which are so applicable to the early history of the Erkes/Arcus family, especially the saga of Nochem Lazer Erkes—who became Nathan Louis Arcus in America. By "early history" I refer to the family back in the old country, with Nochem and his larger family in Czipowitz/Odessa planning for Nochem, his wife and two children to emigrate to America. The resulting saga was of epic proportions embodying the Russo-Japanese War, assassinations, World War I, intrigue, revolution, civil war, pogroms, bigamy, suicide and finally the institutionalization of three young children; but also finally, the establishment of many strong and healthy families in America.

So again, here are the two quotations:

"THE BEST LAID SCHEMES O' MICE AND MEN GANG AFT A-GLEY"
Robert Burns *"To a Mouse"* Stanza 7

"OH WHAT A TANGLED WEB WE WEAVE WHEN FIRST WE PRACTICE TO DECEIVE"
Sir Walter Scott *"Lochinvar"* Stanza 17

"COVER PHOTO: Children Alex and Sam with father Nathan (a.k.a. Nochem) and sister Mary (a.k.a. Manya) at the orphanage circa 1931."

I. NOCHEM

Nochem Lazer Erkes was born in November 1884, the second of three sons of a Jewish family of horse dealers in Czipowitz, Odessa on the northwest shore of the Black Sea, about 200 miles southwest of Kiev, the provincial capital of the Ukraine, part of the empire of the Russian Czars. Nochem had thirteen sisters and two brothers, Meyer and Liebchik.

The family was relatively prosperous in comparison with other Jewish families of the time and place. However, tradition and practicality dictated that the oldest son (Meyer in this case) would inherit the entire legacy to avoid the minute splintering of properties that would result otherwise. So quite early Nochem, as the second son, realized that he would leave the family and its business—which is why he agreed to serve the two-year terms of his two brothers in the Russian army. While conscription was compulsory, one could have another person substitute for him, usually for 400 rubles (about $200). Thus Nochem earned himself $400, which he planned to use for his future emigration to America. Counting his own two years, Nochem spent a total of six years in the Russian Army, entering on October 1, 1902, just a month shy of his 18th birthday.

The family made a birthday party for him before he left for the army because on the day of his actual birthday he would be on his post in the outskirts of Kharkov. His mother and sisters fawned all over him, considering the fact that he was the first male in the family, since his father Chaim ben Yitzhak served in the Imperial Army of Czar Alexander II. His father made a point of saying that the present well intentioned but weak Czar Nicholas II was no Alexander, but he was sure that Nochem would make them all proud regardless. And everyone urged him to take care of himself and to send plenty of letters.

Dutiful son and brother that he was, Nochem made certain to write within the first week of his arrival at the army base outside Kharkov. But he didn't expect his Lieutenant barging in on him so soon after submitting the letters for mailing.

"Hey Erkes, what the hell are these?" the Lieutenant shouted!

Flustered at first, he tried to respond calmly: "Those? Why they're letters—written in Yiddish—which uses the Hebrew alphabet for the Yiddish language."

"Well Godammit Erkes, unless you want to be hauled out and shot for a spy—and me with you—you better write your letters in good old Russian. You know how to write Russian, don't you Erkes?"

"Yes sir, I will sir, thank you sir." And Nochem stooped down to pick up the letters that his Lieutenant had thrown on the floor.

Following his basic training he and his army buddies were instructed to consider what branch of the army services they had preferences for and what skills they possessed to qualify them for their listed preference. There were spirited discussions with soldiers mentioning cooking and baking, metal-working, tailoring, and most giving consideration to that which would keep them out of the front lines and the actual combat.

"Hey Erkes, how come you haven't said anything?" one of his comrades said.

"You learn more by listening" Nochem said sagely.

"Yeah, maybe so, but that's more like taking than giving anything."

"Well, I've spent practically my whole life with and around horses. So maybe I better list the cavalry. At least that way you get to ride rather than march all the time." Nochem said with a smile.

"I think the Cossacks have a lock on the cavalry, Erkes. So maybe you better choose something else," said another soldier.

Nevertheless Nochem did list horses as a particular skill, and as is the case in all armies of the world, his submission was totally ignored.

"So Nochem, what did they assign you to?"

He sighed a heavy sigh of resignation and replied: "Artillery School. They want to make me an artillery-man."

"Hey, that's not so bad. The artillery usually is in the rear lines. Better than being right up front, right?"

THE RUSSO-JAPANESE WAR

Aside from his training in Artillery School, the first two years of army service were routine and boring. Oh there was some interest deriving out of the fact that periodically his unit was transferred to different posts of the far-flung Czarist Empire, including a stint in Kiev, the Capital of the Ukraine, and then from there, farther and farther east towards Siberia. He kept up a regular correspondence with many members of his family, in which he described his visits to many cities and communities.

And then army life was no longer boring! On February 8, 1904 the Russo-Japanese War broke out and Nochem found himself in the thick of it! The train ride all across Siberia via the Trans-Siberian Railway (built in 1891) was long and arduous and seemed to Nochem and his buddies never to have been improved upon.

"Stop complaining" the sergeant told his men inside the coach behind which was the flat-bed cars that were transporting their artillery pieces. "At least you don't have to ride and sleep with the guns and caissons like the cavalry people do with their horses."

"Yeah sure, Sarge! But do you have any idea where we're going."

And the sergeant told them as far as he knew they were heading towards Vladivostok, the chief Russian naval station on the Pacific coast founded in 1860, and they were also to make some stops in between—but the high command failed to inform him of the details, he sneered.

The train stopped at a small settlement along a river and for some inexplicable reason they were directed to unload their artillery field pieces and to set them up on a hill some distance from the body of water.

"Why are we stopping and setting up here?" several of the men asked.

"Yes, and what river is that?" Nochem asked.

"I'm told that that's the Yalu River, someplace in China or close to it," the sergeant replied. The men expressed surprise to be in China when the war was with Japan and the sergeant tried to explain the competing imperialisms that brought Russia and Japan to be fighting a war mostly in Chinese territory. And he finally gave up trying to do so and ordered his men to set up their tents a distance behind the field pieces so that they could sleep and get a good night's rest—which he was certain they would need to be prepared for what presumably was ahead.

As Nochem settled onto his cot in his tent shared with two other soldiers, he was asked if he knew what day it was—because Nochem was known to be keeping a diary and therefore kept tabs on days and dates. And he thumbed through his little black book and announced that he was quite certain that it was Saturday night, April 29, 1904. And then he bid his buddies good night.

As the first rays of the dawn peeked over the horizon on Sunday April 30, 1904, artillery shells began exploding in and over the encampment and dazed but suddenly awakened Russian soldiers dressed hurriedly and rushed outside to greet the day and their Japanese adversaries. It was immediately apparent that their own artillery field pieces were the target of the bombardment because most of the fifty pieces were smashed or overturned or otherwise unusable. Not knowing what next to expect, but conditioned by their training, they grabbed their rifles and formed a skirmish line along a small stonewall which provided them with a degree of cover.

"Christ O'mighty, these little yellow bastards are sneaky, aren't they?" remarked one of the soldiers.

And others nodded or grunted their agreement. "Just keep your eyes open—and yes, here they come advancing across the river on some bridges they slapped together during the night," said the sergeant.

Nochem and his buddies fired round after round at the advancing Japanese, with bullets flying by them. And as the enemy advanced they let out weird cries that sounded something like "Bonsai" or something akin to it. And suddenly Nochem felt a sharp pain in his left wrist and found himself unable to control or operate that hand or arm and then he felt faint and saw only blackness and heard nothing.

When next he opened his eyes he found himself in some sort of barracks in a bed with white sheets and some women—yes women—in white garb. He tried to call out but could only emit a whisper. And then one of the women came to his bedside and welcomed him and asked how he was feeling and he replied that he felt very weak and tired and what the hell happened anyway?

The nurse told him that he had been shot in the left wrist and had lost lots of blood before the medics could get to him and bring him to the first aid station and from there to this army hospital. She added that he was responding well to treatment and it would be only a week or less before he would be discharged and return to his unit and his buddies.

"I'm in no hurry," Nochem answered. He tried to raise his arm and found it very heavily bandaged and thus heavy to lift. "Gee, if it was only a small bullet wound to the wrist, why do I have this mountain of a bandage? Are you sure I still have my hand and fingers?"

The nurse then explained that the bullet just barely missed severing his artery and that he was indeed lucky to be alive and to have his hand, wrist and arm intact!

Nochem nodded and thanked the nurse for her attention and explanations. And he dozed off again.

Back with his unit Nochem pressed his buddies for details of the encounter, which would go down in the history books as the Battle of the Yalu River, won so overwhelmingly by the Japanese. He was distressed to learn that at least a dozen of his comrades were killed and another dozen, including him, wounded. And all because the Russian General Kuropatkin had spread his men out too thin so that the unit at the Yalu River was outnumbered four to one!

"Well, glad that you came through all right Erkes," said his sergeant. "We'll kick their little yellow asses next time, for sure!" he added.

"Yes for sure." Nochem and his buddies agreed.

And then they found themselves on board a train again, with replaced artillery pieces on the flat bed cars behind their coach. And again they were headed towards Vladivostok and Port Arthur. So far the war had not been going well for the Russians, the Japanese winning all of the major battles on land and even on the sea.

Once Nochem and his unit arrived at Port Arthur they discovered that they could go no further towards Vladivostok since the Japanese laid siege to the entire Chinese Amur Province, which included Port Arthur! And as the Japanese advanced, town-by-town they closed the noose around Mukden and their final target, Port Arthur.

On the morning of March 10, 1905 the Battle of Mukden began with a tremendous Japanese artillery barrage—which was met in kind by a Russian artillery barrage. All morning the two artilleries exchanged shell for shell. Nochem and his fellow-artillery-men were taxed beyond endurance, blackened by the cannon smoke, and weary from loading shells and standing back and holding their ears. And suddenly the shelling from the Japanese side ceased and an eerie silence fell on the field. Nochem and his buddies were pleased for the respite and sat on the ground next to their field pieces wondering what good any of the bombardments had done.

"On your feet everyone, up, up!" shouted the commander of the battery. "The Japs have broken through our front lines and coming at us on horses!"

Nochem and his comrades rushed to get their rifles stacked a few yards behind their cannon and as he grabbed his gun and turned he found himself fact to face with a Japanese lancer on horse-back. He tried to use his rifle as a club, but before he could grab the barrel to swing the heavy butt the lance entered his throat on his left side and he fell, he was sure, mortally wounded! But before he lost consciousness he heard a rifle shot and saw his assailant tumble from his horse to the ground next to him.

For a second time Nochem awoke in an army hospital, his neck heavily bandaged and his head throbbing. He tried to speak but without success and limply he waved his hand to attract the nurse's attention.

A male attendant came to his bedside, smiled and welcomed him back to the living.

He tried to smile back but found that difficult too. But apparently his facial expressions conveyed his many questions.

"I know, you want to know what happened, where you are, and what's the prognosis, right?"

And Nochem nodded.

"Well, you've been here about three days, and we were able to remove the tip of the lance from your throat. You were very lucky because the Jap that stuck you was shot by one of your buddies and as the Jap fell his lance broke and failed to pin you to the ground. Yes indeed, you were a very lucky fellow. By all accounts you should be dead now, but as I said, the lancer did not have time to finish his lancing—or whatever the hell you call it.

"Now as to the prognosis, it looks very promising. First, and most important, you'll live. Whether you'll be able to talk again—or even swallow normally—only time and God will determine that. Now, I'm only a male nurse, and what I just told you came from the doctors, so if you want any details you'll have to talk—excuse me—get that from the doctors."

Nochem spent several weeks recuperating at the army hospital and during that time was able to catch up on his correspondence with his family, and to obtain information about the battle that almost did him in, the Siege of Port Arthur and the Battle of Mukden. The battle specifically was horrific in terms of casualties. The Russians lost over 90,000 soldiers while the Japanese lost only half of that, but still it amounted to 45,000 Japanese dead! It was the bloodiest battle in European history to that date. For all practical purposes it ended the war on land, although the war on the sea would continue a bit longer. But before that end came, Nochem had an unusual visit from an unexpected dignitary.

AN UNUSUAL LANGUAGE

"Hello, you are Nochem Erkes I understand. My name is unimportant but we have been impressed with your military record, and—if I may be brutally honest—since the war is not going very well for us, we are compelled to resort to unusual methods. Some time ago your Lieutenant chastised you for corresponding with your family in an unusual language." He paused. "I believe you used Hebrew alphabet characters to transmit Yiddish speech, correct?"

Nochem's first reaction was near panic. He could have sworn that his Lieutenant had dismissed the incident as youthful folly and here was an apparently high government official bringing the matter up—and at such an inappropriate time! "Yes, my name is Nochem Erkes and a long time ago I did, unintentionally do the thing you describe, but I meant no harm."

"No, no, you don't understand, I'm not here to bring any charges against you. I'm here to ask your cooperation in a new government effort at military communication, which will insure maintaining the secrecy of our communications. In plain Russian, helping us to use a system of communication that the Japs especially, or any other enemy, would be unable to decipher. Our thought is to recruit, train and deploy a number of people like you around the country who can communicate in the Hebrew/Yiddish medium. Would you be willing to help us, and participate in such a program?"

Nochem was much relieved, but asked whether this new assignment would be outside the army, because he felt that he still had some years of commitment to the army, but if he could serve in this new capacity and still be considered as officially part of the army, then count him in.

The un-named dignitary had Nochem sign a statement of Intent, thanked him and said he would be in touch. But as the weeks went by, and the Japanese had, for all practical considerations won the war, President Theodore Roosevelt of the United States brokered a peace treaty between the two adversaries Russia and Japan signed in Portland, Oregon on August 29, 1905 and thereafter known as The Treaty of Portsmouth.

LOVE FINDS NOCHEM

Nochem never heard from the unnamed dignitary, which he thought was just as well since he still had another three years to serve in the army: one year to finish his own term of service and two years for his younger brother Liebchik. And the next three years seemed to pass much more quickly for some reason. Following his discharge from the army hospital he and his artillery unit was stationed in posts all over the Ukraine, Byelorussia and finally that third of Poland that had been taken over by Russia when it was divided for the third time in 1796. In Poland he and his unit was first stationed in Warsaw, but when some disturbances occurred in the eastern part of what later would be recognized as White Russia or Byelorussia, he and his unit were moved to the Kletsk/Nesvizh District.

In Nesvizh he chanced upon a young, petite and pretty Jewish girl by the name of Bashya Friedman. He was 23 years of age and she 14, nine years his junior and he thought carefully before daring to ask her out. He wrote to his family in Czipowitz telling them about her and of his dilemma deriving from the disparity in their ages. His father Chaim ben Yitzhak, his mother Malka, his brothers and even all his thirteen sisters were unanimous in urging him to follow his heart. His father reminded him that he had almost lost his life twice and one does not tempt fate too often. His mother reminded him that she was merely 16 when she married his father. And Meyer and Liebchik stressed that he wasn't marrying the girl, just yet, merely inviting her to go out with him. And so he began courting her.

Bashya, for her part, found him to be very good looking, with a pleasing personality, witty and charming and, above all, with his army history, a very romantic and dashing figure. She invited him frequently to her home, where he got to know her mother and her brother Moishe Chaim and two other brothers.

"To tell you the truth, Nochem, our biggest concern is not the difference in your ages but the fact that you are still in the army," Moishe Chaim said to him one evening when Nochem was again visiting.

"But I wont be there much longer" Nochem countered.

"Bashya tells us that you were almost killed twice," her mother pointed out.

"Well yes, but we were at war then. The war is over, so it's not likely that I'll be killed or even hurt now."

"Still, we feel that it's best that the two of you should not consider anything serious until the discharge is about to happen, or better still, after the discharge," Moishe said, looking caringly at his younger sister.

And now Bashya spoke: "Mama and Moishe, I know that you both are looking out for my best interests. But Nochem and I have talked this over and agreed that we will not take any serious steps until he is discharged from the army. So we all agree on that. But there is a more important thing that you should all know. Nochem plans to return to his family in Czipowitz near Odessa—at least for a while and then he plans to go to America. And when we marry he wants me to go with him to Czipowitz and then to America."

Her family members sat as if stunned. "America?" they all asked in unison. Apparently they had accepted the fact that once married she would go with her husband to his home.

But America? The thought evidently had not occurred to any of them.

And then following a long silence, Moishe spoke: "America is a far away place. Once one goes to America, seldom do his or her loved ones in the Old Country see that person again. But if one loves someone, one does not stand in that person's way for happiness. Isn't that right Momma?"

And Momma reluctantly nodded her head.

On October 30, 1908 Nochem was discharged from the Imperial Russian Army having spent six years of his young adult life in its service. Nochem wrote his family that he was going to hang around the Kletsk/Nesvizh area for a few more months courting Bashya. Which he did and in February 1909 they married. He was then 25 and she a respectable 16. And after tearful goodbyes to her family they both returned to Nochem's home in Czipowitz/Odessa.

NOT THE END BUT A PAUSE

Bashya's Uncertain Journey

II. UNCERTAIN JOURNEY

A uthor's note Re. fact and fiction: It's been said that truth is often stranger than fiction. And to more sharply focus a true story and have it hang together more effectively, writers sometimes use fiction or fictionalize some facts—such as the Gypsies and the Displaced Persons' Camp in this story that follows. Likewise, the dialogues employed are, for the most part, extrapolations by the author. Aside from that, this story is totally true. SGA

HISTORICAL BACKGROUND

October 1917: Russian Revolution.
March 25, 1918: Byelorussia Democratic Republic proclaimed in formerly White Russia
April 1918: Pogroms in Odessa, Ukraine, Russia
January 1919: Bolsheviks crush Byelorussia Republic
1919-1922: Civil War rages in Russia and Byelorussia
1920-21: Poland invades Byelorussia; annexes western half.
September 1939: Nazi Germany defeats Poland; starts World War II.
October 1939: Western Byelorussia reannexed by USSR.
September 1945: End of World War II. Byelorussia renamed Belarus.

DATELINE: Czipowitz, Odessa, Ukraine, Russia: April 3, 1918

Rumors of Pogroms have been flooding this predominantly Jewish community for weeks. The "shtetle" inhabitants are concerned with the constant reports of violence and mayhem against fellow Jews in places like Kiev, the provincial capital, and Kharkov, the largest city of the province. Over the centuries it has become engrained in the Jewish psyche, that when things go awry, Jews must be on guard for they are the historical scapegoats. It apparently doesn't matter whether the perpetrators are Bolshevik Reds or Czarist Whites or Separatists in this seemingly endless chaos. No matter which side occupies the region, the Jews are singled out for special persecution. Those that survive the initial assault are left homeless and sent on the road to nowhere. The Red Cross estimates that there are many thousands of such displaced persons, mostly women and children with nowhere to go and no end in sight. End Dispatch.

For the Erkes family in Czipowitz, a shtetl on the outskirts of Odessa, the large city on the north shore of the Black Sea, it didn't matter that they had managed to raise themselves more than a few notches above their fellow Jews. They had built a thriving business raising, trading and selling horses and providing ancillary services for horses and their gentile owners. In fact, they were unusual Jews in that they were the official suppliers for the local constabulary and army outpost as far as horses were concerned. But when things go wrong, such as the First World War followed by the Russian Revolution and the endless Civil War, scapegoats are required.

And so Chaim Erkes, head of the family, convened a family conference in the central house. His wife, Malka and his oldest son, Meyer and youngest son, Liebchik and their wives all were present, as were the five youngest of his thirteen daughter—all still unwed—and Bashya, the wife of his middle son, Nochem who had gone off to America a few months before the outbreak of the Great War. That in itself was a story of ironies for it perfectly illustrated what a Scotch poet named Robert Burns had written that "the best laid schemes o' mice and men gang aft agley." That was Scotch for "going awry or wrong." And another Scotch writer, Sir Walter Scott, had later written; "Oh what a web we weave when first we practice to deceive." But the Erkes family had not really wanted to deceive anyone—just to practice some expediency!

Nochem had sent the money for Bashya and the children to come and join him in America, but Sonia, his youngest sister was causing the family considerable concern because of her running around with gentile soldiers and the family prevailed upon Nochem to have Sonia go to America with the children, using Bashya's passport and visa. It was to be a temporary delay for Bashya, and so she reluctantly agreed to the plan. But her children refused to go without their mother and so Sonia traveled to Nochem in America alone. When some time later, Bashya and the children were again preparing to leave for America, World War I erupted on August 1, 1914 followed by the Russian Revolution and Civil War—all of which prevented travel!

POGROM: April 5, 1918

The Erkes house was a fairly large structure having been added onto as the family grew, with hidden accesses to a large cellar. At first the family considered sending Bashya and the children to her relatives in Kiev, but with all the skirmishing between the Whites and Reds and brigands plundering the countryside, it was decided to try to keep the family together. The cellar was stocked with water and food and when the first sounds of smashing and breaking reached the Erkes house, Bashya and her children were ushered into the cellar, which was then sealed off and the entrance effectively camouflaged and thus hidden.

Bashya and her children could hear shouting, screaming, smashing and then the crackling of flames consuming the upstairs. And they literally held their breaths—and each other—Manya seven and a half and Herschel five years of age.

"Momma what is happening?" Manya asked as Herschel whimpered.

"Sha, shtill!" their mother admonished.

"Will they kill us also?" Manya whispered.

After what seemed an eternity, but calculated by Bashya to be only about three more hours, silence settled on the scene. She waited what she estimated to be another two hours before she dared to venture out through one of the secret accesses, followed by her children.

It was night but they could see the destroyed upper structure of the Erkes house with smoke spiraling skywards from the ruins and Manya asked why this was done to their home while Herschel cried and clung to his mother's skirt.

"Who can say why the goyem do what they do! I want you to take Herschel and go back down into the cellar and stay there until I come back for you."

"But I want to go with you!"

"Do as I say. Now! I must see if anyone else is still alive. I will try not to be long."

And Manya took her brother's hand in hers and led him back down into the cellar.

Bashya first examined the ruins of the house and, to her horror, found nine badly burned and unrecognizable bodies. She knew they were the bodies of her family, but two were missing and she wondered whether the two had been able to flee to safety. All the horses were gone and she wondered about the values of people who murder other people but spare the animals. She next went into the shtetl—or rather what was left of it since not a single dwelling was left intact. Not finding any other survivors, Bashya returned to her children, shared with them what she had discovered and explained that the best thing for them was to try to get to her relatives in Kiev. Manya asked how far that was and how they would get there and her mother replied that she thought it was about 480 kilometers (300 miles) to the north and they had no alternative but to walk. Manya then asked how it was possible for them to do that and her indomitable mother replied; "By putting one foot after the other." They stocked up on provisions from that stored in the cellar, each to carry as much as their size would allow, and waited for night to fall.

"But why do we have to go by night?" Manya protested.

"Because that's when it will be safer from the armies and thieves and murderers."

FROM ODESSA TO KIEV: (April and May 1918)

And so, they traveled mostly—but not always by night to avoid the armies and brigands pillaging the land. She reasoned it was better to go very slowly—but surely—if she was to reach their destination. She was surprised that not all the peasants in the Ukrainian countryside were anti-Semitic and in fact, some were kind and helpful. She would order the children to stay hidden in the fields while she approached the farmhouse to determine the degree of either hostility or friendliness of its inhabitants. And, only after establishing the attitudes of the inhabitants, did she make her next move—reclaiming her children. And in this way, farmhouse to farmhouse, averaging 9-10 km. (six miles) per day, Bashya Friedman Erkes and her two children, Manya and Herschel, inched their way to Kiev, via Nikolayev to Voznesenck to Malayaviska then to Belay Tserkov and finally Kiev, the ancient capital of the Ukraine. It required the months of April and May, to cover that distance, 483 kilometers (300 miles)! The first night was the most difficult, because it was the first step in the proverbial thousand-mile journey that the Chinese talk about. While Bashya attempted to ration their food supplies and water, it was difficult to do with growing children. Fortunately April nights in the Ukraine were pleasant and star-filled and Bashya was able to determine and follow the North Star because she knew they had to head straight north. She also knew that their first community they had to reach was Nikolayev on the way to Kiev. While the most difficult, the first night was also the most productive in distance covered because she was able to imbue the children with the sense of adventure that it, in fact it was. But by the dawn, having traveled almost 16 kilometers (ten miles), they were exhausted and ready to rest. Bashya had the children hide in a wheat field while she approached the farmhouse in the distance.

She had to gently knock on the door three times before an elderly woman opened it. Cautiously she asked directions to Nikolayev and the woman called for her husband. The man, also elderly, pointed to the north and also directed her to look for certain landmarks. She thanked them and then asked if she could have a little water and was invited in for that purpose. They invited her to sit while the woman filled a small jug with water. As she sipped the precious liquid slowly, eyed carefully by the elderly couple, the man asked where she came from and why she was going to Nikolayev. Bashya, having assessed the couple as kind and friendly shared with them that she was from Odessa and was on her way to Kiev. The man wanted to know if she was going alone and now Bashya took a deep breath and confessed that her children were waiting for her in the fields.

The old couple expressed surprise that she would have her children hide in the fields and urged that she collect them and bring them in for some food, water and to be cleaned. Bashya thanked them profusely and hurried to collect her children. The food was solid farm food and filling for children and adult alike. And after telling the old couple a bit more about her recent happenings insisted that they had to be on their way because they had a long ways to go. And adding further to her surprise, the old couple insisted on providing them with some food, consisting of many vegetables, some bread and containers of water.

By the third day/night of their journey they had consumed the food provided them by their recent benefactors and they were compelled to raid farms, and apple and pear orchards. From the farm fields they managed to secure carrots, radishes, cabbages and turnips and also many varieties of berries such as strawberries and raspberries growing in the wild. Manya asked whether what they were doing wasn't stealing and little Herschel ventured that even if it was it was overlooked by G-d because of their situation and his mother commended him for having such understanding.

However, Bashya was not so fortunate in her knocking on other doors, again to inquire directions and hopefully to be invited in for a drink of water and subsequently some food. Many doors would not be opened, but only a voice from the inside demanding to know who it was and what did she want— and then told to be gone. But enough doors were opened, and enough jugs of water provided and even some handouts of food that Bashya was encouraged that her efforts to reach her relatives in Kiev would finally be successful. In the meanwhile, she was perfecting a scheme and a strategy for survival. By the end of the first week they reached Nikolayev.

As had been her strategy from the start, she stayed away from the populated areas, navigating the fringes. It was not her intention of staying too long in such populated places, only long enough to check her geographical bearings and confirm directions to her next objective, which, from conversations with some store owners she determined would be Voznesenck. Also, from the conversations she determined that there were some Jewish families in that town, because of the references to "Zids still living there!"

So, with the falling of night, Bashya and her children were again on the road—or rather going through the fields that were parallel with the road and by the end of the of the second week they arrived in Voznesenck. Finding the few Jewish families was not difficult at all, for Bashya merely went to the most downtrodden part of the village and easily found the very small shtetl. It was indeed a very small affair with only a half-dozen Jewish families, each poor as dirt. But as poor as they were, they were hospitable and intensely interested in her saga. Not only did they share their meager supplies of food, but insisted that the Erkes family have indoor shelter and this was accomplished by one family having each of its four members stay with four other families thus making available its small, but comfortable abode for Bashya and her children.

Bashya was careful not to overstay her welcome and so after a few days of rest she very gratefully accepted the foodstuffs the Jewish families of Voznesenck provided, and was once again on her way, this time to Malayaviska. But, during the third week of their odyssey, Herschel became ill with a very high fever—which slowed them down considerably. Manya relieved her mother as often as she could in carrying her sick brother, insisting each time that he was not really too heavy. As they moved slowly through the dark night, Manya told her mother that she thought she saw some pinpoints of light ahead. At first her mother said that she must be mistaken, but then Herschel coughed and said he saw it also. And then Bashya saw it too.

As had become their routine, the children hid in some bushes on the side of the road as their mother moved slowly and ever so cautiously towards the growing light. She was able to discern some shadowy figures sitting around a campfire but their dress was unlike that of the people of the Ukraine. And then she guessed that this was probably a band of Gypsies—who tended to refer to themselves as Rom or Roma. She remembered that the talk among Jews was that Gypsies were in many ways like themselves, because of their wanderings and subsequent persecutions. And so she decided that she could chance going up to them. And she did so, coming out of the shadows into the light of the campfire. The Roma were startled at first, but seeing only a small, attractive woman in ragged clothing, they all stood, bowed and extended a welcome. In a breathless few words she explained her situation and her destination and told them about her children hiding down the road. And in seconds the apparent leader or chief urged her to reclaim her children and to join them around the fire.

Comfortably seated around the fire, and after some food and drink, the chief introduced himself as Amroc and explained that the tribe was also going to Malayaviska on its way to Belay Tserkov, which was on the way to Kiev. Although the tribe would not be going to Kiev, the chief invited Bashya and the children to accompany it as far as Belay Tserkov where it would then turn and head due west on its way to Romania—an offer which Bashya immediately, gratefully accepted.

Amroc's wife, Cleo, felt Herschel's fevered head and asked Bashya to bring the boy to her wagon-tent where she had some herbs and ointments which she felt would relieve the boy's symptoms if not cure his illness. And Bashya, having an immediate sense of trust of these people carried her son to the wagon followed by Manya. As Cleo removed Herschel's shoes, she commented on how worn through they were and suggested to her husband, Amroc that he do some repairs. Amroc smiled and replied that he would do so first thing in the morning, suggesting that it would be wise for all of them to get a good night's sleep. He produced some bedding consisting of a large straw mattress and blankets and pillows and arranged for Bashya and Manya to sleep alongside his wagon so that they could be close to Herschel now sleeping peacefully inside the Gypsy Chiefs tent wagon. And he promised that more comfortable arrangements would be made in the morning with the assistance of all the other members of the tribe.

In the morning Herschel was looking much improved, but still with some fever and Cleo suggested that he continue to rest after partaking of some broth and tea. Amroc set up his shoemaking bench after breakfast but before starting, asked to also look at Bashyas's and Manya's shoes, saying that as long as he was opening his shoe-repair shop he might as well get all the business he could. Seeing the frightened look on Bashya's face he hastened to add that he was merely jesting and that there would, of course, be no charges.

Bashya heaved a sigh of relief but then added that she was an excellent cook, pardon her immodesty, and she would be very pleased if the tribe would allow her to cook for its members during the time that she was traveling with them.

Before Amroc could dismiss the offer as unnecessary, Cleo called from inside the wagon (evidently having overheard the offer) to say that the tribe would be happy to accept the offer.

A bit startled, Amroc smiled his perpetual smile and said: "She is a very smart woman!"

Many of the tribes-people, but particularly the children, crowded into the wagon-tent to observe Cleo's ministrations of Herschel while others gathered around Amroc as he set up his shoe repair shop.

After looking-in on her son, Bashya returned to watch Amroc repair their shoes—which in fact consisted of a rebuilding rather than mere repairing. Again she expressed her gratitude for the tribe's taking them in—which Amroc dismissed as being of no great consequence—and then she commended him on his apparent skill as a shoe repairman.

He smiled as he concentrated on his work and confessed that he was, in fact an expert shoemaker and repairman. 'We Roma have learned many skills, like working with all kinds of metals including silver, gold and bronze, and carpentry and cabinet-making and shoemaking, over the centuries and in our many travels. We are a lot like you Jews. We are wanderers, often driven from country to country for no other reason than we seem to be, and look, different. People are fearful of anything that is different from what they are. They are afraid of what they do not know or understand."

"That is very true" Bashya replied.

Manya nodded her agreement and then asked: "I thought you people were Gypsies? So why do you call yourself 'Roma'?"

Amroc looked up from his workbench, his smiled broadened and said: "Ah young lady, that is the question that everybody asks. My parents have told me that our ancestors originally came from the southeast or central part of India. We are of many tribes—many more than the twelve tribes of Israel, and our earliest tribes who left India, confused Armenia—one of the first places they wandered into—with Egypt, and in their later wanderings, when asked where they were from said 'Gyptia' meaning Armenia. I really don't know how true that is, but it is a good story, don't you think young lady?"

Manya nodded and smiled and said: "Yes, but not as interesting as our Jewish stories."

To which Bashya retorted: "Sha! That is not polite!"

Amroc laughed and said that that was all right, a person should feel proud of his or her heritage. And then he further addressed Manya's question: "We refer to ourselves as Rom or Roma because some of the many Gypsy tribes spread across Europe, especially Romania. But also because our language is Romany, although, like the Jews, with many dialects. Also like the Jews, because of being in so many different countries, we pick up words from each country and add it to our language, Romany. But unlike the Jews, Gypsies accept the religions of the country they reside in, but frequently mix-in ancient gypsy traditions. And unlike the Jews, we only number about 2 million, and shrinking, whereas the Jews, I understand now are over ten million all over the world."

Bashya said that she couldn't affirm or deny the numbers although she added that with all the pogroms it was unlikely that there could be that number. And then she asked: "Where are your children, if you pardon me for asking?"

Amroc's perpetual smile vanished and his visage hardened. "As I keep saying, we share many of the experiences of you Jews. I don't know if one can call the persecutions of us Gypsies 'Pogroms.' But our loved ones who are killed are just as dead as Jews killed in pogroms. Our 14-year old son was killed when he tried to come to the rescue of his 17-year old sister being raped back in Kharkov. And then, for good measure, they killed our daughter too."

"I'm so very sorry. I can now understand why you have been so responsive to our plight." Bashya said.

"Yes, well that obscenity was over a year ago. But still Cleo and I feel the loss—and you better be careful that she doesn't kidnap your son. Isn't that what they always say about us Gypsies?" he concluded with a return of his smile. He finished the shoe repairs and set about to fulfill his promise of the night before——to provide more comfortable accommodations for Bashya and her children. And he called a council of the tribe and asked members to offer whatever they could to ease the journey of their guests who would be accompanying them at least for part of the distance.

Bashya was amazed at the generosity exhibited because when the council was ended, Bashya found herself with a horse and wagon of her own for the duration of her travels with them. The only "condition" was that Marian, a seven-year-old girl who had taken a shine to Manya, be allowed to travel with them so that she and Manya could spend more time together.

And when Cleo pronounced Herschel well and fit to travel, the tribe—with Bashya and her children part of it—took to the road. And by the end of Bashya's fourth week on the road, they approached a river, which was supposed to have a bridge linking Malayaviska with the south, but the bridge had either been washed out by a cresting river, or been destroyed by warring factions. Bashya felt herself doubly fortunate to be with the tribe and to have a horse and wagon to cross the raging torrents because she realized, that without the horse and wagon, on foot she and her children would have had to make a wide detour further upriver in order to ford shallower water.

As was their custom, the tribe made camp on the outskirts of Malayaviska and a few of them went into town to restock their provisions. And again Bashya was amazed at her being so totally included despite the fact that she was without any funds. Amroc reminded her that her cooking for them was a form of bartering—an ancient Gypsy art and tradition—and thus contributing her fair share.

After a few days the tribe left Malayaviska and Bashya and her children spent a relatively uneventful but comfortable two additional weeks accompanying the tribe to Belay Tserkov where they were to part company, with the Gypsies heading due west, toward Rumania while Bashya and her children were to continue due north to Kiev. The parting was sorrowful and tearful for in the span of four weeks they had became an integral part of the Gypsy clan, which filled a void left by the tragedy at Czipowitz on the one hand and the murder of a daughter and a son on the other. Bashya felt certain that they could not have come so far without the Gypsy tribe. And now they still needed to reach Kiev a good 116 kilometers (72 miles) away—probably at least another two weeks of travel on the road in the old fashioned way—the way they had started—on foot!

But they had no choice but to "put one foot after the other" as Bashya had told Manya when they first began their uncertain journey. So, when the provisions supplied them by their Gypsy friends ran out they repeated the pattern and strategy of the first three weeks; they went from farm to farm, with the children hiding in the fields while their mother knocked on peasant doors asking for directions and water. And, as they experienced in the first three weeks, some peasants were helpful and some nasty and slowly they traveled the 9-10 km (6-7 miles) a day to cover the remaining 116 kilometers to Kiev. It had taken them two months to reach Kiev and their relatives, a distance of only 480 kilometers (300 miles) a journey that even in 1918 would ordinarily take no more than a day or two by car, or a week by horse and cart!

KIEV (June 1918)

Although Kiev, the capital of the Ukraine, had witnessed some skirmishes between rival armies, the Russian Civil War had not yet exploded into its full force and so the city was relatively intact when Bashya and her children arrived. It took a while for Bashya to locate her relatives at the address she had and was relieved to discover that they suffered no harm. But her relatives were, of course, very surprised to see them because there had been no advance notice of their coming. The relatives had heard about the pogrom in Czipowitz, Odessa but didn't know whether Bashya and her family had survived or not.

"Bashya! Thank God you and the children were spared! Did any of the others survive?" her Uncle Shmuel Friedman asked.

"No all killed except maybe two. But I couldn't tell which two because all of the bodies were so badly burned. We were spared because we hid in the secret cellar. It was horrible to find all the burnt bodies!"

"When did you leave Odessa?" Uncle Shmuel's wife Blema asked.

"Right after the pogrom, in early April. We traveled six days a week, but not on the Shabbos. Sometimes we were fortunate to find a kind family that would allow us to rest on their back porch and to pick some potatoes and other vegetables. And sometimes some would even give us soup and after that, bread to take with us. But mostly there were those who were cruel, or at least insensitive and would tell us to go away." And then Bashya told them of meeting the Gypsy tribe and of its kindnesses.

"That was quite an adventure!" Uncle Shmuel noted. "But what are your plans now? As you can see, our apartment is so very small even for my wife, our four children and me. Of course you can stay with us until some alternative can be worked out." And Tante Blema nodded her agreement.

Thus it was agreed that they could stay with their relatives in Kiev until they could make alternative arrangements, either with Nochem in America or with her family in Nesvizh, in Byelorussia. So, Bashya—who had never learned to read or write and whose in-laws in Czipowitz handled all her correspondence—had her uncle Shmuel write letters to her mother (his sister) and family in Nesvizh and also to Nochem in America. But there were two problems in corresponding with Nochem that at the time were unknown to any of them. Nochem, having read accounts of the pogroms in Russia and the Ukraine, had written to Bashya in Czipowitz and had his letters returned with a stamped notation that the address and it inhabitants were no longer "Reachable." And shortly after he was informed that his entire family, including Bashya and the children, had been killed in the Odessa/Czipowitz pogrom! And secondly, many immigrants to America, when being processed through Ellis Island, New York, experienced involuntary name changes because of language difficulties.

Nochem Lazer Erkes was one of those, becoming Nathan Louis Arcus when being processed through that gateway to America! His family in Czipowitz was aware of this but not wanting to confuse or upset his wife, failed to inform her of this fact. They reasoned that all of that would be taken care of once Bashya and the children joined Nochem/Nathan in America. But when her relatives were murdered in the pogrom all Bashya had was his original name and address. What was it that the Scotch poet, Robert Burns said about "the best laid plans?"

Within two weeks a reply was received from the family in Nesvizh expressing "thanks to G-d" for their survival and inviting them to "come home." But after almost a month, the letter to Nochem in America was returned with the stamped notation: "Addressee unknown."

With Nochem and America ruled out as an alternative for now—the two families quickly learned that they needed to take another look at their options, particularly since three additional people in the Kiev apartment was causing overcrowding and increasing tensions.

Uncle Shmuel lamented that, with all the political turmoil going on in what was formerly White Russia but now called Byelorussia, commercial transportation to that region was nonexistent and he worried about Bashya and her children having to travel what he estimated was another 400 km (250 miles) to Nesvizh on foot. Perhaps she should consider renting a small place nearby in Kiev, he suggested.

Bashya replied that she had neither the money nor the time nor the desire to delay going to her mother and family in Nesvizh. She added that she and her children were now experts in foot travel and that they probably could reach her family in Nesvizh well before winter set in.

Uncle Shmuel suggested that he might be able to subsidize part of her rent costs (and received a dirty glance from his wife for his audacity) and then quickly added that Bashya's skill, as a cook surely would insure her getting a job as such.

"And what will my children do while I'm off cooking for strangers?" she asked. And following much back and forth, considering all the angles, there was agreement that Bashya was correct in desiring to reach her family in Nesvizh.

Her aunt and uncle hoped she was right that she could reach her goal before the onset of winter and gave her what little money they could spare in addition to some provisions of fruits, dried meats, breads and jugs of water. Uncle Shmuel said that he would write his sister, Bashya's mother, to tell them that she and the children were on the way and should arrive within several weeks or months. And after the kissing of cousins and aunt and uncle, Bashya and her children left to continue their only slightly less uncertain journey.

"Make sure to let us know when you get home!" Uncle Shmuel called after them.

SURPRISE AT THE BORDER (July 1918)

So in early July 1918 they were on the road again, their first major destination being the border between the Ukraine and Byelorussia about 145 kilometers (90 miles) away. Bashya's estimate of three weeks proved correct as they moved slowly and carefully from Irpen then to Malen and then Korostan, stopping at farmhouses near each village to verify her route.

Not certain of the political situation, Bashya decided that it was best to cross the border under the cover of darkness and so that night they entered what she believed to still be a province of Russia, not knowing that earlier in the year (March 25, 1918 to be exact) the province had declared itself the independent Byelorussia Democratic Republic. They came to Stolin, the first significant village on the north side of the border. And by first daylight, they were apprehended.

"Who are you and what are you doing in Byelorussia?" demanded the leader of the border patrol.

"Isn't this White Russia?" Bashya asked deferentially.

"It was but now it is the Byelorussia Democratic Republic, no longer part of Russia."

"I'm sorry, I didn't know this."

"Where did you come from and where are you going?"

"We came from Kiev, but before that, Czipowitz near Odessa. And we're going to my family in Nesvizh near Kletsk."

"How did you travel?"

"By walking." Bashya instinctively thought it best not to mention the Gypsies.

The officer raised his eyebrows, as if to challenge her, but then, apparently remembering that most displaced people traveled by foot, resumed his questioning:

"Where is your husband? Is he dead?"

"No he is not dead, he is in America."

"America? Then why don't you go to him in America? We still have too many Jews in Byelorussia despite the pogroms" one of the patrolmen laughed.

"I can't go to him. It's over the water. And I don't have my passport or visa or any of the other things you need to go to America, especially money."

"Well then, you'll stay here at our camp for Stateless and Displaced Persons and you can write to him," the captain said, casting a disapproving glance at his subordinate.

"I do not know how to write—or read." Bashya replied, her head bowed.

"Well, that's all the more reason you need to come and stay with us. We will have someone to do the writing. You will tell that person what you want to have written and it will be done," the captain said with a disarming smile.

And so Bashya, Manya and Herschel were taken by horse cart to the camp for Stateless and Displaced Persons located in Pinsk, 64 km (40 miles) to the northwest.

PINSK: CAMP FOR STATELESS PERSONS (August through December 1918)

At the Camp Office a clerk wrote down their names, ages, nationality, religion, their place of origin, the route they had traveled and their nearest relatives—which Bashya listed as her Uncle in Kiev and her mother in Nesvizh, since Nochem in America was far from near. She was also asked what skills she had because every adult in camp was expected to perform some chores to help maintain and operate the facility. She listed her skills as cooking and soon found herself assigned to work in the kitchen cooking for hundreds of displaced persons.

Following the intake interview they were assigned to a small tent erected on a wooden platform in which was three cots, a table with a kerosene lamp, three chairs and a small stove and told that this would be their home for the duration of their stay at the camp. For their lavatory and toilet needs they were to use an outside common latrine. In response to Bashya's question about when she could have her letters written, she was told; "All in good time."

While families had their private sleeping quarters such as the tents on wooden platforms, everything else was done enmasse, such as eating in a large mess hall, and separate religious services and educational activities for the many denominations and religions. In fact, it was as a consequence of this that Bashya and her children discovered that there were other Jews at camp, in fact, enough to support a minyan for religious services and to set up a cheddar, or Jewish school. And this was a great comfort to her and her children. But despite the disappointing results of the efforts made from Kiev, she still yearned to be in touch with her husband, Nochem in America and her family in Nesvizh.

Finally, three weeks after their arrival the day came when the camp secretary had the time for Bashya to dictate a letter, and Bashya started to give the name and address of her mother in Nesvizh and the secretary looked puzzled and announced that she had been informed that the letter was to go to her husband Nochem Lazer Erkes in America.

"But why can't I write to both?" Bashya asked. "I want my family in Nesvizh to know that we are all right." And then she explained about the letters to Nochem written from Kiev.

And the secretary replied that Bashya would have to take that up with the Commandant. In the meanwhile, did she want to write to her husband or not?

And so Bashya dictated a letter addressed to her husband at the only address that she had for him, informing him that they were alive and in fairly good health in this camp and would soon be on their way to Nesvizh so that it was wise for him to have that address as well. And after dictating her letter she went to see the Commandant, who was too busy and she was told that she would have to make an appointment to see him. Which she did, although it was two weeks away.

When her appointment time came she made certain that Manya and Herschel were in Cheddar and she went to the Administration building. Inside she sat across a huge desk looking at the Commandant, a heavy-set, middle-aged man with a bushy mustache and baldpate. He seemed to be an amiable enough man, one that one could talk to. And when he smiled and asked what he could do for her, she directly asked: "Why can't I send a letter to my family in Nesvizh?" And she again told of the returned letters from Nochem sent from Kiev.

Still smiling, the Commandant flipped through some pages, apparently familiarizing himself with the details of her situation. "Missus, we assume that you would want to rejoin your husband in America, rather than remain in such unsettled times and places. And with our government facilities I'm certain we can locate your husband and also be helpful in securing the necessary papers you will require. There will be time enough to contact your family in Nesvizh once we have all the facts and possibilities of your situation. Wouldn't you agree?"

His reasoning seemed reasonable, albeit a bit rigid, she thought. And so. After a while she answered, "Yes sir."

However, after many additional anxious weeks, the letter to Nochem was once again returned stamped "Addressee Unknown" and Bashya again had a conference with the Commandant, who assured her that they would continue trying to track Nochem down using resources that only a government, such as Byelorussia possessed. Still she pressed for at least one letter to her family in Nesvizh informing them that she and her children were all right and the Commandant relented and authorized one such letter.

"After all, we don't want to jeopardize our main efforts, do we?" he again cajoled.

Despite Bashya's insisting that the family in Czipowitz/Odessa had been wiped out efforts were made by the camp personnel to contact the family in Odessa in the hope that they might have a more current address or information regarding Nochem. But each time the letters came back as undeliverable because the address had been demolished or people demolished or moved away.

Bashya marveled at the persistence, if not the obstinacy, of the bureaucrats. On the other hand, she received a reply from her family in Nesvizh decrying the long delay in her writing to them. They had received the letter from Uncle Shmuel saying that she and the children would arrive in a few weeks, and it was now a few months but in any event, she would find enclosed some money to help pay for her travel costs. Except, even though she turned the pre-opened envelope inside out, there was no money to be found.

The Commandant explained that the money had been expropriated—and he had to stop to explain what that word meant—to cover the costs of her and her children's stay at the camp. She argued that she was led to believe that her cooking was taking care of that and he retorted that was hardly the case, and continued endlessly about how much it cost to care for each and every person. But he agreed to allow her to send another letter to Nesvizh, although he feared that that one would have to be the last to that community. They had to concentrate their efforts on uniting Bashya and her children with her husband. After all, she was very fortunate to have a husband who was not only alive but in America and by now probably a millionaire!

The last remark raised for Bashya the suspicion that the Commandant might have other items on his agenda and so she expressed them at a gathering of fellow Jews following a Friday evening service: "Is it not possible that once he connects with Nochem that he would ask for a ransom for us?"

"Of course it is possible. The corruption of officials in positions like the Commandant's is well known. Each one runs his agency like his own personal little Empire," one minyanaire said.

"But even if that is so, the important thing is for him to be successful in locating and contacting your husband so that you could begin the process of rejoining him, don't you think?"

And everyone began nodding their agreement with the last speaker except Bashya, who protested: what if Nochem did not have the kind of money they would be demanding? And the man who focused on "the important thing" responded "you cross that bridge when you come to it. First things first," he concluded. And this time everybody, including Bashya, nodded in agreement.

Still, the weeks went by, expanding into months and there was no success in locating the whereabouts of Nochem Lazer Erkes in America. And there was no way of their knowing that the reason for that was that Nochem Lazer Erkes was now Nathan Louis Arcus, who had made several moves in the City of New York. So after five months of this frustration—six months after leaving Kiev—Bashya and her "captors" (which she regarded them to be) determined that she had no alternative but to resume the odyssey to Kletsk and Nesvizh.

"Missus, are you sure you want to start out now to go to Kletsk and Nesvizh. It's now December, the heart of winter and there is still a lot of unrest out there. The Bolsheviks are attacking the Byelorussia Democratic Republic and want to replace it with a Soviet Republic." the Commandant pointed out.

"I know nothing of politics and care even less" Bashya replied. We have done nothing wrong so why should you continue to keep us prisoners. All I want is to return to my family in Nesvizh and be with them. And we have withstood the Russian winter before."

"Why not stay here and go in the spring? Think of your children." The Commandant persisted.

But Bashya was adamant and although the Commandant had it within his power to restrain her, he also thought of the Bolsheviks who had a reputation of demolishing camps such as his and drafting the males into the Red Army and putting the remaining people in labor camps.

PINSK TO NESVIZH *(January to Early March 1919)*

In the first days of January the camp authorities provided her and her children with warm clothing, food, water and other provisions and directions. They told her that her destination was to the northeast of Pinsk and provided her with a list of towns and villages along the way, which included Gorodische, Doborslavska, Gantsvevichi, Sinyavka, Kletsk and finally Nesvizh a total distance of about 322 km (200 miles). To her surprise the Commandant joined the circle of Jews and other well-wishers and presented her with an envelope saying that it was just "a little going-away present from the camp staff." Her first thought was that perhaps Nochem had been reached but when she opened the envelope she found money inside and looked at the Commandant with a bewildered expression.

"It's the money your family from Nesvizh sent a few months back. I think you could use it now, don't you think?"

Impulsively Bashya threw her arms around the man's neck and kissed him on the cheek. "Yes! Thank you!" she shouted.

The Commandant disentangled himself from Bashya's embrace and said: "Ahem, well yes, you're very welcome. We will write to your family in Nesvizh to tell them that you are on your way—again." And he instructed that Bashya and the children were to be driven by horse and wagon a few kilometers to the road that would eventually lead her home.

THE ROAD TO NESVIZH

Fortunately the winter thus far had been mild with a minimum of snow and sleet. And so making their way to their first objective, Gorodische was uneventful. But as they left the environs of Gorodische—for again Bashya used the strategy of avoiding the communities themselves but circling around them—to head for Doborslavska it began to snow. It was a light snow at first, but as they trudged on towards Doborslavska it became heavier and heavier slowing their pace to that of a snail. And by the end of the third day, when they arrived in the town exhausted, it had become a full-blown, White Russian winter snowstorm. And a very tired Bashya realized that she would have to reassess her strategy and plan, particularly as her children—who were not prone to complaining—now were complaining of being very tired, cold and hungry.

She discovered that Doborslavska had a bus terminal from which rickety, ancient buses ran irregular schedules to Gantsvevichi, Sinyavka and all the way to Kletsk! So she inquired as to costs figuring on using some of the monies the Commandant had returned to her. She insisted that Herschel—who was small for his young age—was only three and would sit on her lap and finally compromised on his being four and paid out all but a few Zlotys which she determined to keep in reserve. The fare would take her as far as Sinyavka, some kilometers shy of Kletsk, which itself was only 16 km (ten miles) away from her destination of Nesvizh! They were indeed getting closer! And after allowing a porter to stack their improvised knapsacks on top of the bus they boarded the half-filled vehicle and went to the back, which seemed to provide roomier space but certainly protection from the snow and inclement weather outside. Such luxury!

"Mama why didn't we take the bus before?" Herschel wanted to know.

"Because we didn't have any money before, silly boy," his sister Manya retorted.

"Sha! Don't talk so loud about money!" their mother chastised them in a stage whisper.

"So when does the bus start to move?" Herschel wanted to know.

And Manya and Bashya agreed that it was a good question so Bashya got off the bus and went inside the terminal to ask that very question and was told that it would begin to move when it had filled with passengers. So she returned to the bus and conveyed that exact message to her sleepy children and then suggested that they might as well just relax and even sleep a little. It did not take long for all three to drop off into a deep sleep.

The lurching of the bus caused Bashya at least to awaken. Manya and Herschel, although turning and stretching, remained fast asleep. Bashya asked a neighbor passenger what had happened and where were they? And he replied that the bus had skidded on the icy road and slammed into a snow bank and all the male passengers had been asked to go outside to help to shovel the vehicle out of its predicament. And as far as their location, he was assuming they were not far from Sinyavka because they had stopped at Gantsvevichi about two hours ago. And he excused himself so that he could get out of the bus and help the others to dig the bus out.

It took several hours for the bus to be freed from its snow bank imprisonment, with men taking turns coming back into the interior to warm up before returning to the task. But finally it was freed and able to resume its journey to Sinyavka where Bashya had to wake her children because this was as far as their fare had provided for. The bus driver expressed his regret that they could not travel further with him, but the company frequently planted spies among the passengers to make certain that there were no violations of rules or passengers exceeding their destinations. But he advised her that she could stay out of the winter weather inside the café and saloon which also served as the bus terminal, at least until the weather moderated. He retrieved their baggage and wished her good luck and bon voyage and she, in turn, thanked him for his courtesy and consideration. Inside the café she used some of her dwindling funds to purchase three bowls of heavy soup and bread and they retreated to a corner of the establishment, eating and waiting for the sun to come up and the weather to moderate. And then she became aware of what appeared to be three soldiers at the café counter, one of whom in particular was becoming loud and rowdy. And so instinctively she retreated with her children into the deeper recesses and shadows of the facility.

"Ho what have we there?" the rowdy one shouted as he spotted Bashya moving back. "Hey lady, yes you—what are you hiding, huh?" And he lurched towards her in the shadows, with his two companions on his heels. "Boris, no, stop it!" the taller of the three shouted.

But Boris was not to be deterred. He came up close to Bashya, so close that the vodka on his breath was evident. 'Pretty lady, what are you hiding?" and he reached to pull her aside while Bashya stiffened and braced herself in front of her cringing children. "Well all right, don't' show me, I think I like you better than what you're hiding anyway. You are a pretty little thing."

"Boris, stop it, now!" the tall one repeated and reached to grab his companion, only to have Boris duck and reach for Bashya.

"Come now, just a kiss, one little kiss, pretty one" Boris hissed.

"Get away from me you drunken coward!" Bashya shouted.

"Leave my Momma alone!" Manya shouted, and was joined by Herschel shouting and crying: "Leave my Momma alone!"

The entering of the children into the fray caused Boris to momentarily back off, but then he lurched forward again, more insistent than before, his arms seeking to envelope his quarry.

Bashya struggled to free herself and at that moment the tall soldier smashed a full bottle of beer over his companion's head and Boris slumped to the floor senseless.

The tall soldier turned to his other companion and directed him to take Boris back to their barracks and treat the bump on his head. And then he turned to Bashya: "I'm terribly sorry lady, Boris is usually a good man when he's sober. But we're all under a lot of pressure these days and times."

"Thank you for your interfering" Bashya said. "I see that you are soldiers. In which army if I may ask?"

He brushed his long blonde hair away from his eyes and laughed. "It's a good question because sometimes we're not even sure ourselves with all the upheavals taking place. By the way, my name is Aleksei Bronstein and we are in the Red Army, of course."

"You are Bolsheviks? What are Bolsheviks doing in Byelorussia?" Bashya asked in disbelief. And Manya and Herschel looked wide-eyed at a real live Bolshevik!

Aleksei asked if he could be seated at their table, and with Bashya's permission sat himself between Manya and Herschel. "I don't pretend to understand all the politics involved, but I was drafted into the Red Army of the Russian Soviet Republic. They sent us to crush the Byelorussian Democratic Republic because it is so corrupt and really is part of Russia."

"You said your name is Aleksei Bronstein. Are you, by any chance Jewish? My uncle in Kiev told me that Leon Trotsky, the big macher—that is important person—along with Lenin—well his name was originally Lev Davidovitch Bronstein."

"I know, he's my uncle. We came from Yanovka, but Uncle Lev—I mean Leon—went to Boy's School in Odessa and then went on to become a revolutionary."

"Odessa! We are from Czipowitz, which is really a part—

or was until it was destroyed—of Odessa. We may be related!"

Aleksei laughed again. "If you go back far enough, all Jews are related. And you asked if I was Jewish. Well, I certainly was born a Jew. What I am now, I'm not sure. Except I'm sure I'm a soldier, even if a reluctant one. But what are you doing here, and where are you going in the middle of winter with two small children?"

And Bashya quickly recounted her story, concluding that she was heading for Nesvizh to join her family there.

Aleksei listened intently and deep in thought. After a moment of silence he said that he had some leave coming and had thought about visiting his relatives in Kletsk, which as she knew, was not too far from Nesvizh. He had a horse which he was sure his superiors would allow him to take on his leave and he would very much want to accompany Bashya and her children, at least as far as Kletsk—where she could delve more deeply into the extent of their relationship. It would take a day or two to firm up matters and he would guarantee the Café payment for allowing Bashya and the children to stay there for those days.

Bashya was so overcome with the offer that she was speechless, but Herschel could not contain himself from asking whether he could ride the horse, joined a moment later by his sister asking the same question.

"Well it looks like the children have made a decision for you. I'll be back in at most two days and we can then continue your odyssey."

"What is an odyssey?" Bashya asked.

"Exactly what you've been doing for the past 9-10 months."

As promised, Aleksei was back within two days with his horse Aleksander and Herschel and Manya were ecstatic to once again be near a horse remembering that their grandfather had operated one of the most successful horse-businesses in the Odessa region before the pogrom. And within minutes they were ready to travel. Bashya declined to ride the horse because she did not have the proper "attire" so Aleksei accompanied her on foot while Manya and Herschel rode astride the magnificent Aleksander for most of the distance from Sinyavka to Kletsk. Even with a horse it took them two days to reach Kletsk, because, after all the horses could go only as fast as those accompanying it on foot.

In Kletsk, Aleksei's aunt, uncle and cousins greeted him effusively and then very warmly greeted their guests and possibly newfound relatives. But it only took a few hours of comparing and exchanging recollections of relatives to confirm the fact that they were, indeed second or at least third cousins. As Aleksei had said; if you go back far enough all Jews would be found to be related.

Although Bashya was eager to travel the remaining five and a half to six kilometers (9- miles) to Nesvizh immediately, Aleksei and his family prevailed upon them to at least spend the night and get an early start in the morning. While Aleksei did not require his family's urging for him to accompany Bashya and the children, Bashya was pleased that they did so because it was therefore a unanimous decision. She protested, albeit feebly, that it wasn't necessary but when Aleksei explained that it was an opportunity for him to meet his relatives in Nesvizh, just as she had the opportunity of meeting her relatives in Kletsk, she gratefully accepted the offer.

GHOSTS FROM THE PAST

Their arrival in Nesvizh caused a stir. Bashya had left Nesvizh eight years ago as a new bride to go live with her husband's family in Czipowitz/Odessa. And her family in

Nesvizh had also heard the news about her and the children having been killed in the Pogrom of April 1918. But then they heard from Shmuel in Kiev that they had arrived there. And Shmuel wrote them again telling them that they were on the way, but months went by and no news. And then they heard from Bashya telling them she was in a Displaced Persons Camp and that she would be coming home soon, and again months went by and no Bashya. And now she was back with her two children—and brought along a long-lost cousin in the bargain!

She shared with her family, now consisting of her aging mother, one sister and two remaining brothers, a quick summary of her odyssey and the frustration in trying to reach Nochem in America and her family consoled her and assured her that the connection would be made and for now she and the children should rest and settle down to live with them.

"It's taken a very long time for you to come home." Her mother said.

"Yes, too long. We left Odessa in April 1918 and it is now early March 1919. That's more than eleven months!"

And Aleksei pondered: "You know, it's really only about 885 kilometers (550 miles) from here to Odessa, only a few days by motor car and maybe a couple of weeks by horse cart."

"I thought it was a million kilometers!" Herschel piped in, and everyone laughed.

And then everyone thanked Aleksei and urged him and his family to stay in touch and bid him a fond adieu.

NOT THE END—ONLY ANOTHER PAUSE

III. CHUTZPAH UNDER FIRE

("Tis the sunset of life gives me mystical lore; and coming events cast their shadows before")
From: "LOCHIEL'S WARNING"
By Thomas Campbell (1777-1844)

Herschel Erkes and his older sister Manya were part of a single-parent household in Nesvizh, Poland headed by an indomitable and persevering mother, Bashya, whose two surviving brothers and one sister and aging mother constituted the extended family necessary to provide some support network.

Herschel, Manya and their mother had come to Nesvizh in early March 1919 following a pogrom in Czipowitz/Odessa in Ukraine, Russia in April 1918 when Manya was seven and a half and Herschel a mere five years of age. It had taken them eleven months to travel the 550 miles from Odessa to Nesvizh! It was now 1926, seven years later with Herschel approaching his Bar Mitzvah. When they first arrived in Nesvizh, it was still located in Byelorussia, but while Russia (of which Byelorussia was again a part) was consumed by its Civil War Poland used the opportunity of invading Byelorussia and annexing most of the western half of the province. And so the Erkes family in Nesvizh found themselves citizens of Poland!

Herschel had no memory of his father who had gone to America in 1912 when Herschel was only two-months old. But he heard about him, although not in the most laudatory terms. Herschel did know two of his four uncles quite well; Moishe Chaim Friedman, the oldest, was married and had a daughter, Schlamme. When he was 7 or 8 years old an angry gentile hit the youngest of the four brothers, Label Friedman, over the head and thereafter he was unable to hear or to speak. However he was able to become a tailor and thus supported, not only himself, but also his mother with whom he lived. A third brother was killed serving in the Russian army while a fourth lost touch with the family after going off to some distance place in Russia.

Enroute from Odessa to Nesvizh Bashya had made attempts to contact her husband, Nochem in America, first from Kiev while at her Uncle's home and again while she was at a Displaced Persons Camp in Pinsk and each time the efforts failed because of two vital factors: first, Nochem had read accounts of the pogrom in Czipowitz/Odessa and attempted to contact his family there only to have his letters returned as undeliverable and shortly thereafter was informed that his entire family in Czipowitz/Odessa had been wiped out; and secondly, because of language difficulties at Ellis Island Nochem Lazer Erkes became Nathan Louis Arcus, who had moved several times. Since Bashya was unable to read or write, all correspondence went through her in-laws, who did not want to confuse or upset Bashya with such news and hence failed to share it with her. When they were murdered in the pogrom at Czipowitz that information died with them.

In the spring of 1919, once settled in Nesvizh, Bashya, assisted by her mother and brother Moishe Chaim, enlisted the help of the venerable Rabbi in unraveling the mystery of why she could not connect with her husband Nochem in

America. The Rabbi had many contacts with other Rabbis especially in New York and he utilized them to the fullest. The Rabbis in New York, in turn utilized all the organizations and agencies in that area to the fullest, including examination of the records of the Immigration and Naturalization Service, the agency that operated the Ellis Island entrance facility. Within a few months, the venerable Rabbi of Nesvizh had the answers, and he arranged a conference with Bashya and her family.

"The reason why your efforts to reach Nochem Lazer Erkes failed is because his name is now Nathan Louis Arcus and he moved several times. Didn't you know that my dear Bashya?"

"No I did not! Because of my inability to read or write, all his letters to me came through his parents. Perhaps they knew about it, but if they did, they never said anything to me. But why would he change his name? I don't understand that at all."

The Rabbi explained that such things happened frequently to immigrants because of the language problem. He doubted very much that it was Nochem's doing.

"Did the Rabbis in New York contact Nochem—or now Nathan?" Moishe Chaim asked.

"No they did not. They believed it only proper to provide you with his name and current address. And now that you have it, you can write to him and tell him the good news of your being here in Nesvizh. And in good time you will finally be able to join him in America."

Which is what Bashya did—with Moishe Chaim, of course, doing the writing.

Having written to Nathan Louis Arcus in May 1919, Bashya Friedman Erkes and her family waited impatiently for a reply—which didn't come until a month later, in June of that year. In it Nathan expressed his surprise at hearing from

Bashya saying that he had written to them after reading about the pogrom but the letters came back and that he was informed that she and the children had been killed along with the rest of his family. He thanked G-d for the fact that they were still alive. However, believing that she and the children were dead, he had remarried and been blessed with a son and another child on the way. He further wrote that he had discussed their dilemma with his Rabbi in New York, who granted him a "get" (divorce) retroactive to the presumed date of Bashya's death on the condition that he (Nathan) would do everything in his power to assist Bashya and the children. And this he promised to do. And to prove that vow, they would find some American dollars enclosed. Which they did.

Just as Nathan's receiving the letter and the news of Bashya's and the children's resurrection must have been a bomb blast, so Bashya's receiving the letter and news from Nathan was another bomb blast. She sat stunned, and her children, Manya now almost 16 and Hershel going on 13 also sat silently. Bashya's aging mother wiped her eyes and muttered that G-d works his wonders in mysterious ways and it was not for them to question G-d's ways, while Moishe Chaim gritted his teeth and said that he hoped Nathan would continue to fulfill his pledge to help out financially and there was nothing for them to do now except to try to make the best of things.

For a while money from Nathan in America arrived regularly every month, accompanied with small newsy notes about Nathan's family. He told about the tragic death of his firstborn Solomon who swallowed pieces of broken glass but in later letters he told about the birth of his next son, Alexander, and thirteen months later of the birth of his son Sholom. But then the letters, and the money, came less frequently and irregularly, with an explanation that he had lost his highly remunerative job as a "mole" digging the new Holland Tunnel connecting New York with New Jersey and it had taken him a while to find another job as a presser, which paid considerably less than the tunnel job.

And Bashya, in her replies kept Nathan informed of the progress of Manya and Herschel telling of Manya's interest in Zionism and her expressed intent to make Aliya to Palestine; and of Herschel attending the Talmud Torah in Kletsk because, even though Nesvizh had many shules, each catering to the people of a particular trade such as "schneiders" (tailors), the butchers, the bakers, and the "blechers" (roofers), it did not have its own Talmud Torah and Herschel needed to prepare for his upcoming Bar Mitzvah the next year. With her brother's prodding and help Bashya wrote Nochem about their educational system, which was unlike the public school system in America with each shule receiving some small subsidy from the Polish government, but required to include at least two hours of instruction in Polish language and history in addition to the teaching of Jewish history, culture, Torah and Hebrew language. So the Jewish boys, including Herschel were in school from 8:00 a.m. to 8:00 pm!

Moishe Chaim's opinion to the contrary, Bashya felt that Nathan would be interested in knowing about the exclusion of Jewish girls from this system because the initial prevailing attitude amongst Jews was that girls did not require any formal education. But as attitudes changed, the girls were given some instruction in the reading and writing of Yiddish—which the Polish government did not recognize and hence provided no subsidy. On the other hand, since the shule (and later the Talmud Torah) that Herschel attended did not provide any instruction in Yiddish, it was left for Manya to teach her brother the reading and writing of that essential language.

KLETSK TALMUD TORAH

Herschel had a difficult time in shule and later in Talmud Torah. He found the teaching by rote intolerable. He was an energetic and rebellious "trumpernick" full of questions, mischief and impatience. He loved sports (especially soccer and swimming which he learned from the goyem), but 12 hours of rote learning was hard to take especially for Herschel. But that was how things were taught and he had to grin and bear it, his mother Bashya and uncle Moishe Chaim kept telling him. Nesvizh did not have a Talmud Torah, so when Herschel was ready, at age 12, for Talmud Torah he was sent to Kletsk, 14 km (9 miles) south of Nesvizh.

Bashya and Moishe Chaim's brother-in-law (their sister's husband) in Kletsk allowed Herschel to sleep on a rickety cot, which he had to fold up each morning and put into a shed. It wasn't that his uncle and aunt in Kletsk were harsh people, only very poor people. Herschel had no place to wash—either himself or his clothes—and so he quickly became infested with lice, along with most of his classmates. Which was why swimming became so important for them; it served in place of bathing! While he had a place to sleep, eating was another matter and he would make the rounds of the Jewish homes, literally begging for odd jobs in exchange for food.

His mother had suggested that he try to look up their cousin Aleksei Bronstein who had been so helpful in their getting to Nesvizh seven years ago. Herschel clearly remembered that part of their journey because of the horse Aleksander. And he was disappointed to learn that they had gone to America a few years ago—without the horse. So, after three years, of being always hungry, itchy from lice, and bored out of his skull, at age 15 (having already been long barmitzvahed) he decided he had enough!

Herschel started his day as he had all his previous Talmud Torah days for the past three years by folding his cot and putting it into the shed, walking to the creek, taking off his clothing and, despite the chilly temperature, swimming several laps in the creek and running a few laps to dry off. Dressed, he went down the road, knocked on the farmer's door and asked if he could chop some wood for some eggs and coffee. His appetite partially sated, he walked the three miles to the Talmud Torah, arriving in time for the 7 am class and took his seat on one of the long benches alongside the long table. As the lessons droned on he found himself particularly edgy and impatient and by 10 am it had become intolerable. While one of his classmates was spewing forth something from the Mishna, he found himself rising from his bench and saying, "Excuse me, I have something important to say." And then he told them how it had been nice to know them, and he loved them but it was now time for him to get on with his life. He then walked up to the startled Rabbi, took his limp hand in his own, shook it vigorously and told the Rabbi how much he appreciated everything the Rabbi and the melamuds (teachers) had taught him and walked out the door to begin the 14 kilometer walk back home to his home in Nesvizh.

Enroute home he encountered three Polish farm boys who, recognizing him as a "zid", (the Russian equivalent to "kike" or Jew) and demanded money from him.

Herschel scanned the faces of the three boys surrounding him, all three taller than he, who at age 15 was still of short stature. "I'm sorry, but I have no money" he answered truthfully.

"Go away, Zids always have money, don't they guys?" said the apparent leader, as the other two nodded."

"No, it's the truth, I don't have any money."

"Well, if you don't have money, we'll just have to beat you up." Said the leader.

"Hey, you don't want to do that—it's three against one. But anyway, I better tell you that I'm pretty good at soccer." "Soccer? Who's talking about playing soccer? First you don't want to give us any of your money and now you're talking about playing soccer—just like a Zid!"

Herschel realized that his warning had fallen on deaf ears, and that he could not wait any longer. So he aimed a swift kick to the groin of the leader, which felled him, and as the other two bent over him, Herschel delivered a second kick to the stomach of a second would-be assailant and then a third kick to the head of the third, ending the encounter. "I tried to warn you!" he shouted over his shoulder as he continued on his way home to Nesvizh.

Mama Bashya knew her son well and made no effort to have him return to the Talmud Torah in Kletsk. Instead, she paid a local tailor $10 (American) to take her son on as an apprentice.

(A tragic footnote to the Nesvizh/Kletsk saga: On October 26, 1941 all the Jews of Nesvizh were rounded up by the Nazis, and—except for some artisans—shot! In Kletsk 4,000 Jews were killed near the Catholic cemetery; and on July 21, 1942 the Germans set the Kletsk Ghetto on fire and another 1,000 Jews perished!)

FAST FORWARD TO WORLD WAR II

(Note: In the spring of 1929 Manya and Herschel Erkes came to America to join their father, Nathan Louis Arcus. Manya became Mary Arcus and Herschel became Harry Arcus in the United States.)

From June 1942 to September 1946 Harry found a home in the U.S. army, serving in the European theatre of operations. Because of his knowledge of Yiddish (a Plattdeutsch dialect of German), Polish and Russian he was called upon to serve as a translator when American and the Russian forces linked up in Germany in April 1945. A few weeks after that he was designated to serve as a Courier to deliver important messages between the American and Russian armies.

As he rode relatively leisurely in his Jeep Harry ruminated on the twists and turns in his life. He wasn't too far from the American lines, having finished delivering his dispatches to the Russkies, and he was looking forward to his hard-earned leave. Suddenly something whizzed by his right ear and plunked into the ground ahead of his Jeep. Then another zinged by his left ear.

He quickly realized that they were not mosquitoes and began zigzagging his vehicle. But the volleys intensified and he thought it best to stop and turn over the Jeep for better protection. He did so, and determined that the source of the gunfire as coming from a clump of trees. Crouching behind his Jeep for protection his mind raced through the possible alternatives he faced.

Every once in a while he would stand and let loose a volley from his automatic and then crouch down again for protection. "Shit, this ain't good, gotta do better than this," he mumbled to himself. And so the next time he rose to fire a volley he also shouted in his Yiddish/Plattdeutsch dialect: "I'm point man of a big American convoy coming up fast behind me. Surrender now or be wiped out!" And he punctuated his remark with another volley.

To his surprise, there was silence, as if the Germans were debating the merits of his suggestion. But they seemed to be taking an awful long time in making a decision. Perhaps they needed an exclamation mark to his announcement. So he rose from behind his protective Jeep, fired another volley and repeated his demand, adding: "You don't have much time, they're only about five minutes behind me when you shot at me." And then he ducked back behind the Jeep.

The silence continued for another long while, and then he heard a shout: "Amerikan, Amerikan, we're coming out." Cautiously he looked over the fender of the Jeep and sure enough he saw what appeared to be five Germans coming out of the woods carrying a white flag of surrender. Swallowing hard, he rose from behind his protection and, cautioning himself to be very alert for any tricks, began walking towards the Germans. A few feet from the Jeep he stopped, thinking it best for them to come all the way to him, with his Jeep within reach. As they came closer he could see that they were very young, almost just boys, except for the sergeant who must have been all of 25 and that they had apparently left their rifles behind in the clump of trees from where they had ambushed him. And that was a good sign, he thought.

As they neared him, keeping the white flag high and visible, they kept asking. "You are sure they are Amerikans and not Russians, Ja? Amerikaner, Ja. Russkies, nein!"

And Harry responded: "Ja, Ja, Amerikaner, nicht kein Russkies." And he noted that they kept looking in the direction from which he had come, expecting to see the dust of the oncoming big American convoy and he knew he had to do something clever and daring since the odds were five to one—much greater than the odds of three to one he had encountered at Kletsk. He had the Germans put his Jeep right side up and then commanded them to remove their pants belts and throw them on the ground.

The Germans were perplexed and the Sergeant asked why that was necessary and Harry retorted that because he had ordered them to do so.

The Sergeant then argued that without belts they would have to use their hands to hold up their pants and thus would be unable to keep their hands raised in surrender.

"You got that right man." And then he translated it for the Germans to understand and sat behind the wheel of the Jeep directing the Germans to walk in front. With his rifle on the dashboard at the ready, he moved his captives as a shepherd moves his flock, slowly covering the few miles to the American lines. He could hear grumbling from his captives as they realized they had been duped and that there was no big American convoy coming up the road.

FOOTNOTE:

My oldest brother Harry Arcus received a Presidential Citation for that chutzpah. And years later, in talking with him about it, his response to my question of "How come you came up with such a ploy?" his answer to me was: "Hey, when you're Jewish, you find a way."

ANOTHER PAUSE

IV. ONE SMALL STONE

It was February and 1929 had so far been a good year for some people on Wall Street—a sharp contrast with Willett Street on New York's lower East Side where our tenement flat was filled with much activity, bewildering for a 7-year old just returned from school together with his eight year old brother, Alex. Neighbors and strangers were milling about babbling in Yiddish and English, but mostly "Yinglish."

I looked at Alex: "What's goin' on, Alec?"

He shrugged his shoulders. "I dunno. Let's ask Mama, and he disappeared into the milling mob.

But Mama was nowhere in sight. I thought I caught a glimpse of Papa and Tante Sonia. What was Papa doing home at 3:30 P.M.? And why was Tante Sonia here? I tried to follow Alex but being a small 7-year old, I couldn't push through the jungle of legs and thighs. So, I scrunched up against the nearest wall and waited—and listened.

"What a terrible tragedy. Did she really jump or did she fall? God will never forgive her if she jumped." Said Mrs. Stein our fat, upstairs neighbor.

"Who knows if she jumped or fell? But does it make a difference?" a stranger replied.

Somebody fell or jumped off something, that much I gathered. Now I listened even more carefully so as not to miss a single word.

"Such a young woman. How old was she, thirty eight?" another neighbor asked.

Mrs. Stein shook her head. "Nein. She was thirty-four, only a year younger than me. And she didn't have any family. At least I never met anyone from her side. Ach, terrible, terrible!"

Who was she talking about? I edged closer to hear better and they suddenly became aware of my presence.

"Sha, shtill! Sholem is listening to every word we're saying," Mrs. Stein warned.

Which was true, and it didn't matter whether they spoke in English, Yiddish or Yinglish since I was fluent in all. My smile faded, however, as they began speaking in Russian which I did not understand. So I returned to my wall and slunk to the floor to wait, for what I didn't know.

Finally Papa and Tante Sonia (yes, they were there) cleared the apartment and I rushed to hug him but he put me off with a curt: "Later Sholem." His blue eyes were red from crying and he kept biting his lower lip.

I clutched his hand and shouted: "Papa what's happening and where's Mama?"

He shook his head and replied: "You stay here in the parlor with Tante Sonia." And he went into the parent bedroom with Alex, where I spotted my two-year old sister, Henrietta, surprisingly still asleep. The door closed and I was alone with Tante Sonia. She sat down at my side, took my pudgy hand in hers, but said nothing. Her blue eyes were tearful, her reddish hair all mussed up.

"Where's Mama?' I asked.

She bit her lower lip (just like Papa) but didn't answer.

I repeated my question. "Where's Mama?"

She blinked back her tears. "Mama went away—far away." I felt my hand being squeezed.

"Why? Where? When will she come back?"

The tears streamed down her pretty face and in a choking voice said; "She is not coming back. Never!"

Still I persisted. "But where did she go? And why isn't she coming back?'

"Sha!" she exploded. "So many questions!" And she ran into the bedroom where Papa was with Alex.

And I was all alone with my mounting fears. And I thought; Mama must be very sick because lately she had been behaving as if in great distress, even more than usual.

I remembered coming home from school one day and found Mama sitting in a dark corner with a faraway look in her eyes. She did not even greet me or ask about Alex (who had gone directly to Hebrew School), and Henny was sitting on the floor in the opposite corner, very quiet.

"What's the matter, Mama?" I asked.

She looked at the two of us as if trying to remember who we were and then, suddenly she scooped Henny into her lap and clutched me to her bosom, squeezing the breath from me.

"Oh my darlings, my little ones," she sobbed. "Why must I suffer so?"

I managed to pull away and again asked: "Mama, what's the matter?"

"Memories—and ghosts, my darling. God is punishing me," she answered.

"Why? What did you do?" I kept asking.

She started to speak, paused and then said; "No, you're a child, you wouldn't understand. You shouldn't know anyway. Come, have some milk. And it's time for Yenta to have her nap."

When I heard her refer to Henny as Yenta' I knew my mother was back with us that time.

Papa, Tante Sonia and Alex came out from the bedroom and Papa said that he had to take care of a few things and put on his coat and left. Tante Sonia went into the kitchen to prepare supper and for the first time in hours I was alone with Alex in the parlor.

"Alec, where's Mama?"

"Mama is dead," he replied sadly.

"What do you mean dead?" I pressed him.

He looked at me, not certain what to make of the question, then replied: "Dead is dead. No more! Finished!"

I looked at my brother. He was only a year and a few months older and while we got along most of the time, we also quarreled a good deal. I didn't like his answer—probably because I didn't understand. Many times while playing "Cowboys and Indians" we would shout, "Bang, bang, you're dead." And Alex would fall down 'dead' or I would fall 'dead.' And still we would always get up and continue to play—or otherwise go about the business of living.

He stared back at me annoyed and repeated: "Mama won't be coming back, never Because when you're really dead, you're dead a long, long time!" He did not cry nor otherwise betray any feeling, so how could I believe him?

Nevertheless, I asked: "How did she get dead? Did someone shoot her?"

"Naw," he replied matter-of-factly, she fell outta window. Papa said she was sick and fell outta a high window."

Sick? I knew it! Mama was sick! But the falling out of a window? Hey, the neighbors had been talking about my mother!

"How did she fall outta a high window?" I asked.

Tante Sonia suddenly interjected. "Nein! Not so! Your Mama didn't fall out of a window. She threw herself off the roof'!"

"Papa said she fell," Alex retorted. 'Papa is not a liar" He glared at her and I glared also.

"Oy, your poor Papa. Look what your Mama did to him. She threw herself off a roof. She didn't care about her children. She didn't care about my poor brother. She killed herself!"

Alex looked like he was going to explode, when Henny emerged from the bedroom crying and rubbing her eyes. Tante Sonia tried to pick her up and comfort her but Henny looked around and called out: "Mama! I want Mama!"

Tante Sonia burst into tears, dashed into the parent bedroom and slammed the door, while we three sat quietly looking at each other confused.

Finally Papa came home and we all rushed to him, bombarding him with questions: "Why did Mama throw herself off the roof? Huh, why?

"Who says this?" Papa shouted.

"Tante Sonia,' we answered all together and pointed to the bedroom into which his sister had run.

He ran into the bedroom and we heard shouting. Then quiet—and brother and sister came out, red-eyed, holding onto each other.

"All right," Papa said. "I finished all the arrangements for tomorrow's funeral. So, let's eat and go to sleep."

We ate a light supper and went to our tiny bedroom. But Alex and I, lying in the same bed, could hardly sleep. I pestered him for whatever information he had and he whispered the following: Mama left Henny with Mrs. Stein and walked over to Orchard Street supposedly to do shopping. For some reason she walked up the four flights of the Orchard Street tenement and either fell or jumped from the hallway window or the roof. An ambulance took her to the hospital where, with her last breath, she identified herself. The police got the address where Papa worked and brought him home.

"Stop talking in there and go to sleep!" Papa shouted through the tissue thin walls separating our bedroom from the kitchen.

"Yes, Papa. Goodnight, Papa," we replied.

But still we could not sleep and we could hear Papa talking with Tante Sonia: "It's not only that our first-born Solly died so horribly swallowing pieces of glass—ugh."

"It was an accident," Tante Sarah said. "As a mother I can understand how terrible it was, especially for Mollie. Normal people pull themselves together and go on living, but no, not your Mollie. Nathan, you must admit she was becoming more and more peculiar: always so moody and depressed. You told me yourself the arguments were getting worse."

"That's true. But now I realize she couldn't help herself. It wasn't just Solly's death that was eating at her."

"You mean finding out about Bashya and the other children?" Sonia asked.

"Yes. How would you feel to suddenly discover that your husband's first wife and two children were still alive in Poland? And that, in your mind at least, you were living in sin?"

"Nathan, that's nonsense! Everyone believed the reports about Bashya and the children being killed in the pogrom in Odessa. Who could know that a year later they would show up in Nesvizh, Poland—nearly 600 miles away. Besides, the Rabbi absolved you and Mollie and granted you the divorce from Bashya. Nathan, those things had absolutely nothing to do with Mollie throwing herself off a roof without a thought for her husband and children"

"Wow, did ya hear all that?" Alex whispered, poking me in the ribs.

"Yeah," I whispered back. "But what's a pogrom? And where's Odessa?"

"I dunno. But I know Tante Sonia's a big liar," Alex said, his voice rising above a whisper.

"Yeah she is," I agreed, also above a whisper.

"Aren't you two in there asleep yet?" Papa shouted. And probably he and Tante Sonia realized they better stop their own talking. The sliver of light under the kitchen door disappeared so we knew that the kitchen light had been turned off and then we heard fading footsteps out of the kitchen and Alex and I lay in total darkness listening to each others' breathing. After awhile I asked, "Alec, you sleeping?" And as an answer, there was only the deep breathing of one asleep.

But I couldn't sleep. My mind churned. Suddenly, I understood an experience about a year before involving Mama, broken glass and me. We had gone to the roof to hang out the laundry. Henny was asleep with Alex as babysitter. It had rained and there were glistening puddles galore all over the pitted roof. The sun raced from puddle to puddle and I raced the sun across the slippery tar. I slipped and fell—my arms outstretched to brace myself against the fall. My right hand crunched into something jagged and sharp—a broken bottle. Bright red blood gushed forth.

I was more frightened than hurt at first, but quickly a dull, aching pain spread from my hand up through my arm to the shoulders. And all the while the blood continued gushing.

"Mama, Mama" I yelled. "I fell on glass. My hand hurts!"

Mama's eyes and mouth were wide open and she stood very still for a moment and then yelled: "No! No God! Not again!" And she picked me up and raced down the four flights to Dr. Friedman's office. It was a good thing that he was in to give the necessary first aid; a half-dozen stitches in the right hand opposite the thumb, a little below the vein and artery of the wrist. I had never seen my mother look so white and wide-eyed. She wrung her hands, moaning and rocking herself back and forth.

"Now Mollie, relax," Dr. Friedman said. "Sholem is very lucky. Another inch higher and he would have cut his artery and that would have been very bad. But everything is all right now."

Mama moaned and rocked. "God is reminding me. He is punishing me. He will never let me forget."

"Don't be foolish," Dr. Friedman replied. "Be grateful to God for sparing this child."

Mama shook her head and we returned to our flat. I was delighted with Alex's attention to my heavily bandaged hand and with his interest in all my details of what had happened. Mama settled herself into what was now her favorite corner and swayed back and forth moaning: "Why don't you leave me alone—please stop; please leave me alone." And Alex and I stared at each other but said nothing.

I lay in bed upset by the recollection. Alex began to snore but I hesitated to poke him awake as I usually did. I wasn't in the mood to start a fight. The things Tante Sonia said about Mama also troubled me: about Mama becoming more and more peculiar. And yet...Tante Sonia wasn't the only one who felt that way. I recalled another incident not long ago.

Mama and I were down in the candy store on the street level of our tenement—the social center for the entire block. Mama was very careful in dealing with the proprietor. "Max, what can you do for us today?"

"How about a nice egg cream, Mollie," Max answered.

Some older boys in the candy store whispered, giggled and pointed to Mama.

"Hey Mollie! How are you today?"

Max warned the boys. "Behave yourselves or get out!"

But they kept it up. "Hear any voices lately, Mollie?" one asked.

"Is the bogeyman after you, Mollie?" a second boy followed up.

Mama looked hurt. "Stop it. Why don't you leave me alone?"

"Ha, ha—Meshugeneh Mollie. Ya, ya, crazy Mollie."

"That's enough!" Max said. "Out—get out! From Jewish boys yet! You should all be ashamed. I'm very sorry, Mollie."

Mama nodded and got up, took my hand and we returned to our apartment both of us very upset. She went to her usual corner to moan and rock back and forth and I went to my bedroom bewildered.

I lay in the dark still bewildered. And I must have dozed off after all for the next thing I knew Alex was shaking me ordering me to: "Getup! Today is Mama's funeral."

"Mama's funeral?" I repeated. Funerals are for dead people. Oh, yeah. Mama is dead; she's not coming back, I thought. And the next thing I knew, Clara Stein, our upstairs neighbor's fifteen-year old daughter came down to baby-sit Henny while the rest of the family went to the funeral.

The funeral parlor was located at the corner of our block on the opposite side of the street. It filled rapidly with friends, neighbors and our handful of relatives.

"You notice that the relatives are all from Nathan's side of the family? Nobody's here from Mollie's side," one of the neighbors whispered.

I wondered: Was it really possible that Mama was all alone in America except for Papa? Didn't every "greeneh" have to have a sponsor? Who was Mama's sponsor? Why wasn't he here? I turned to my brother, "Alec, is the whole family here?"

"I dunno. Let's ask cousin Harry."

To get to Harry, Tante Sonia's 12-year old son, at the opposite end of the funeral parlor, we pushed through lots of adults moving around and passed a narrow, six-foot long wood box placed in the middle of the room—which was in everybody's way.

"Hesh, is the whole family here?" Alex asked.

Cousin Harry, short, brown-haired and blue-eyed replied: "Well, the family in America is here. Those in Russia ain't here."

"Russia? Who's in Russia?" I asked.

Harry answered that at one time there were grandparents, two uncles and thirteen aunts back in Russia. But whether any of them were still alive after the World War, the Russian Revolution and Civil War and all the pogroms—he wasn't sure. "I'll ask my mother," he said. He started toward Tante Sonia who suddenly let out a shriek and hurled herself upon the long, narrow box. "Mollie! Mollie! What have you done? Why, Mollie? Why?"

Cousin Harry stopped short, open-mouthed. Alex and I stared, too. I asked Harry: "Why is she doing that, Hesh? What's in the big box?" And he looked at me like I was so dumb.

"That's the coffin your mother is in, you dope," he answered.

I shook my head. No, it couldn't be.

Papa, eyes red and puffed, tried to console his sister and to pry her loose from the coffin. But Tante Sonia continued screaming: "Mollie, why did you do this to my brother? And to your children? To me? Mollie . . . Mollie Why?" Her shrieking started a chorus of wails, moans and screams and the pulling of hair and beating of breasts.

Frightened, I clutched Alex's arm and saw tears streaming down his cheeks. Everyone was in tears—except me! Mrs. Stein's fat, hulking frame suddenly stood over me: "Sholem, why aren't you crying? Your poor mama lies in that coffin and you just stand there. For shame! What kind of son are you?"

Now filled with fear and shame, I started to cry while Mrs. Stein walked off satisfied.

Alex put his arm around me. "Aw, don't listen to that fat dope."

Having witnessed the episode, Cousin Esther Gold, from Philadelphia, came towards us. She smiled, sat on a nearby chair and gathered the two of us around her. "Boys, do you know what has happened? Do you understand what is happening now?"

Alex nodded so I started to nod too, but caught myself "No!" I blurted. "Why did Mama hafta die?"

Esther blinked back the tears. "Your mama's gone to heaven to be with her parents, her Uncle Moishe and your little brother, Solly."

"Who's Uncle Moishe?" Alex asked.

"He was your mama's sponsor. He died shortly after she married your papa." And then Esther cleared her throat and pulled us closer to her. "Your mama became very sick because of so many bad things happening."

"Like Solly swallowing glass and dying?" I asked.

Esther nodded. "Yes, that amongst other things."

Then Alex asked Esther if she knew about Papa's first wife and children.

Her eyes widened. She looked at her husband, Ben, standing behind her and then back at us. "So you know about that, too? Well, you might as well hear the whole story." She cleared her throat again and continued: "You know, there was this poet, Robert Burns, who once wrote that the best plans often go astray—they don't work out. And I'm afraid that's what happened to your papa. He came to America from Odessa—that's in Ukrainia—a part of Russia—alone, without his wife Bashya and their two children, Manya and Herschel."

"Why didn't he take them with him?" I interjected.

Alec elbowed me and said: "Why don't you stop interrupting and let Cousin Esther tell the story'

"It's a good question." Esther said. "Most immigrants couldn't afford to take their families. So, like your Papa, Nathan, they came alone, worked very hard and saved every penny to bring over their families. But, in the year that Nathan worked and saved in America another problem developed in Odessa with Nathan's youngest sister, your Tante Sonia. The family convinced Nathan to have Sonia go to America on his wife's visa and passport. Naturally the children wouldn't go without their mother, so Sonia came alone to Nathan in America.

Now Alex interrupted with a question: "What was the problem with Tante Sonia?"

"Well, that's not important right now. The important thing is that everybody thought this would be only a short delay for Bashya and her children and nobody expected the Great War, the Russian Revolution, Civil War and all the pogroms; the one in Kharkov wiped out your Momma's entire family. She was lucky to have gone to America before the war. And the pogrom in Odessa killed most of the Jews there. Your papa was notified that his whole family, including Bashya and the children were killed. And when Nathan went to a Memorial Service, that's where he met your mother, Mollie. And they married—maybe too quickly, because about a year later Nathan heard from Bashya's home town in Poland that she and the children showed up"

"How come they weren't killed in the pogrom?" Alex asked.

"Yeah, and how come it took so long to find out?" I chimed in.

Cousin Esther fidgeted in her chair. "Well, I don't know everything. But we were told that Bashya and her children were put into the secret cellar that the family in Odessa had built and they hid there for more than a day before coming out. The whole house was burnt to the ground. It was very dangerous so Bashya and the children hid during the day and traveled only a few miles each night. And even though Nesvizh, her home town in Poland, was only 550 miles away, it took almost a year to get to her home."

The wailing and weeping ended as Esther finished her story. "The services are about to begin so you boys will have to sit in front with your Papa," she said.

The story of Bashya and her children was sad. But it also raised my hopes. See—everyone thought she and her children were dead—and they weren't after all! The same was probably true of Mama. I went with Alex to join Papa sitting up front beside the casket. Behind us sat our small American family; neighbors and friends filled the other chairs. The cantor sang the "Song of the Dead" and the weeping began again, but not as loud this time.

The Rabbi, a short man with a long white beard, large square skull cap and long black coat covered by a full prayer shawl spoke softly in Yiddish and Hebrew: "What is man? In the morning he ariseth—only to be cut down at night."

I didn't understand. Mama was not a man. And who cuts down? And why? "Papa, what is he saying?" I asked.

"Sha—shtill" Papa commanded.

The Rabbi continued: "Such a young woman—in her prime—what are we to believe? We are created in God's image. To destroy oneself is to destroy God! I want to believe that Mollie would not want to destroy God."

What is he talking about? I knew my mother would never want to destroy anyone, least of all God. All these words.

The voice droned on. "And so dear bereaved family..." I looked at Alex. He was looking at the long, narrow box—the coffin. Hesh said my mother was in there. She couldn't be. It was so narrow—and looked so very uncomfortable.

And then the Rabbi's voice boomed: "But there remains a bereaved husband and three helpless children—who will care for them?"

And suddenly Tante Sonia screamed: "I will care for them: Yes—I will look after all of them—my brother and his children. Your children, Mollie! I will care for all of them!"

The Rabbi looked surprised as if he didn't expect a direct answer to his question. "Of course my dear Sonia, of course!" And then he adjusted his prayer shawl and continued as Papa comforted his sister. "Who is to say what God has in mind?

Who is to question his ways? The Almighty is merciful and he will forgive. We will go to the synagogue to ask his understanding."

The Rabbi stepped down, the coffin was wheeled out and put inside a black automobile, which was called a hearse, and it moved so slowly down Willett Street around the corner to the large synagogue on Orchard Street. And we walked sadly and very slowly—because the hearse was moving so slow—behind the hearse until it came in front of the shul. But the coffin was not carried inside but left in the hearse with its rear doors left open. The Rabbi walked up a few steps and turned to explain that because there was some question of Momma's killing herself—suicide I think he said—the casket could not be brought into the sanctuary itself.

And now Papa was very angry and he yelled: "Nein, it was an accident! It is not right what you are saying and doing!"

Cousin Esther calmed Papa down and the Rabbi nodded and went on. "The Almighty is compassionate. He understands and he forgives. We will now recite the Kaddish," which is the mourner's prayer Cousin Esther whispered to us. And the Rabbi said the prayer with Papa, Tante Sonia and everybody joining in. Even though Alex and I did not know the words to the prayer we mouthed the sounds. Then the back doors of the hearse were closed and from around the corner a few larger, black cars came to take us to the cemetery.

I had never been inside a cemetery. It was not a pretty sight. There was one row after another of headstones, some large, but most very small, close together, crowding upon each other just like the East Side ghetto tenements. Was it deliberately designed so that those coming to their final resting place could be in familiar congested surroundings?

We left the limousines and walked past a few rows of monuments to a freshly dug hole, on one side of which rested the coffin. I looked around the circle of faces, red eyes and tear-stained cheeks. Papa bit his lower, quivering lip. His right hand clutched Alex, who, in turn held my hand. Tante Sonia, her husband Chaim, and their three sons stood stone-faced around the grave. And rounding out the family were cousins Esther and Ben. Behind them were the Steins and some other neighbors. Suddenly it began to rain and I thought that even the sky was crying for my mother. The men with the shovels shifted from one foot to another, as if they were impatient.

Someone from Papa's Landsmanshaft Fraternal and Burial Society came forward and said some things and I felt Alex poking me in the ribs and saw him pointing to the casket being lowered into the hole in the ground.

It was then that I felt the fill impact of my mother's death and a panic seized me as I burst into tears. Lower and lower went the coffin! My mother was in that coffin! "Mama! Mama! Come back, Mama!" I shouted in Yiddish and lunged towards the open grave.

Papa grabbed me. "Sha mein kind," he whispered hoarsely. "Be strong-and happy. Mama now goes to heaven."

"I want Mama!" I cried. But the casket now rested on the bottom and Papa, to my horror, stepped forward, took a shovel, loaded it with soil and threw it into the hole! The thud of the soil and pebbles hitting the coffin sent shivers through me. Uncle Chaim followed Papa's action and then Cousins Ben and Esther took their turns

Tante Sonia scooped up a handful of soil and threw it in. Then Alex threw in his handful. Now it was my turn. But I refused!

"Sholem, you must do this!" Papa commanded.

"I don't want to!" I cried.

"You must" everyone yelled.

Frightened, I gave in. I picked up one small stone and

dropped it gently into my mother's grave. It hit the casket with a dull thud, and Mollie, my mother, found her eternal rest.

THE END

"This story first appeared (with minor modifications) in the book 'The Hebrew National Orphan Home; Memories of Orphanage Life'. Edited by Ira A. Greenberg, Richard G. Safran and Sam George Arcus. Published by Bergin & Garvey of the Greenwood Publishing Group of Westport, Connecticut in November 2001."

V. MOLLIE'S PERSPECTIVE

Heaven is a nice place, Mr. Interviewer, but I would have liked a few more years in the YENNERVELT...the OTHER WORLD...to spend with my children and my husband. Only a few more years, even though YENNERVELT gave me more than my share of grief. Believe me, more than my share. You see, I was only 34 years old when it happened and even in 1929 that was considered quite young. Yes, only 34 and with three young children: Alex 8 and 1/2, Sholem 7, and Henrietta—we nicknamed her 'Yenta'—a mere baby of only 2 years.

You want to know what the "it" was? Well people down there argued for a long time whether I jumped or fell—whether it was suicide or an accidental fall. I'm not sure myself now. I'll admit, I did go there to end it all. But when I stood there on the roof of the Orchard Street tenement on New York's lower East Side, looking down, I thought of my children—and yes, even of my husband Nathan and I think I changed my mind. It's all so hazy now.

You know, even though one has tzores—you know, troubles and problems, still being apart from one's children is an even greater agony. As I stood on the ledge I saw my poor, sweet innocents, without a mother. I thought: Who would care for them, my husband, Nathan? Oh he's a good man, for the most part; a good father who tried so hard to be fair to everyone. But he's a man—a father, not a mother. So who—my sister-in-law Sonia? How could I trust HER after all the troubles she caused?

I'm not a learned woman, but I know that since we are created in God's image, to kill oneself is to kill God. And I did not wish to kill anyone, especially the Almighty—even though he had not treated me kindly. Yes, I had sinned, but it was unknowing and unintentional. And God's punishment was much too severe. I thought about all these things, as I stood there dizzy and swaying, looking down into the dirty backyards of the tenements.

"Jump and be done with it!" a voice in my head said.

"No! No! Think of your children, of your family. You are a young woman. The problems will press themselves out," another voice said. It was all so confusing!

You ask: 'What could drive a person to kill herself?" Mind you, I still can't say for sure whether I did commit suicide. But I assure you that people can be driven to destroy themselves because life on Earth can be a living hell.

What? Are you sure you want to hear about it? Well, as a child in Kharkov life was very difficult for my two brothers, my dear parents and me. We were very poor, and yet the goyim—the gentiles, you know—taunted and persecuted us, day in and day out, year after year. So we were very happy to hear from Uncle Moishe in America that he had saved enough to bring at least one of us to America. He wanted Mama—his sister—to come first, but Mama and Papa and my brothers all insisted that I should be the first one to go. I didn't want to go alone, or be the first, but they insisted because the persecution was becoming worse with more killings and raping. I was an attractive girl—pardon my immodesty—and my family feared for me. So I came to America alone.

I was happy living with Uncle Moishe but I was also lonely for my family in Kharkov. We worked hard scraping together the pennies that would now bring over another member of my family—this time, Mama for sure. And then The Great War broke out in 1914. There was nothing to do but wait and pray—and we prayed, believe me, we prayed!

But as if the Great War wasn't enough, then came the Russian Revolution and after that the Civil War and the war with Poland and the pogroms, always the pogroms. And then... then. Oh God, I'm sorry. I cannot go on, please excuse me Mr. Interviewer while I compose myself.

All right. As I was about to say, then came the pogroms, by White Russians, and Red Russians, by Poles and Ukrainians. Does it matter by whom? When it comes to slaughtering Jews you must get in line. My mother, father and two brothers were butchered! For no reason except that they were Jews. And I was alone, except for Uncle Moishe, in a big, strange, goyishe land. I felt that somehow I was to blame. At least Mama would be alive if Uncle Moishe had his first choice. I came in Mama's place. Mama was dead and I was alive. Uncle Moishe said I was a silly girl. That it was bashert, ordained by God. It was God's will and that he worked his wonders in mysterious ways. And who was I to question God's will. So, I wiped my eyes and blew my nose and tried to accept God's strange will.

I met Nathan at a Delancy Street Memorial Service for the victims of the pogroms. We had something in common. He lost his wife and two children in a pogrom in Odessa—a place in Ukraine on the Black Sea. Such a terrible thing to have in common! He was a fine looking fellow, well built, with sparkling blue eyes, a big grin and thinning brown hair. Even then I knew he would be bald, but still I found him attractive.

He seemed to have overcome his grief more quickly than I and was helpful to me in my pain. We married within two weeks. His sister, Sonia, her husband, Chaim and their three boys came to the wedding, as did Uncle Moishe. It was a small and simple affair, and for the first time in years I felt happy. It was a strange feeling.

But then, as if God couldn't stand my being happy even for a moment, a run-a-way truck killed Uncle Moishe. Right on the sidewalk! Why? What had he done to deserve such a terrible fate? What had I done? Was I not entitled to a little bit of happiness? Again I was told that it was bashert. I was tired of things being bashert and I guess I was becoming difficult—and even a little envious of Nathan. Yes, envious. After all, he had his sister Sonia, brother-in-law Chaim and three nephews. And here I was all-alone in the world. Nathan tried to be helpful; he said his family was my family. I really tried to believe that but it was not really so, especially with Sonia. She acted like my friend in front of people, but I began to feel that she really resented me and talked about me behind my back. I couldn't understand this—until much later.

Anyway, Nathan and I began to quarrel a lot. Until we learned that I was pregnant with Solomon and peace and contentment settled in. And after Solomon was born we lost no time in my again becoming pregnant. "We have to make up for the loss of many," Nathan said. And I was again happy with my husband, my little Solomon and the new life in my womb. And I thought, finally a new world was beginning for us.

And again God intervened with his mysterious and painful ways! One day when Solomon was just two months old, Nathan received a letter from Neshvizh, a place in Poland. I tell you I will never forget the look on Nathan's face as he finished reading that letter. It was as if someone had stuck a knife in his belly.

I asked him "What is the matter? What does the letter say?"

He didn't answer but only staggered to a chair and dropped into it. His mouth was open and his eyes staring into space.

"Nathan," I said, "you're white as a sheet. Who is the letter from and what does it say?"

He still said nothing but just gave me the letter.

"But Nathan," I said, "You know I can't read—or write. Why do you embarrass me so?" And I handed the letter back to him.

He shook his head. "I'm sorry. I forgot. Well the letter is from a Rabbi in Nesvizh and he says that my first wife, Bashya, and my daughter Manya, and son Herschel suddenly returned to Neshvizh—Bashya's home town in Poland—after spending almost a year traveling only 600 miles from Czipowitz, my home town near Odessa. The Rabbi also says that I'm a very fortunate man and that the Almighty is very compassionate."

I couldn't believe my ears! "But I thought they were murdered in the pogrom!" I said "And why did it take a year for them to travel only 600 miles?" I asked.

"I was so informed. And so I believed. And I don't know why it took so long for them to travel that distance." Nathan answered. And then he sat like a golem, eyes wide and mouth grim.

I remember screaming: "Another one of God's mysterious wonders!"

"Don't blaspheme!" Nathan shouted back at me. And we had a terrible quarrel. Oh my head hurts from remembering.

Nathan went to our Rabbi on Willet Street, who issued him a divorce from Bashya... how do you say it... ? Well yes, I guess that's the word...retroactively... to when he learned of her so-called death. And that seemed to solve everything... at least for Nathan, Sonia and everyone. But it solved nothing for me. How can a piece of paper say something was not so when the reality showed it was so? We quarreled constantly, violently. Even though he was officially divorced from Bashya, he started sending money to Poland because our Rabbi said he should because it was part of the agreement. Money we could hardly afford. And that was cause for more arguments. And nothing anyone said could convince me that I was not living in sin. And one day God proved it by working another of his mysterious wonders.

I left Solomon alone with his glass of milk while I went to hang out the wash at the kitchen window. He was nine months old, old enough to hold the small glass. Suddenly I heard him scream and I rushed into the bedroom and found him in a pool of blood; blood coming from his mouth and his hands. Blood everywhere. I picked him up and rushed down the street to Dr. Freedman, who wasn't in. I rushed up and down the street: "Someone... help me! Please! Help me!" But no one would help. Everybody held back, afraid because of all the blood. Then it was too late! My baby died in my arms from swallowing broken glass! My sweet, innocent baby...to die so horribly. Was not God punishing me? For living in sin, he took my first-born!

Everybody tried to tell me it was a tragic accident. Suddenly it was not bashert but only "an accident". All the earlier tragedies were bashert, preordained, God's will. Now we merely have a "tragic accident." Ah, Mr. Interviewer, can we stop for a while and do you mind if I get up and walk around? It relieves me to do so. I thank you.

All right. I'm ready to continue. So, a few months after Solomon's tragic death my son Alexander was born. We called him "Elek" a beautiful baby. Nathan wanted other children and we quarreled about my resistance in bed. But how do you deny a robust man his needs? Sholem was born a year and a half after Elek. And all the time, the letters from Poland kept coming and Nathan kept sending money—which I felt—I'm sorry but I must say it—which was coming from the mouths of my children. I didn't think it was right to have more children. So, how does one not have children? In those days, who of us orthodox Jews knew anything about controlling birth—other than abstinence? Was I wrong? Well, the quarrels grew more heated.

And then there was Sonia! She joined her brother in urging me to have more children. "You need a daughter, Mollie," she said laughing.

But for me it was not a laughing matter. "How can I be sure to give birth to a daughter?" I asked her. "Knowing God's will, I'd probably give birth to triplet boys." And so I continued to resist. And that's when Nathan began staying out late—sometimes all night! And the arguments grew worse. Oh, now I realize I couldn't really blame him. As I said, a robust, vibrant man must have his sexual needs met, one-way or another. And finally I realized that he was right. I had to behave like a wife. And so, five years after Sholem's birth I delivered a daughter, Henrietta, or "Yenta" as we nicknamed her. Such a joy! Perhaps having a girl was a good omen, we thought. And so, again for a short time we were happy.

But still the letters from Poland kept coming. The money going to Poland made it very difficult for me to make ends meet, because now there were five mouths to feed, and five bodies to clothe. Nathan could not—or would not—understand this.

"Why are you such a poor manager?" he always yelled at me. "What happens to all the money I give you?"

"If you didn't send so much to Poland, I'd be able to manage better here." I felt terrible saying such things. I knew Bashya and her children were barely surviving. Still, this was not my doing. And why should my children suffer? This last I did not say, but only thought it—and I felt ashamed for even thinking it.

"A good wife would be able to manage with whatever she got. Your trouble is you brood too much. You can't manage either the money, or the children!" Nathan yelled at me one day.

What did he mean about "managing" the children? He was referring to Solomon, wasn't he? I was shocked.

"You are blaming me for Solomon's death? All along it was a tragic accident, and now you are blaming me!"

Now it was Nathan's turn to be surprised. He suddenly calmed down and came to me and tried to embrace me. But I shuddered and moved away.

"No, no, Mollie. I wasn't even thinking of Solomon. I'm not blaming you. It was not your fault. It was an accident. Please believe that."

I ran into the bedroom and slammed the door and cried and cried. Because you see, I really felt that it was my fault.

Well, things went from bad to worse between us. It's true; Nathan had a short and violent temper. But he was also quick to cool while I tended to pout and seethe inside. Unfortunately, the children overheard our many arguments. How could they not? The walls were tissue thin on the lower East Side. Worse, the children sensed my unhappiness and increasing despair. But I couldn't help myself. The many tragedies kept coming back to haunt me. Do you know what it is to live with ghosts, Mr. Interviewer? I feared getting up in the morning. I feared going to bed at night. I feared everybody and everything. I literally shook. Neighbors noticed my condition and the neighborhood children poked fun at me. They called me "Meshugeneh—crazy—Mollie." I couldn't walk down the street without being taunted: "Ya, ya, Meshugeneh Mollie! See any ghosts today, Mollie? Hear any funny voices today, Mollie?"

Perhaps I was meshuga in some ways. Aren't we all? Certainly I was very upset. And Nathan was hardly understanding. He would explode: "Pull yourself together. I've told you many times Solomon's death was an accident. Nobody's blaming you. Take care of the three lovely children we have now, instead of brooding all the time over our first-born."

As if I had suffered only that one tragedy—although that one alone would be enough to drive anyone to despair. No! He completely dismissed all the terrible things I had suffered, all of God's mysterious wonders! Oh Nathan, where was your understanding, your compassion or even your love?

Sonia? You ask about Sonia? I finally realized that she was playing both ends against the middle. She had her own guilt to handle. Yes, guilt! Didn't I tell you? Well, If it weren't for her, Bashya and her children would be in America and who knows whom I would have ended up with. You see, Nathan had scraped together the money for Bashya and the children to come to America. But Sonia had become involved with a Russian soldier—a goy. The family had always had trouble-controlling Sonia. So they persuaded Nathan to allow Sonia to use Bashya's visa and passport to come to America. But naturally, the children (Manya and Herschel) refused to go without their mother. So, for Bashya and the children it was to be only a temporary delay. But before Nathan could send for them the Great War broke out followed by the Russian Revolution and Civil War and the pogroms—like I told you before. So, how do you think Sonia felt at the news of Bashya's and her children's' deaths? And then how do you imagine she felt about the news of their being alive? Yet somehow, all of her feelings were directed against me. Sonia was always a vain and self-centered person and one who twists things around. What? Yes, manipulative is the word. She pushed Nathan to marry me so quickly after we met at the memorial service. But later, when she heard of Bashya's being alive, suddenly I was the one who tricked her brother into a quick marriage. And remember, she was the one who urged me to have a daughter. Oh, that Sonia! We argued a lot—as if the arguments with my husband—her brother—were not enough!

I so wanted her to be my friend. Sisters-in-law should be friends. But I suppose that was not bashert. Only the bad is bashert. So, I was fighting with my husband and my sister-in-law. I was the butt of the neighborhood. My own children were becoming more and more frightened of me. The letters from Poland kept coming—and the money kept going. Everywhere I turned I was trapped. The past, and present and even future were closing in on me. I was alone, Mr. Interviewer. So alone! Do you know what it is to be alone, really alone? I was so frightened. So very frightened. I went to Orchard Street. I walked up the four flights to the roof. I was tired, lonely, guilty and afraid. Yes, I did want to end it all. I wanted to join my mother, father and brothers—and my Uncle Moishe and my baby Solomon. I stood on the roof ledge. I looked down. It was dizzying. And then I thought of Elek, Sholem and Yenta. Yes, even of Nathan and Sonia. No! I would not do it! God must work his wonders in other mysterious ways using other people for a change. And that's all I remember. Did I jump? Did I fall? God only knows.

THE END FOR MOLLIE

VI. TANTE SONIA'S STORY

No one feels more sorry for my sister-in law Mollie's sudden death than me. And certainly no one is more upset about what her death did to my brother, Nochem—Nathan— and to his three lovely and now motherless children. As you may know, I tried to look after them after Mollie's death— which I still believe was suicide in spite of what my brother and others think or say. Yes, she threw herself off the roof of the tenement on Orchard Street because she could no longer stand her torment—which she told me about many times. There is no question that it overwhelmed her. Another strong person might have coped with it, but Mollie was, unfortunately not a strong person. And I don't say this to blame her—it's just that's the way she was.

I do believe we were friends, because she did confide in me and I tried to be helpful to her. She was a tall, thin but attractive woman who was also very tense and nervous. And here again, she had good reason for that, since her whole family was wiped out in the pogrom in Kharkov and then her Uncle Moishe was killed suddenly by a runaway truck so soon after she married my brother. I know she kept expressing her guilt over the fact that she had come over to America in place of her mother and so when her mother was killed in the pogrom she felt that somehow she was responsible. She was alive and her mother was dead.

But we all had tragedies like that happen to us. For instance, Nochem—Nathan and me—we lost our whole family in Czipowitz/Odessa around the same time! I was with Nathan when he received the official news that our entire family—mother, father, two brothers and 12 sisters and Nochem's first wife Bashya and her two children, all were murdered in the pogrom there! But we picked ourselves up and went on living. But Mollie, poor soul, would spend hours grieving and holding herself personally responsible. And if it wasn't over her mother and family in Kharkov it was over the terrible accident with her first-born Solly dying from swallowing broken glass. Oy! Poor Mollie would sit for hours in a corner in her apartment swaying back and forth and moaning. I know because my dear brother Nochem would tell me about her doing such things.

And then Nathan unexpectedly heard from Nesvizh—that's Bashya's hometown in Poland. He got a letter from the Rabbi, saying that she and her two children Manya and Herschel had arrived from Czipowitz/Odessa after nearly a year traveling. They had not been killed in the pogrom there after all! Wasn't that wonderful news? But when Nathan told Mollie about it, she went almost completely mad, screaming that she was married to a bigamist and that her three American children were bastards! Normally a person would be pleased to learn that people first thought to be dead were actually alive and that person would shout "praise be to G-d!" I would think.

What took them so long in traveling only about 500-600 miles? I don't know. And yes, as you say, that long delay, together with our believing the official reports of their deaths in the pogrom probably did contribute to Nochem's quick marriage to Mollie. Mind you, I told my brother not to be in such a rush, but like me, once he makes his mind up there's no stopping him from doing what he wants. And yes, I can understand Mollie's thinking of herself and her children as being illegitimate and initially reacting the way she did. It was indeed a problem.

Well, the Rabbis in New York finally solved that problem by giving Nathan a divorce effective as of the time when Bashya and her children were reported dead, and he readily agreed, generous soul that he always is—to send whatever money he could to help them over in Poland. And even though I could understand Mollie's upset over having money go out of her household, I thought it strange that she would begrudge Bashya and her children such little help.

What? Yes, that story about me coming over to America using Bashya's visa and passport is true. But I believe that the story about the how and why has become very distorted and I think now is the time for me to tell you what really happened over there at that time.

SONIA'S STORY

Bashya and I were not only sisters-in-law but also very good friends. As you probably know, I had twelve other sisters and I was the youngest who also happened to be the same age as Bashya—about 18 or 19. Our family was quite prosperous, certainly for Jews. The family had a horse business; buying, selling, trading horses and everything that went with that. In fact, the Erkes Horses became the official service establishment for the local constabulary—something unheard of for Jews before then. And it meant that our family had more gesheft—business or contacts with the goyim than Jews generally did.

Well, you know, being a part of a very large family had its advantages but also it had its disadvantages. Especially with so many girls, I think there were more disadvantages than advantages. It's hard to explain, but let me try; you see, among us Jews, especially in the Ukraine, there are all these rituals and customs about courting; you know going out with boys and such. And the most important of these customs is that a younger sister should not start courting before an older sister! It simply is not regarded as proper. So, imagine my situation being the youngest girl of the thirteen! Added to that, courting was not permitted to begin before a shidach—you know, a match—was arranged by the matchmaker. And with many older sisters before me, I saw myself as being a very old lady before my time would come according to the prescribed rituals and customs. And added to that I was, pardon my immodesty, a very attractive girl. And as I've already told you, I was eighteen going on nineteen! There had to be a better system, I argued with my parents and most of my older sisters. My three brothers agreed with me, you should know, but not all my sisters.

On top of all this, my parents were very particular about accepting matches proposed by the matchmaker. After all, we were the "rich" Erkes horse dealers and really above the rest of the community. So where do you find the appropriate young Jewish men for all the Erkes girls? And as I already explained, our family had more contact with the goyim than the average Jewish family. And since I was helping out in the store selling horse feed and supplies, I met many non-Jewish people, including many of the soldiers who came into the store for supplies.

I see that you are smiling. Perhaps you are thinking: "that's not such a terrible problem what with all the other problems Jews faced." And in a way I have to agree with you. Except, at the time, for me it was a great problem—because who can control where the heart connects? Yes, my heart connected with a very handsome and loveable young soldier in his majesty's army. He came in regularly, every week for his supplies and as we talked we were attracted to each other. And one day our hands touched on the counter and my face must have become red as borsht and he laughed and apologized. But then Mikhail—that was his name—managed for our hands to touch often. He would linger in the store and we would talk. He told me that there was Jewish blood in his veins since his grandfather was Jewish but converted and married a shikse—a non-Jew.

My mother noticed what was happening and she cautioned me not just once, but also several times. I told her about Mikhail's grandfather having been Jewish and she thought about that for a while and said she would talk with my father about that. But my father dismissed the whole idea as being out of the question. Jews trace their being Jewish through their mothers. Having a Jewish grandfather who converted out of the Jewish religion was worse, as far as he was concerned, than being a goy for generations! And besides, there were still seven of my older sisters needing to be matched! And after being matched, to begin courting.

NOCHEM GOES TO AMERICA AND SONIA'S SECRET COURTSHIP

Again my three brothers, especially Nochem, were more sympathetic. But then Nochem took off for America, leaving Bashya and Manya, then a little more than two and half years old and Herschel, only a few months, old behind. The plan was for him to work in America, save the necessary money and then send for Bashya and the children. It was a good plan, one that many Jews were doing. Although, frankly I wondered why he had to do it the hard way when our family was so prosperous. But then Papa never discussed business with girls or women. Meyer and Liebchik, my other two brothers, tried to explain to me that since the decision to go to America was Nochem's, then it was only fair that he pay his own way rather than have the family do so. But the reason why Nochem decided to go to America in the first place was because it was the tradition that the oldest son—in our family that is Meyer—should inherit the entire property and business because otherwise it would mean constantly splitting up the inheritance among so many children with the result that very little would remain. And because the family would not pay for Nochem's going to America, he agreed to serve the two-year terms in the army for both his brothers in return for $200 from each of them. That's why Nochem served six years in the army and saved $200; and that plus the $400 from his two brothers gave him the $600 he needed to go to America. So, even though it's all tradition, I still don't understand why it wasn't fair to help Nochem with the expenses of going to America and yet fair for one person to inherit everything a family has! But then, I'm only a woman.

But you're right; I'm straying from my main story—my falling in love with the Russian soldier who had a Jewish grandfather. Well, you can guess that my parents forbid me from continuing to have any gesheft—dealings—with Mikhail. But they couldn't prohibit him from coming to the store. Well, Mama or one of my other sisters serving him solved that! But we did see each other secretly whenever we could. Which was not so easy, since he was still in the army and didn't have so much free time. But I swear we didn't do more than kiss and caress each other and I must admit this took a lot of self-restraint on both our parts.

This secret courtship went on for about a year or so. But when I say "secret" I'm not sure it was a secret from anybody. Although none of my family every caught us in any of our secret meetings, the whole family knew that we were seeing each other. Papa forbade me over and over again not to continue seeing Mikhail, but since they could never actually find us together there was little more that they could do.

And then one day Nochem wrote from America and sent money for Bashya and the kids to come to join him there. In expectation of that, they had arranged in advance to have their passports and visas ready. And now Papa suggested that I go to America in place of Bashya, and that it would be only a slight delay for Bashya. Naturally I refused to agree to do this. And I know that Bashya was not eager to do this, because she and I spoke about it and she told me so.

But Papa wrote to Nochem and—I don't actually know what he said to him in the letters, but after a while Nochem wrote to Bashya telling her that she would be doing a mitzvah—you know, a good deed—if she agreed to the plan. I'm not sure, but he also wrote something in the letter about Papa paying for my fare and expenses, so that the money sent for Bashya's fare and expenses could be saved for when it was time for her to come and join Nochem, me and the children in America. And so Bashya finally agreed to do what Nochem asked her to do.

But I still refused to be part of the scheme and Papa then threatened to turn me out of the house if I didn't agree to it. So what was I supposed to do? Mikhail and I talked about it a lot and he said that I should comply and that I should write to him from America and once he was discharged from his remaining year of service in the army he would make an effort to join me in America. In America, he said we could make a new life. It was a new country, with new ideas and this scheme could therefore be seen as a blessing in disguise. With Mikhail explaining it in this way, I finally agreed to the plan.

Except, now Manya and Herschel refused to go without their mother, Bashya, so I found myself on the ship, alone, going to America to join my brother Nochem!

SONIA IN AMERICA

What? Why should I feel guilty? You mean hearing about Bashya and the children's deaths after coming to America? Of course I was terribly upset when I heard the news, but I never felt it was my fault—like Mollie always felt it was her fault when her mother was killed in the pogrom in Kharkov because she came over in her mother's place. I'm a strong person. That's one of the differences between Mollie and me; although, as I said, we were friends. Sisters-in-law should be friends.

You ask what happened with Mikhail and his joining me in America? Oy! He was killed in an army training exercise and I was beside myself with grief. Nochem tried to console me with the nonsense about everything being bashert—you know, preordained, and that it was G-d's will. But maybe he was right after all, because, in America I met my first husband Chaim Bronstein and with him I had three sons. But again, I'm running ahead of the story.

Someone once said, or wrote, that even the best plans that people make don't always work out. What's that—a Scottish poet and writer? Yes, what did Robert Burns write? Oh, the best made plans of mice and men often don't work out? I don't know what mice have to do with it; it's bad enough that the plans of men and women don't work out. But we agree. Now as to how that applied to us in America and Bashya and her children in Czipowitz/Odessa. First of all, Bashya had to go and get a new visa and passport and tell the story that either she lost hers or that it was stolen. They decided to claim that the papers were stolen. Big mistake! Because she was told she had to report the theft to the police and only after the police completed their investigation—or reclaimed the documents, should Bashya come back to the immigration office.

Well, you know how such bureaucrats work! The case dragged on for months and naturally they could find nothing! And it was too late to go back and claim that the papers were lost and not stolen! And Bashya was still waiting for her new passport and visa when the Great War broke out in 1914. Which of course meant no more immigration from Russia, or all of Europe! And then, as you know, came the Russian Revolution and Civil War and worst of all, the pogroms!

And that brings us back to what we started talking about—Mollie's suicide. The arguments between my brother and my sister-in-law became more frequent and loud and many times Nochem—Nathan would come over to my apartment on Delancy Street, just around the corner from where he and Mollie and the children lived on Willett Street, to get away from the arguing. And he also complained about Mollie refusing to fulfill her wifely function yelling that she did not want to bring any more bastards into the world! And, being a man, he'd have to go elsewhere to have his needs and desires met. Oy, it was a very difficult life that my poor brother was living. And then Mollie threw herself off a roof somewhere on Orchard Street. I do not wish to speak ill of the dead. But poor Mollie killed herself without a thought for what this would do to her husband and her three lovely children!

After the funeral and burial, I tried caring for Yenta especially. She was only 2½ years old. Nochem—Nathan made arrangements for Elek and Sholem to stay and play in the after school program so that they would leave school about 4 pm. and then go eat at the corner delicatessen because their father came home from work as a presser after 7 pm. But even though I tried very hard to also check on the boys as well as care for Yenta, it was really too much and after a few months we had to put the boys in an orphanage way up in the countryside in a city called Yonkers and Yenta—whose real name was Henrietta—had to be put into the Israel Orphan Asylum right here in New York. And oy, that was not very easy either, I can tell you. My poor brother; that's what his wife Mollie did to him! And to her children! Mind you, I can understand what she must have been going through and I do not wish to speak ill of the dead...but poor Mollie and poor Nochem—Nathan and my poor nephews. What will happen to all of us?

END OF TANTE SONIA'S STORY

VII. NEW ARRIVALS (COMING TO THE HOME)

(A version of this first appeared in my book: *Deja Views Of An Aging Orphan*)

For a few months after our mother's death, in February 1929, our father, Nathan, tried to hold his American family together by having his sister, Tante Sonia, look after our two and a half year old sister Henny and arranging with a local delicatessen proprietor to feed Alex and me while he was off working as a presser in a garment factory. Alex was nine and I was 7 ½ years old. But these arrangements proved to be unsatisfactory and so in April 1929 Papa placed Alex and me in the Hebrew National Orphan Home located in an isolated, rural outskirt of Yonkers, and Henny in the Israel Orphan Asylum for infants and toddlers in New York City proper. This separation of brothers and sister was necessary because the HNOH accepted only boys beginning at age six.

The trip to the HNOH from 65 Willett Street on New York's lower east side took over three hours. The Home's social worker, Claire Fiance, accompanied us on this long, tortuous journey, which involved taking the Broadway/Seventh Avenue Interboro Rapid Transit (IRT) all the way to the end of the line at Van Courtland Avenue; then taking a trolley (streetcar) to a village known as Nepperhan; and from there slogging along an unpaved street called Tuckahoe Road for over two miles until we came to the four-storied, square, U-shaped, red brick building which formerly housed the German Odd Fellows Home.

Germans? Odd Fellows? That was not very reassuring. And why so far out? Ms. Fiance explained that it had been determined that fresh, country air was much superior to dirty ghetto air. As for the inconvenience for relatives in visiting their kids, well that was part of the price paid for the advantage. And on this bleak April day it rained all the way on our journey up Tuckahoe Road, so much so that the street was a sea of mud, and we boys took turns asking our father: "Papa why are you putting us here? Papa why can't we stay home? Papa, I'm wet and cold!"

The separation of father and sons at the HNOH orphanage was heart-rending, and the trip back to an empty apartment on Willett Street for Papa must have been unbearable. It could have been that at this time the thought occurred to Nathan Louis Arcus that all his problems could be resolved by the simple—although subsequent developments proved it to be other than simple plan of bringing Bashya (his first wife) and her children from Poland to America. And then we kids could be taken from our respective orphanages to join one re-created big, happy family! The Arcuses and the Erkeses together at last! (The family's name in Europe was originally Erkes. It was involuntarily changed at Ellis Island because of a failure to communicate—an all too common experience.)

As we (Papa, Alex, Ms. Fiance and I) approached the massive, fenced building on 407 Tuckahoe Road, trudged up the colonnaded front steps and entered through the heavy double doors, we encountered the portrait of a stern-looking personage in black robes and gold rimmed glasses peering down on us. Justice Aaron J. Levy, long-serving president of the Hebrew National Orphan Home, didn't even greet us with a smile.

We were brought into the office of the superintendent, a Mr. George Goldenberg. He at least greeted us with a smile and proceeded to sign some papers given to him by Ms. Fiance, while Papa, Alex and I stood by frightened and perplexed. Mr. Goldenberg returned the signed papers to Ms. Fiance, who then turned to Papa and said; "We better leave now Mr. Arcus, it's a long trip back to the city."

While we boys clung desperately to our father—who reciprocated with a bear-like embrace—a strange man and a woman entered the office. The man helped Papa disengage himself so that he could, ever so reluctantly, leave, his eyes filling with tears as we boys wailed our protests! With Papa gone, the man now took Alex by the hand and gently, but firmly, pulled him from my clutches. As he left, Alex turned to me to say: "Sammy, if I don't see you again, remember you have to say Kaddish (the mourner's prayer) for Mama."

Not knowing what was to happen next, I nevertheless answered that I would remember, adding, "Goodbye Alec" as he disappeared up the huge central stairway with his supervisor. And now the woman, Mrs. Rubenstein, took me by the hand also up the mysterious staircase to my dormitory, Company "E" on the third floor of the east wing of the massive building, passing the portrait of the still unsmiling president Levy. En route I pondered the loss of my mother and my baby sister and of my father and now my brother! I asked Mrs. Rubenstein where the man had taken my brother and she told me that, being older, he was assigned to Company "C&D", on the same floor but in the west wing. While relieved to learn that Alex was still in the same building, I wondered why we had been put into what seemed to be some kind of army place even though we were such small, young boys.

Mrs. Rubenstien and I arrived at the Company "E" dormitory—a long, narrow, hall-like room with one row of 30 army cots along the window wall and another 30 beds against the opposite wall with a narrow space of about five feet between them serving as the center corridor of the dormitory. I would learn that this was the smallest of the three dormitories, housing only 60 boys in contrast to the 130 each of the other two. I was assigned an iron-frame cot, told my number was #180 (which I would keep throughout my stay at the Home) and to watch the other boys and do as they did. At a given hand-signal, all of us stood rigidly at attention in front of our beds. At another hand-signal half the dorm went across the hall to the washroom to clean hands and faces.

On their return, the other 30 boys went to the washroom to do likewise, while the first 30 stood rigidly at attention in front of their cots. Upon the completion of this ritual, we all 60 of us, marched, in twos and in size-place down the stairs to the synagogue directly below our dorm for the afternoon/evening services. I thought I caught a glimpse of Alex in one of the rows of pews—but I couldn't be sure. When it was time for the mourners to come to the front of the synagogue to recite the Kaddish, however, Alek and I were momentarily re-united.

Only to again be separated as each of our companies marched separately to the dining hall for our supper, each company being segregated in its own section of the hall. Here too I was compelled to become quickly oriented to the regimentation and discipline of orphanage life. I was assigned to my table of eight and required to stand stiffly behind our respective chairs. At the hand-signal we all sat down. At another hand-signal we recited the prayer giving thanks to "The Lord Our God Who Bringest Forth the Bread From the Earth." And now we could eat—but not talk! Being famished from the long trip and the long day, I quickly devoured my small portion and looked for more. But rather than more food there was to be more prayer—again to thank the Lord for what we had just devoured.

And then Company "E", being the youngest and closest to the exit doors, rose in a body and marched out again in double file and size-place, silently, down to the Old Gym, to march endlessly around the six columns supporting the massive building. This was as punishment for some boys having violated the "no-talking-while-eating" rule and because it would help us to digest what we'd just eaten. Companies "A&B" and "C&D" marched to their respective dorms to receive a form of detention known as "Standing On Line"—something I would soon become very familiar with.

Such was my first day and evening at the Hebrew National Orphan Home. As we wearily trudged up the stairs to our dormitory, a boy whispered to me that it used to be worse when "The Colonel" was at the Home. I was told I was lucky because he had left about six months ago. I pondered my luck as I stood at attention in front of my cot, putting on my pajamas at the authorized hand-signal, going to the washroom at another signal, and finally climbing into bed at still another signal. And I wondered if we were nothing more than trained dogs. When the lights went out, so did my life's future—so it seemed. And then it all came crashing down on me as I began sobbing uncontrollably, trying to understand what was happening and why. Then Mrs. Rubenstein was there, comforting me. She stroked my head and brushed the tears from my cheeks and softly assured me that—in time—I would get used to it.

And in time, I did. I spent nearly 12 years at the HNOH and for most of those twelve years I kept hoping for that one, big happy family—which would only become a reality upon my marriage and the births of my son, daughter and later three granddaughters and one grandson.

A HAPPY ENDING IN THE FUTURE

FOOTNOTE:

For those interested in a fuller treatment of what it was like growing up in the HNOH read: *DEJA VIEWS OF AN AGING ORPHAN: Growing Up In The Hebrew National Orphan Home* by this same author; Xlibris Publishers, Philadelphia, PA. Also *The Hebrew National Orphan Home; Memories of Orphanage Life*; Edited by Ira A. Greenberg with Richard Safran and Sam George Arcus, Bergin & Garvey; Greenwood Publishers, Westport, CT.

VIII. COMPLETED JOURNEY

In March 1929 Bashya Erkes Friedman received a letter from her former husband Nochem (Nathan) in America telling of a very tragic and significant event that he and his children experienced the previous February.

Bashya and her children Manya and Herschel had been erroneously reported as having been murdered in the Czipowitz/Odessa pogrom of April 1918 and shortly after receiving this report Nochem/Nathan remarried and proceeded to have another family in America.

But Bashya and her children, having survived the pogrom, undertook a dangerous and uncertain journey from Czipowitz/Odessa to her family in Nesvizh, originally part of Belorussia but later a part of Poland—a distance of 550 miles which took them eleven months to cover! Once in Nesvizh Bashya again made efforts to contact Nochem/Nathan, this time with success, only to receive back a reply informing her of Nathan's second marriage and second family. He promised, however to help financially as best he could and for a time he kept his word. But after losing a well-paying job and having to settle for one paying much less, his financial support dwindled to a pittance or nothing for months. And so the correspondence between them also dwindled.

Bashya—still unlettered and unable to read or write—handed the letter to her daughter Manya to read. Manya was now 18 and still had intentions of making Aliya to Palestine despite her mother's protestations.

"So what does the letter from our undependable father say?" asked Herschel, now 16 and still apprenticed to the tailor in the village.

"Sha! Don't talk that way about your father. He does what he can when he can."

Manya's brow wrinkled and she scowled as she skimmed the letter quickly to herself and then announced: "The letter says that Papa's second wife, Mollie was very disturbed and upset for a long time and because of that she threw herself off a roof and died. He tried to care for his three children but then had to put them in orphanages. His Rabbi told him that G-d indeed works his wonders in mysterious ways and suggested that perhaps this was the time to reunite with his first wife, Bashya and her children." Manya paused in her reading and couldn't resist interspersing her own comment: "Such chutzpah"

"Never mind your opinion, finish what the letter says," her mother chided.

"Yes, what more does our great supporter say," added Herschel who then averted his mother's glare.

"Well, he goes on to say that if you think the idea has merit, then he would be very pleased to send the money for our passage and we should begin to make the necessary preparations including obtaining the needed visas and passports." And then she again added emphatically "That is chutzpah!" and handed the letter to her mother.

Bashya held the letter in her hands as tears filled her eyes and she then pressed the letter to her bosom, clearly indicating that she still loved the man! "He may not have been the best father, but he was, and still is my husband. I'll want to talk about this with my mother and brother, Moishe Chaim. He is always an intelligent and sensible man."

Manya noted her mother's comments, nodded and said to her brother: "No more cracks out of you. Go find Bubbie and Uncle Moishe Chaim."

When Bashya's mother and brother were assembled the discussion began in earnest. They examined the issue from every conceivable angle, with Moishe Chaim stressing that concern for their mother—Manya and Herschel's grandmother—should not be a determining factor because, he assured them that he and his wife and daughter Schlamme would look after the aging woman. Also, he stressed that while he was not a total believer of letting "Bygones be bygones," still one had to look ahead and not backwards.

Bubbie agreed with her son, acknowledging that she had only a few more years left to live and her daughter should not allow this new opportunity for her and the children to go to America—which they were supposed to do 15 years ago, in mid 1914 before the Great War. And besides, it provided an alternative to Manya's wanting to make Aliya to Palestine, and she winked at her daughter Bashya.

Bashya smiled back at her mother and then looked to her daughter. "So Manya, what do you say to that?"

"I haven't had a chance to even think about it, so what can I say to you?"

And suddenly Herschel exploded: "Doesn't anyone care about what I think?" And without waiting for anyone to ask him what he thought he told them what he thought: "I think it would be a good way to repay the man for all the years of neglect by accepting his offer. The important thing is that we can get to go to America."

"Fine, you go to America and I'll go to Palestine." Manya said. And that announcement shook Herschel in particular because he was very close to his sister.

"Oh come on, you're not really serious are you? You'd go in the opposite direction from what Mama and I would go—to America?"

"Of course, anything and any where, to get away from you because you can be a pest sometimes."

And then after some more good-natured banter Manya finally agreed to accompany her mother and pesky brother to America. Uncle Moishe Chaim offered to reply to Nathan's letter telling him of their decision, but Manya insisted that she was capable of handling that task.

The decision having been made that Bashya, Manya and Herschel would all be going to America, they now proceeded to make the necessary arrangements which involved applying for their passports and visas which, unfortunately could not be done in Nesvizh nor, for that matter even in Kletsk, both communities being too small to accommodate such prestigious governmental functions. Minsk, the capital city of the province—which was now a part of Poland after Poland invaded Byelorussia and annexed most of the western half of that country in 1920-21——certainly provided such functions as well as the consular offices of most of the foreign countries. But Minsk was 100 kilometers (62 miles) to the northeast of Nesvizh—which did not have any public transportation connections to the capital, whereas Kletsk was 114 kilometers (71 miles) to the northeast and did have such connections.

From their inquiries, however, they learned that Baronovichi, 54 to 55 kilometers (34 miles) due west of Nesvizh, provided Polish governmental services three days a week, which would allow them to obtain their Polish passports. But they would still have to travel to Minsk to obtain visas from the United States Consular Office there.

Bashya commented that she could not remember the process being so complicated 15 years ago when she obtained

U.S. Consulate in Minsk an effort would be made to sort out the matter.

"What are they talking about?" Manya and Herschel demanded to know, while Bubbie and Uncle Moishe Chaim remained silent, seemingly remembering something from long ago.

"Oy! I think I know what they are talking about" Bashya said. And she proceeded to relate the story involving her sister-in-law Sonia, who back then was causing her family much concern because of her running around with goyishe soldiers and so the family prevailed upon Nochem to have Sonia come to America using Bashya's visa and passport! But the children would not go without their mother and so Sonia went alone. It was supposed to be only a temporary delay of at most a few months, so Bashya reluctantly agreed to the plan. But before they could complete the plans for Bashya and the children to make the trip (including reapplying for another visa and passport) the Great War broke out in August 1914!

Bubbie and Uncle Moishe Chaim nodded their remembrance of the event—which Bashya had reported to them at the time—while Manya and Herschel couldn't believe their ears.

"So where do we go from here?" Manya demanded. "Is there no end to the problems this man, our father, and his family inflicted on us?" she added bitterly.

"Sha! You don't know what you are talking about. You were both very young children at the time. We lived with 'his family' as you called it and were happy until the pogrom put an end to it. 'His family' paid a very heavy price, all being murdered! So bite your tongue young lady" Bashya said as she wiped the tears from her eyes.

"I always say that G-d works his wonders in mysterious ways and who are we to question those ways?" Bubbie said, getting up and walking over to comfort her daughter.

"That is true, Momma" Uncle Moishe Chaim said. "As to where we go from here, dear Manya, my guess is that it could take a very long time to straighten out this mess, especially when you deal with bureaucrats. I suggest that we write to Nochem...I mean Nathan and explain what has happened and arrange for Manya and Herschel to make the trip without Bashya. And this time, you children, being much older of course, should not decline to go without your mother."

Both Manya and Herschel laughed at their uncle's characterization of the situation and both agreed—if it was allright with their mother.

Bashya shrugged her shoulders and looked at her family: "I've waited this long to make this trip so I guess another— what is it—-month or months or years . . . ? But there is no other choice. The children should go and with G-d's help, it will not be too much longer. After all, Moses never entered the Promised Land, but I'm sure I will!"

On December 29, 1929 Manya Erkes and her brother Herschel sailed into New York harbor, on the SS Lithuania of the Baltic/American Line docking at Ellis Island the processing center for all new immigrants to the United States. Manya was 18 going on 19 while Herschel had just turned 16 the past October. Considering the fact that she was just two and a half and Herschel only a few months old when their father left for America in October 1912, there was no remembrance of what each looked like! So Manya had sent copies of their passport photos to Nathan, and Nathan had gone into a fotomat and had photos taken of himself, which he sent on to Nesvizh in Poland.

As the two of them left the vast processing hail, dragging their heavy baggage behind them, they scanned the sea of faces of relatives waiting to greet their loved ones from the Old Country "Do you see him?" Herschel asked, since his sister was taller than he and had a better view.

"No, not yet. I hope he's wearing the hat that he had on when he took his picture. So many people!"

passports and visas for herself and her two children and were planning to leave from Odessa in the Ukraine, Russia to join Nathan in America.

The official in the Polish passports office in Baronovichi smiled indulgently and explained that first of all this was Poland and not the Ukraine, Russia and secondly, yes it had become necessary, since the Great War, to tighten up the emigration process. And then she went on to explain that, although there were no consular offices in Baronovichi from where they could obtain their visas—those could only be obtained in Minsk—it was important for them to know about visas. The most common type was the entry visa, which signifies that the bearer of the passport to which the visa is affixed has received official permission to enter a country of which he or she is not a citizen. The consular office of the country that one wishes to enter issues the visa.

Bashya, Manya and Herschel listened intently as the official continued her explanation: "There are two types of entry visas; the passport entry visa, which is for a limited stay; and the immigration entry visa, which is for persons intending to stay permanently in the new country. And some countries were now requiring exit visas to control the flight from their countries of large numbers of their citizens or subjects." The official stressed that when they went to Minsk for their entry visas they should be certain to stress that the visas should be the immigration entry visas. And Bashya thanked the official for her courtesy and the invaluable information, which she was certain, would save them time and aggravation.

"Boy, that was some megillah (Story of Esther and the Purim celebration)" Herschel commented as they left the office with their respective passports to return home to plan their trip to Minsk.

"Maybe so, but the information she gave us will probably help us to avoid mix-ups and mistakes, I'm sure. So don't be so critical." Manya said.

In the United States Consular Office in Minsk they presented the necessary documentary evidence of who they were, including birth certificates (or in Bashya's case affidavits from the Rabbi) along with their new passports with their small photographs attached. They were told that it would take about two weeks for everything to be processed and the visas would be mailed to their home address in Nesvizh. And now even Herschel was beginning to feel the excitement and the expectation.

Bashya had Manya write to Nathan that the process had begun and that it would be only a matter of a few weeks before they would be ready to depart for America. In the meantime he should make the necessary transportation arrangements and send some money.

Nathan answered promptly that he had accumulated the necessary funds for the trip and was now looking into the various steam ship lines available and as soon as they had all their papers, including the immigration entry visas, they should send him a collect telegram and he would send the monies. In the meantime he was sending some cash.

Two weeks later, letters arrived from the U.S. Consular Service in Minsk for Bashya, Manya and Herschel and they waited to open them until Bubbie and Uncle Moishe Chaim joined them so that they could all celebrate the event. Manya and Herschel's letters included their immigration entry visas—which they were directed to paste inside their passports—but Bashya's envelope contained only a letter, which Manya proceeded to read. It politely stated that an immigration entry visa could not be issued to Bashya Friedman Erkes, because the United States Immigration records showed that the named applicant had immigrated to the United States in May 1914! And if the current applicant would come to the

"Well maybe he'll see us before we see him" Herschel said as he sat down on his bag to wait for that possibility as his sister joined him.

They watched in envy as relatives connected, hugged, cried and walked off together; but still no sign of their father, Nochem—now Nathan. And they waited.

"Excuse me young lady and young man. Are you Manya and Herschel?" asked a middle-aged man with a gray fedora hat wearing a nervous smile.

"Poppa?" Manya asked. And as he nodded, she tentatively took his hand to shake it.

"Are you my father?" Herschel stood up and asked. And as the man again nodded, he took the man's other hand to shake.

Suddenly Nathan embraced them both exclaiming: "Oy, that is not the way to greet a father—this is the way to greet a father!" and he hugged them even more tightly. And he burst into tears as Manya joined him in the shedding of her own. "How is your mother?" Nathan asked.

"She is well, but eager to straighten out the mess so she can join us, hopefully in a few months. She asked me to give you this letter which Uncle Moishe Chaim wrote for her."

Nathan took the letter and put it in his pocket. "I'll read it later, after we get home. You both look so... so... so big!" he exclaimed.

"And you don't look as tall as when I last saw you almost 17 years ago" Manya replied.

"Yes, yes. It has been a long time. But now we will be able to make up for lost time."

"And I don't remember you at all," Herschel said, just to remind his father that he was a mere infant of several months of age when Nochem left to go to America in December 1912.

"There's no way that you could even though I sent some pictures of myself to Bashya and the family. But all of that is behind us. Now we can build a new life and a new one big happy family. I think you both will like your new brothers and little sister," he said.

"Do Elek (Yiddish for Alex), Sholem and Yenta know of our coming?" Manya asked referring to Nathan's children by his second, deceased wife Mollie.

"Yes they do and they are anxious to meet you both. But let's get started home. It is a long ride, by ferry and then subway."

"What's a subway?" Herschel asked.

"You'll soon find out," his father replied with a laugh.

"It's a train that rides underground. I read about it in school." his sister told him.

On the ferry ride from Ellis Island to Brooklyn Nathan explained that in America everything was faster and more crowded and that "greeneh" ("greenhorns" or newcomers) made every effort to assimilate as quickly as possible. It was only a suggestion, mind you, but they would be wise to consider using other than their Yiddish names. For example, Manya would be called "Mary" in America while Herschel would be called "Harry."

"So call me 'Harry' Herschel" quickly responded eager to demonstrate how quick he was to become an American.

Manya thought about it for a moment and replied that publicly she would respond to the name "Mary" but within the family she still preferred to be known as, and called Manya—at least until she became more settled.

And Nathan realized that his daughter had a mind of her own. He would find out that was also the case with his reunited son.

At the Brooklyn apartment they met their aunt Sonia and her husband Bronstein (since that was all that his wife called him although that was their last name) and their three male cousins. And after the embraces and exchanges of greetings, they all sat around the dining room table in the parlor.

"Isn't she the one that... " Herschel, now Harry, whispered in his sister's ear, only to have Manya poke him in the ribs with a curt "Not now!"

Following the departure of Tante Sonia and her family, Nathan explained that after a few days rest, Mary—excuse him, Manya—could begin her job as a sewing machine operator in a clothing factory in Manhattan while Herschel—he meant Harry—could begin his job with a distributor of the *FORWARD*, the most prestigious of the Yiddish language dailies. But since the distributor lived and worked out on Long Island, it was desirable that Harry live with him out there to avoid the very lengthy commuting that would otherwise be involved. Harry could, of course, come home weekends.

Both Manya and Harry were ambivalent about the plan for Harry, but Manya urged him to try it for a while. Harry, while a very independent-minded young man, was receptive to his sister's suggestion—although he complained that it would be hard to get to know his father living so far away from him. And how was he to get to such a far away place?

Nathan explained that Harry's employer was willing to come and pick him up for the first time. And thereafter would assist from time to time in the commuting.

My brother Al and I met our new sister for the first time when she accompanied our father, Nathan in visiting us one Sunday at the Hebrew National Orphan Home located in the outskirts of Yonkers, New York. It was early January 1930. Harry could not attend because he had been unable to get home that weekend. Al was 9 and ½. I was 8 and Manya (Mary) 18 going on 19 (See picture on book cover).

She was all charm and love and evidently delighted to have two new, young brothers. She gave me a small mirror with a picture of herself on the front and told me, in Yiddish of course; "Sholem, whenever you get tired looking at yourself, turn it over and I'll be there for you."

Harry, who as a child in Poland had learned to be quite self-reliant, began to clash with his father almost from the very beginning. Nathan's attempt to exercise the role of the authoritarian father—"Ich bin der Tate!"—clashed with Harry's independent streak. In addition, with his father's encouragement he sent home almost his entire weekly paycheck, keeping only a few dollars for expense, expecting that his father would be banking it for him for his future needs. Instead he was horrified to learn that his father had been spending the money, using as his rationale that it was reimbursement for Harry's travel expenses to America! So, the "one big happy family" was off to a shaky start!

In addition, the few months that they thought it would take to straighten out Bashya's problems with the Consular Service and the visa dragged on for another three years and it wasn't until November 1932 that Bashya arrived in the United States to join her children, her first and soon-to-be third husband and hopefully a one, big, happy family involving Mollie's three children. She was supposed to have joined her husband in 1914. It was now 18 years later!

One Sunday in December 1932, Papa came to the HNOH without Manya. He had with him two wrapped boxes of candy, one for Al and one for me. But it was not for us to eat. We were to bring them along with us as he took us to Brooklyn to meet his first, and soon-to-be third wife, Bashya, now to be known as Bessie.

The meeting was stiff, anxious and tense for everyone. Papa did the introductions; he introduced Alex and then me and then said (in Yiddish of course) "Kids, this is your new mother. Give her the candy."

Many years later Bess confided to me that that was one of the most difficult times of her life. She had mixed feelings about taking on the care of three strange children—two of whom were pubescent or pre-adolescent. She was very nervous and uneasy—which came across at the time as her being cold and aloof. And she was unhappy to find that Harry was not getting along with his father. Being an honorable woman she was determined to uphold her end of the bargain.

But fate decreed that she would not have to do so, because the 'one big happy family' envisioned would never come to pass. Instead there would be many smaller, happy families.

END OF COMPLETED JOURNEY

IX. ABORTED JOURNEYS

What follows herein is totally non-fiction. I grew up in the Hebrew National Orphan Home, a New York City, all-boys Jewish institution located in the outskirts of neighboring city, Yonkers, New York. I spent nearly 12 years there; from age 7½ till almost age 19. When I first arrived, April 1929 together with my older brother Alex, Mr. George Goldenberg was the superintendent, but after a few years Mr. Harry Lucacher replaced him, serving ten years before being struck down by a massive heart attack.

In my previously published book *DEJA VIEWS OF AN AGING ORPHAN: Growing Up in the Hebrew National Orphan Home* (Xlibris Corporation, Philadelphia, PA. 2000) one of my columns "guestimated" that the total number of boys cared for by the institution over its nearly 50 year history was between 1500 to 1800, making the HNOH a small institution, certainly in comparison with its contemporary orphanages of the time, such as the Hebrew Orphan Asylum of NYC and the Brooklyn Hebrew Orphan Asylum. And I concluded that particular column with the following:

"But the smallness was in numbers only. In terms of bonding and fraternity, there was no institution superior to the HNOH, so say most of us alumni…. What I'm saying is: THERE WERE NOT THAT MANY OF US OVER THE

NEARLY 50 YEARS! Which is why we do feel so close to one another, especially as we grow fewer and fewer!" When the United States was propelled into World War II, as a consequence of the Japanese attack on Pearl Harbor on December 7, 1941, many of our Homeboys were called to serve in our armed forces, with many being wounded and others killed. The following material deals with the tragic untimely death of Harry Lucacher and with just two of our alumni "brothers" killed in that Great War.

HARRY LUCACHER (1883-1938)

On March 23, 1938 I (Sam Arcus) was 16½ going on 17, sleeping ever so soundly, when a shriek, followed by an eerie wailing, pierced the Junior dormitory——my province of responsibility as one of its monitors. The shriek and wailing emanated from the White House, the domicile of the HNOH's superintendent and his family. It was about 4 am. Later we learned that Ida Lucacher, wife of Harry, our then superintendent, had discovered her husband lying dead from a sudden massive heart attack and the shocking discovery produced her shriek and wailing.

Harry Lucacher spent half of his 54-55 years in the service of orphaned and dependent children, first as business manager and fund-raiser and finally as superintendent of the Hebrew National Orphan Home from 1930 to 1938.

Harry Morse, an older alumnus in his late eighties, in his segment of the *HNOH ORAL HISTORY* recalls the five bar mitzvah banquets at the Commodore Hotel he participated in (as a member of the HNOH band) where Harry Lucacher kept pitching for funds to eliminate the $100,000 mortgage—which was a very sizeable sum at the time.

And Charles "Chick" Baker, in his segment of the same *ORAL HISTORY*, tells of the incident in Harry Lucacher's office—wherein Abraham Lewin, HNOH Vice President in charge of religious education, asked a boy (who had come to inquire something of Mr. Lucacher) whether he had prayed that day. At which point Harry Lucacher impatiently interrupted with: "Abe, why don't you ask him if he ate today?"

I'm not sure what events compelled Harry Lucacher to abandon his business management and fund-raising roles to take over as the HNOH superintendent in 1930, succeeding Mr. George Goldenberg. But his assuming that responsibility had a significant impact on those of us who were in the HOME at the time. While not immediately, there was a gradual lessening of the regimentation and disciplining so common at the time. For which we kids were grateful.

It was after all, the depth of the Great Depression and money was hard to come by. Yet, despite the desperate times Harry Lucacher nevertheless found the time and wherewithal to "rescue" alumni like Charles "Chick" Baker and Murray Julius who were having difficulties in managing on the outside and weathering the bad times. And simultaneously he attended to his charges in the institution, protecting them against the rigidities of the well-intentioned Abraham Lewins. Chick was "hired" as the athletic coach and relief supervisor, and Murray as waiter and orchestra leader and later as the Freshman supervisor with Lucacher promising to pay them whatever, and whenever, he could.

While not a professionally trained childcare worker (like Reuben Koftoff who succeeded him a year after his sudden, premature death) Harry Lucacher brought to his superintendent job an uncanny and intuitive application that captured the hearts and minds of most of his charges. So much so that, about 2 years after his death, a group of HNOH alumni (and some soon-to-be-alumni-like myself) organized the Harry Lucacher Alumni Society (HLAS) on January 2, 1940, to perpetuate his memory and his ideals. His wife, Ida agreed to serve as Honorary President, as did the new HNOH President, Samuel Fields—who had succeeded the venerable Honorable Justice Aaron J. Levy. Charlie Vladimer was the HLAS President and, I'm pleased to say, I was its Vice President. The HLAS unfortunately survived only a few years as many of its members moved out of NYC to work in the war industries in Baltimore and elsewhere or were drafted into the US armed services.

The impact of Harry Lucacher's sudden death in 1938 is best captured in the HNOH's publication, THE HOMELITE in the following story of June 1938:

HUNDREDS MOURN HARRY LUCACHER'S PASSING: BOYS ARE PALLBEARERS

By Lewis Zedicoff

As hundreds from all walks of life overflowed the Gutterman Funeral Chapel to pay their last respects and as two hundred boys of the Home acted as honorary pallbearers, a most touching but simple service was conducted for Harry Lucacher, superintendent of the Home he served for the past quarter of a century, and commemorating an entire lifetime spent in charitable work. After the services his remains were buried in the Mount Hebron Cemetery in Flushing. Mr. Lucacher died suddenly from a heart attack in his fifty-fourth year on Wednesday morning, March 23, 1938 at the Home.

Herbert Immerblum, sixteen-year-old resident of the institution, in attempting to speak at the funeral on behalf of the boys, became so overcome with grief that he was unable to carry on. Rabbi Morris Sandhaus, spiritual leader of the Home, and Rabbi Harry Halpern of the East Midwood Jewish Center of Brooklyn, conducted the impressive services, which were characteristic of the role Harry Lucacher played through life. Most of those present were unable to control themselves and wept bitterly while the hundreds of mourners, most of them prominent charitable workers, stood in tributary homage. Mr. Justice Aaron J. Levy, president of the institution, attended but could not speak, owing to his depressed feelings. Mr. Lucacher was in Judge Levy's company several hours prior to his passing.

Prior to his untimely death, Mr. Lucacher had been warned by his doctors to discontinue his work because of failing health. However, seeing the importance of his work for the upkeep and maintenance of the institution, he carried on. Two years ago he was involved in an auto, accident that disabled him for sometime, but he arose from his sickbed to resume his activities for the Home.

When the news of Mr. Lucacher's passing reached the boys, they folded into small groups and spoke in low murmurs as though each and every one of them had lost a personal and devoted friend. For two days the boys remained home from school and the flag in front of the building was flown at half-mast in a silent tribute.

Irony also played its part with his passing. On May 15th Mr. Lucacher was to celebrate his 55th year with the birthday boys of May, sponsored by the Yonkers Ladies Auxiliary. Also, it was the first time that money was donated by the boys and members of the staff for his annual birthday party.

His wife, Ida and his son, George and two daughters, Emma and Sylvia, survive Mr. Lucacher.

END HOMELITE ARTICLE.

DEDICATIONS

Of the Home's six or seven superintendents over its nearly 50-year history, the two most memorable and outstanding—in the opinion of most alumni—were Harry Lucacher (who served during the depths of the Great Depression and insured the institution's survival) and Reuben Koftoff who picked up the fallen baton and carried it to the finish line—and the end of the HNOH existence. It was fitting that both were memorialized with Dedications, both in the *DEJA VIEWS OF AN AGING ORPHAN* and another book dealing with the Hebrew National Orphan Home, edited by Ira A. Greenberg, Rick Safran and Sam George Arcus, titled *THE HEBREW NATIONAL ORPHAN HOME; MEMORIES of ORPHANAGE LIFE* (Greenwood Publishing Group, Westport, CT. 2001).

END HARRY LUCACHER SEGMENT

And now we come to two of our alumni brothers killed in World War II whose lives, and journeys were aborted at much younger ages than our beloved Harry Lucacher. They are Arthur "Spike" Schiller and Seymour Kasonsky (Kaye).

ARTHUR "SPIKE" SCHILLER

Authors Note: One of the earliest references to Arthur Schiller in the Home appeared in the form of a poem written by him and published in THE ORACLE on March 5, 1933. THE ORACLE was the boy's newspaper at the time, preceding THE HOMELITE.

A TRIBUTE TO JUSTICE AARON J. LEVY

(HNOH President for many years)
By Arthur Schiller (age 12)

> I have searched the world for a man, who can help an orphan lad.
> And I found that the one who can, is the man who can make him glad.
> There is such a man and I know it, I know who he may be:
> Someday that man will in heaven sit; He is Justice Aaron J. Levy.
>
> I am an orphan lad, and have been in his home for many years;
> He has made me glad, and helped me lose my fears.
> I'll surely remember that man, as others surely will too;
> And I'll try to do all I can, to show him what I can do.
>
> I'll do anything to please that man; whatever it may be.
> I'll do anything I can, to please Justice Aaron J. Levy.

The piece was typical of Arthur ("Spike")—always thinking the most positive of people and speaking well of them. He was of my (Sam Arcus's) generation, both of us being in the Bar Mitzvah class of April 1934, so he must have been born in 1921, as I was. And even though the memory is fading, I still recall him as being soft-spoken with a ready smile and a very friendly disposition.

He was next mentioned in the April 15, 1934 HNOH BULLETIN (another predecessor of THE HOMELITE) along with some other boys who, because of their "good work and good conduct were placed on the P.S. 403 Honor Roll: Murray Feierberg (4B), Samuel Arcus (7A), Arthur Schiller (7B)..." And later, I spotted him in a picture taken in 1937, in his band uniform with his clarinet, together with Walter Lewis, Charlie Vladimer, Irving Pincus and Walter Felder.

He also played a part in our school's production of HMS PINAFORE in the early 1930s, handling the role of the one-eyed sailor sporting a black eye patch. But that wasn't Spike's sole effort as thespian. He was a member of the Dramatics Club, usually fulfilling small, supporting roles, like a reporter or detective and then doing considerable work in the background. Again typically Arthur Schiller.

Arthur attended Commerce High School in Yonkers, where he pursued a business and commercial curriculum and where he also joined the band and orchestra. The December 16, 1936 issue of THE HOMELITE mentions Arthur, together with Isadore Berman, Phil Pincus, Ben Liebowitz and Meyer Adelman as being the mainstay of that school's musical efforts.

Arthur "Spike" Schiller's literary endeavors were not confined to poetry. As early as 1936 he was listed as a reporter for THE ACCOMPLISHER and after that went under, he worked on THE HOMELITE, first as INQUIRING REPORTER and then as writer of the KALEIDESCOPE column as well as serving as an Associate Editor thru 1938.

In June 1939 Arthur left the Home to live with his brother, Harry, four to five years his senior and his only family as far as was known. Presumably he finished his high school senior year outside the HNOH, since his name was not listed in the 1940 Commerce graduates. We learned of his being drafted into the army and over the years there were varying stories regarding his death during World War II. One version described his drowning when the Nazis torpedoed his troop ship en route to England. Others said he died in the fighting during the invasion of France begun on D Day. But in recent years his older brother Harry put the record straight: Arthur's ship was torpedoed in the English Channel. And he had been married only a month when he was drafted. In any event, a journey and a life aborted.

I've been asked many times: where did the nickname "Spike" come from? I've discussed this with Charlie Vladimer, another friend of Arthur's and a band companion, and we both agree-no one truly knows. Some say it was because he was so tall and thin, like a spike. Others say it derived from a character in the OUR GANG COMEDY series—the skinny kid with the cowlick refusing to stay down and with the continual grin and cheery demeanor. I'm afraid we'll never know for sure because the one who could definitively tell us is not with us any longer.

Arthur "Spike" Schiller was a well-liked boy growing up in the Home. He played ball, acted in plays, played the clarinet in the HNOH band and Commerce orchestra, and got along well with everyone. But he was denied the opportunity of making his mark in the world with America's entry into World War II and had his life cut short. Who knows how far he might have gone had he but had the chance. Our guess (Charlie and mine) is he would have gone very far and would have been a leader among men.

God rest your soul, brother "Spike"

END ARTHUR "SPIKE" SCHILLER

SEYMOUR KASONSKY
(As Remembered by Sam George Arcus)

THE HOMELITE issue of November 26, 1939 featured a BRIEF BIOGRAPHY of Seymour Kasonsky, written by then cub reporter Ira Greenberg (Later Editor of THE HOMELITE and after leaving the HNOH, numerous academic works as well as the Senior Editor of the recently published *THE HEBREW NATIONAL ORPHAN HOME; Memories of Orphanage Life).*

"Seymour Kasonsky entered this world on January 22, 1922 in a little hospital in Brooklyn. He spent his first six years in Brooklyn, after which he entered our abode on June 14, 1929. He is now a member of our Senior Dorm and is one of the fortunate boys chosen to occupy the newly—constructed room in the Senior Dorm. Seymour is a senior at Roosevelt High School. He is a member of the Home's orchestra 'The Star Dusters' and also captain of our HNOH band. Seymour likes to see green and brown and doesn't care for sweets. He is a member of the Social Club and enjoys dancing to a great extent. Seymour hopes to become a musician playing the trumpet or cornet and perhaps a crooner." (End reprint).

Seymour was, as the saying goes, of my generation. I was born October 19, 1921, just three months earlier. And my brother Al and I entered the Home in April, also three months prior to Seymour's arrival. While we were not in the same public school classes, we did both attend Roosevelt High School and graduated in June, 1940 together with Hy Chartove, Harry Mandelkern, Marty Miller, Jack Passin, Jack Ross, Abe Roth, Sol Sklar, Sam Prince, Irving Rosenbloom, Paul Schrenzel and Jerry Tobias. You wonder at my remarkable memory? Well I must confess, reviewing my copy of L'ENVOI, the Roosevelt High School Year Book, bolstered my recall.

Seymour Kasonsky was a very handsome lad: so much so that when PS.403/404 put on its Gilbert & Sullivan operetta (HMS Pinafore) and needed a female lead opposite the captain (played by Hy Furman) it utilized Seymour. He was also always very athletic playing baseball and basketball being part of the 1935-36 Public School Athletic League (PSAL) Westchester champion team coached by Chick Baker; which also involved Albert Fleischman, Martin Miller, Sid Kotlick, Morris Padover, Pinky Liebowitz, Jack Shapiro, Ted Greenberg and Ben Liebowitz.

While of the same generation, we nevertheless moved in different cliques because of differing interests. I had to drop out of athletic activities because of my chronic osteomyelitis and hence veered towards the artistic and literary endeavors, such as the Arts & Crafts and Home newspapers. So while Seymour was doing his impersonation of the captain's daughter in HMS PINAFORE, I was working with Chick Baker in creating the scenery for the production.

For readers of this volume who may still be unaware: HNOH was an all-boys institution (the only such Jewish orphanage in the New York metropolitan area). And when female roles were required for the plays and operettas, boys had to be used for the parts. For HMS PINAFORE, for example, there was an entire chorus of females required and thus fifteen of our cutest kids were dressed in female garb, had lipstick and rouge applied and expected to perform their female roles. What the teachers had not expected however, was—you could dress boys up to look like girls but you could not make them WALK LIKE GIRLS! As a consequence the actors were urged to MOVE AS LITTLE AS POSSIBLE across the stage.

Although Seymour was only three months younger than I, we were not in the same Bar Mitzvah class. As mentioned earlier, I was born October 1921 whereas Seymour was born January 1922. The Home organized its Bar Mitzvah classes according to the calendar years. So I was in the 1934 class whereas Seymour was in the 1935 one. So again, while of the same generation, we moved in different circles.

Ira Greenberg's BRIEF BIOGRAPHIES described Seymour's wanting to become a crooner. In fact, from his earliest boyhood at the Home he liked to sing—at first in his boy-soprano voice and, as he entered puberty and adolescence and his voice cracked—in a more tenor tone. But he sang frequently, in the freshmen, then junior, and finally senior dorms amateur hour performances. So it wasn't just his good looks, which cast him in feminine roles. He did have a good voice, which added authenticity to his female portrayals. And hence it wasn't so fanciful for him to think about becoming a professional singer, in addition to being a trumpet player.

As another matter of fact, Dave Fruchtman (Fredrics)—who ran all sorts of enterprises in the Home—signed Seymour to a contract with his F&F Talent Agency focused on Seymour's crooning. F&F stood for Fruchtman & Furman (another very enterprising fellow). The contract actually used Seymour's selected stage name, i.e. Sy Kaye. We joked about it back at the Home in 1940. But fate decreed that events would never allow the premise to be truly tested.

As with so many American young adults, the Japanese attack on Pearl Harbor cut short ambitions and aspirations and HNOH boys were drafted in droves into the armed forces; Seymour Kasonsky went into the army. Unlike many army boys who never reached England because their troop ships were torpedoed and sunk in the North Atlantic—Seymour "Kaye" Kasonsky made it to England. And from there to France, as part of the invasion of Normandy. He was killed in the very first wave of that assault!

Seymour Kasonsky, a beautiful person with a beautiful voice and matching charm and personality, never had a chance to entertain the world, either as a musician or crooner; or to become a husband and father. I don't know what family he had—outside of us at the HNOH. In my copy of L'ENVOI, 1940 Seymour wrote: "Best of Luck to a life-long pal and fellow grad." And now, looking back over the 59 years I can truly say, he was more than my "life-long Pal." He was my Home brother!

END ABORTED JOURNEYS

X. PARACHUTE

(This story first appeared in my book *Deja Views Of An Aging Orphan*)

Danny Melzer was a little peculiar. He always seemed to be in trouble of one sort or another, being the prime suspect whenever there was some thievery going on in the ORPHAN HOME. Usually the mystery was rather quickly solved when an "interrogation committee" of the larger, better-muscled fellows would take him into one of the storage rooms, and in short order encourage him to produce the purloined item.

While Danny's stealing was bad enough, we were even more disturbed by his predilection for harming defenseless animals. One time, before anyone of us older boys could intervene, Danny tossed a kitten out of the third story dormitory window—to see if it would land right side up—he explained when smashed up against the wall by several of us.

"Cats always land on their feet," he protested, as we roughed him up.

"You dumb jerk," came the retort, "even if they did, they'd have no feet left after falling down three stories."

We made him go down, pick up and bury the remains of the poor creature, thinking that perhaps he had now learned something. And he had—but not enough for the next thing we knew, he was experimenting with homemade "parachutes," made out of handkerchiefs. While the chute opened, it only slowed the fall, cushioning the impact enough so that the attached kitten was not killed instantly, but instead lingered in its suffering, requiring some of us to put it out of its misery.

We now met to consider what next steps to take. How could we reach and "educate" Danny? More beatings would probably not achieve the desired results since Danny was by now "slug-nutty." No, the "education" had to be more than intellectual, or even "physical".

And then we hit on it. Two of our huskies "invited" Danny to accompany them up to the roof of the HOME. Jerry and I preceded them to do some preliminary work. We stretched out a large, heavy muslin sheet. To each corner we attached ropes, each rope leading to another circle of rope, which was designed to tie around a person's waist. The image was quite clear.

Danny's eyes surveyed the scene, darting from the homemade chute, to each of us nervously, questioning. "What're you guys gonna do?" he asked with mounting anxiety.

"We're going to try an experiment of our own, Danny. We want to see if you'll land on your feet, using a parachute," I answered as the other three fellows proceeded to tie the rope around his waist.

Danny struggled, but was no match for the muscle and brawn. "You guys are crazy!" he shouted. "I'll be smashed like a bug"

"Or like a cat, more likely. But don't be so sure. After all, you have a bigger, stronger chute than what you gave the kitten," replied Jerry as the four of us lifted Danny onto the roof's parapet.

"Yeah, but what if the damn chute doesn't open? Huh. What if it doesn't?"

"It opened for the kitten, didn't it?" I reminded him.

"Yeah. But even if it does open, I'll probably break my legs—Hey, don't push! C'mon" Danny whined.

"Ready?" Jerry asked.
"Yep," the rest of us answered. "Let's get on with it."
"Hey, you guys are joking! Aren't you? Well, aren't you? C'mon, fellas! Please fellas Please!"

THE END

XI. NORMAN'S FIRST JOURNEY

Our son Norman was born December 21, 1947 while I was still attending the Columbia University School of Social Work and we were living in the cold water flat on Riverdale Avenue in the Brownsville section of Brooklyn. With a newborn son it became imperative that we obtain a larger apartment, preferably one with central heating. Housing was still very tight a few years after the end of World War II and when my sister-in-law, Blanche, heard of a ground floor, two-bedroom apartment on Livonia Avenue, just a few blocks from Riverdale, all we needed to do to get it was to pay the on-site manager $200 "under the table." And while $200 was a lot of money in those days, it was worth it, because the apartment was definitely an improvement, even though its location was inferior to the Riverdale Avenue flat.

Directly over Livonia Avenue ran the elevated Interboro Rapid Transit (IRT) system; perpendicular and almost parallel to our apartment, was the elevated Brooklyn/Manhattan (BMT) system; and under that was the Long Island Railroad (LIRR) coupling yards, a two-block-wide river of tracks and trains coupling and uncoupling at all hours. In other words, if the IRT ran east and west, the BMT (and LIRR) ran north and south. To allow pedestrians to get over the LIRR yards a two-block Walkway had been constructed with wire mesh on each side to protect any overly–curious pedestrians from falling into the congested and ever-active yards. But the yards served another function—they served as the boundary-separation between Brownsville and the East New York sections of Brooklyn. In any event, we heard trains constantly, day and night! But it's surprising what one can get used to and what one can tune out. To our amazement—and relief—after the first few days, Baby Norman adjusted to, and accepted the roar of trains overhead from the IRT and/or the BMT systems, and the clanging of trains being coupled and uncoupled in the LIRR yards.

As Norman rapidly grew, I neared completion of my social work courses and field work that would earn me my Master of Social Work (MSW) degree. Between my studies and my part time job at the Brownsville YM-YWHA (as arts and crafts instructor and club leader) I had little free time, but what free time I had was devoted to playing with our son. He especially loved "Hide And Seek" and was quite proficient, for a toddler 19 months old, in finding places to hide in what was still a small apartment. He hid in closets, under the beds, under the kitchen table by pulling the tablecloth down in front and even in the small bathroom and toilet closet.

"Now—your turn, Daddy," he would announce.

And I would protest that I was really too big to find any hiding places in our small place.

But he would insist and so, while I could not crawl under any beds or hide behind any of our sparse furniture, I would hide in a closet or sit in the bathtub and close the shower curtain while he came looking for me and would shout his delight once he found me.

The other passion of Norman's was our visitations to my sister Mary's house and family in Brownsville on Legion Street. It was about a mile or mile and a half away and in good weather we would usually walk the distance pushing Norman in his baby carriage that had been given to us by my cousin Davy Bronstein—whose last child had outgrown the thing.

Norman loved the visitations because he was the newest and youngest child in the family and was the object of everybody's attention including Mary's children Nathan and Rosie, Mary's husband, Uncle Joe (whom he called "Unca Yo" being unable to pronounce the "l" and "J") and most especially Bubbie Bessie, formerly known as Bashya in the old country.

Unca Yo was popular with Norman because he drove the only car in the Brownsville families and was always ready to give Adele, Norman and I, and his own kids, Nathan and Rosie rides either around the block several times, or even to Pitkin Avenue, which was the Times Square equivalent of Brownsville.

"Go faster Unca Yo, faster!" Norman would squeal with delight almost jumping out of my lap and hands as we sat in the front passenger seat.

"I'm going as fast as the law allows," brother-in-law Joe responded in his heavy Yiddish-accented English.

But when the weather was inclement, and this meant most of the winter months when the snow was on the ground, we would use the IRT, boarding the train at the Rockaway Avenue station, only one block from our apartment on Livonia, and ride to the next stop at Saratoga Avenue. Norman loved the train ride even more than Unca Yo's car rides especially having us go to the front of the first car alongside the engineers closed cab and make as if he were the train engineer.

Norman was a very inquisitive child, poking into every nook and cranny of the apartment. And frequently he would disappear for varying periods of time, playing "Hide And Seek" by himself when I said I was too busy trying to finish a school assignment and his mother, Adele, was too busy doing her never-ending chores. But he would reappear periodically to announce that he had found himself and did either his mother or I now have time to join him in the game. And sometimes I would take a break from my assignments or Adele would break away from her chores to participate with him and he would be one happy little boy.

"Have you seen Norman lately?" Adele asked me one Saturday afternoon as I sat at the kitchen table writing out some field reports in long hand in preparation for Adele's later typing them.

"No, I thought he was with you in the bedroom helping you fold clothes.

"He was with me until about a half hour ago. I thought he came in here to be with you."

"Well, yes he came in here, said 'Hi daddy' and then I thought he went back to join you."

We looked at each other, our mutual consternation infecting each other. And then we began a thorough search of the apartment, looking under the bed in our room and the crib in his, in all three closets, the bathroom, even under some piles of soiled clothing waiting to be taken to the Washateria on Powell Street, just around the corner. He was nowhere to be found in the apartment, and we clutched each other for support.

Then Adele's eyes caught something: "Is the front door really closed?" she asked. And she went to more closely examine the lock mechanism of the front door. As a safety precaution we had the landlord install a deadbolt lock along with a chain attachment, which would allow the resident to open the door but still have it chained against any forcible entry. The chain had not been put into place and the dead bolt not actually locked. In short, the door, while closed, had not been locked!

"Didn't you lock the door?" Adele asked.

"I thought you did," I answered. And then the thought

hit us both simultaneously that Norman must have been able to open what we presumed to be a door too heavy for him to open by him-self and wandered out of the apartment to Livonia Avenue!

Hastily we put on some jackets, since the October climate had turned chilly, and went out to Livonia Avenue. "I think it's better that we split up, so you go up that side of the street and I'll go this side. He couldn't have gone too far, so let's check back at the front of the apartment within five minutes, OK?" I said.

Eyes tearful, Adele agreed, saying: "Oh Sam, we've got to find him."

We scoured the length and breath of Livonia Avenue, on both sides of the street and when next we met at the front of our apartment building, several of the other tenants joined us in continuing our search. It was agreed that we now search all the side streets, including Powell Street, Junius Avenue, Rockaway Avenue and all the others.

"Have you seen a little boy about a year and a half old?" became the standard question of the searchers as we entered stores, or encountered street vendors. Some said they had and gave the information they possessed, but the child they had seen turned out not to be the child we were looking for. And after a half hour of this we all again gathered in front of our building.

"Maybe you should notify the police" one neighbor suggested.

But I had one more idea, which I wanted to pursue before involving the police. "He loves the trains" I said and rushed over to the Rockaway station and up the stairs to the change booth and breathlessly asked the attendant if he had seen a little boy alone within the last half hour.

When he answered in the negative, my heart dropped and I returned to my wife and our neighbors ready to involve the local police. But when I reached the group, Adele excitedly told me that a passerby, seeing all the commotion and told what it was all about, said that he had just come across on the Walkway from the Van Sicklen side and he was pretty certain that he saw a little boy fitting the description ambling along at a leisurely pace, now and then peering down at the coupling yards watching the trains being hitched and unhitched. The man said he tried to engage the boy in conversation; to ask him why he appeared to be all alone and where were his parents, but the little boy rebuffed him, his parents apparently having told him never to talk to strangers; and so he would not talk and hurried off alone towards Van Sicklen. The man apologized for not being more aggressive and offered to go with me to find the kid and point him out.

I thanked him profusely and said he would really have to hurry to keep up with me. And as we climbed the steep steps to the Walkway I wondered how a little boy like Norman could have climbed them. The man, being much older than I, excused himself and said I should hurry and not wait for him. Which, of course, I did, running the two-block long Walkway to the other side, and then practically leaping down the steep steps on the other side which landed me on Van Sicklen Avenue.

Next to the steps leading up to the Walkway was an enclosed newsstand, and I hastened to ask the vendor, who was evidently Jewish, whether he had seen a year and a half old boy. The man appeared to be nearly sixty with a white beard and weather-beaten face, several missing teeth in front and a broad grin.

"Vell, I vas vundering ven yu vud finally get here," he said with an almost toothless grin. "Boychik, I tink yur pappa iz here" he added, addressing someone not visible to anyone at the front of his stand.

Then a little head popped up, its face smeared with what looked like Hersheys chocolate. "Hi Daddy," it said.

I almost swooned from relief. "Norman!" I shouted. "What are you doing here?"

"I wann'd go to Unca Yo but id wuz the wrong steps" he tried to explain.

The old Jew smiled and urged me not to be too hard on the child. He explained that he spotted the boy coming down the steps of the Walkway all-alone and he surmised that this was a lost child. He had an old stuffed teddy bear, which he held out to catch the boy's attention and once he had that, he further enticed him with some candy, and then into the booth where he would be warmer while awaiting the inevitable arrival of a parent. And then he added that as the time passed, and there was no parent, he was becoming anxious and thought about calling the police. But he had no phone in his booth and he thought he would ask some passersby to call the police because although the boy was adorable he was quite a "trumpernick"—an active child—and he, the vendor, was beginning to run out of ideas of how to keep him occupied and happy.

I thanked Moishe—which was his name—expansively and collected my son, after taking a handkerchief from my jacket pocket and wiping his face. As I carried him towards the steps leading up to the Walkway, which would bring us both home to the other side of the divide—I first smacked his bottom and chided him for being a "bad boy" and then bear-hugged him tightly, explaining how frightened we were and how much we loved him, thus delivering a totally confusing message to the boy!

THE END

XII. THE SET-UP

So far, so good, Solomon Wise thought as he made his daily tour of the "Y" building. He was glad there were only two stories to the place, considering that it lacked elevators and was a fairly strung-out facility occupying almost an entire city block in the town of Essex, New Jersey. Yep, so far so good. This was Friday, his fifth day on the job as the Assistant Director of the "Y" and everyone so far had been friendly and helpful.

On the second floor he came to the door marked ESSEX COMMUNITY COUNCIL and he hesitated. He thought it strange that his boss, Harry Lazar, hadn't taken him inside to meet the Council people when he took him around on his first day. Harry had merely said that the Council was housed in the building and that he, Sol, would meet "those people in due time." Sol had the strange feeling then that this office and its occupants were somehow "off limits" and now he was again getting that "verboten" feeling. He peered more intently at the lettering on the door: ESSEX COMMUNITY COUNCIL and directly under that; "Lawrence Kagan. Executive Director."

Suddenly the printing fell away as the door opened and a six-foot, curly-haired, bespectacled man attempted to exit. "Whoops! I thought this was a doorway. Sorry," said the figure.

Sol recovered his balance and replied: "No, no, my fault. I should be apologizing since I was blocking your doorway."

145

The man appraised Sol in a glance. "Oh, hey, you must be Solly Wise, Harry's new assistant. I'm Larry Kagan. I was wondering when Harry would allow us to meet. Where's Harry?" He strained to look over Sol's shoulders.

Sol backed up several steps. This unplanned meeting left him flustered but also curious. Why did Larry Kagan use the word "allow"? But still, Sol stammered his reply: "Uh, Harry's not with me. I'm alone. I mean I'm on my own-uh—just making my rounds. Oh hell! I'm sorry I busted in on you!"

Larry Kagan's smile broadened as he adjusted his horn-rimmed glasses. "Well, I'm not sorry. See, God works his wonders in mysterious ways. C'mon. I'm on my way to the John, why don't you join me in a welcome leak."

Sol liked Larry immediately. He was so friendly, outgoing, unpretentious and so...so...so what's the word? Yes, irreverent. As they walked to the Men's Room, Sol again wondered why Harry had not introduced Larry earlier. Oh well, it probably wasn't important and he'd find out soon enough. In the Men's Room, Larry observed: "I love the graffiti in these places. Take this one for example: 'we aim to please. Your aim will help too.'"

Sol chuckled. "Yeah, mine says: 'Tuck your tie in when thru.'"

Larry nodded. "Talking about 'thru'—why don't you join me after work for a little 'Happy Hour'?"

Sol blinked. "Happy Hour? Oh, you mean drinks and stuff. I really don't know. I should be getting home."

"Just a couple at my place. Think of it as a kind of informal welcome to Essex. But not to worry, either I or my wife will drive you home."

Sol squared his shoulders and replied: "Why not? I'll call my wife and tell her I'll be delayed in getting home.

"Make yourself at home," Larry said making a beeline for the kitchen and the Happy Hour ingredients while Sol settled into a living room chair and paused in lighting his cigarette. D'ya mind if I smoke, Larry?"

"Not at all. Say Sol, your folks had fun naming you Solomon, didn't they? I mean considering your last name and all?"

"Yeah, I get kidded all the time about it. But you don't know the full of it. My middle name is David. So if anyone refers to me as 'Solomon D. Wise' you can hear lot's of chuckles." Sol looked around the room and asked, "Where's your wife?"

From the kitchen fixing the drinks Larry answered: "Well, Solomon the Wise, dear Helen works in Newark as a bookkeeper. She should be home any minute now."

"Do you two have any kids?" Sol followed up.

Larry poked his head into the parlor. "Nope. You've got two, haven't you?"

"Yes, a boy, Louis, six and a girl, Shelly nearly one. I Hope Eisenhower settles the damn Korean mess before my boy is old enough to be drafted!"

Well I for one don't like Ike. But I think he'll keep his '53 campaign pledge. But, to hell with national politics. How was your first week on the job?" Larry asked as he re-entered the living room with a tray containing a pitcher of newly mixed martinis and two chilled glasses.

"Pretty good, Larry. Everyone is friendly and cooperative."

"Glad to hear it," said Larry filling the glasses with the mixture. "Here, try this."

Sol sipped the drink, his eyes widening as the cool liquid seared his throat, ignited his chest cavity and settled warmly in his belly. "Wow! What proportions do you use?"

"Four to one," Larry grinned. "I like it extra dry. Hell, after a week at that ulcers factory, I need something to help me unwind."

Sol studied his companion and host. He looked tired, older than his announced 31 years.

"What's the problem, or isn't it any of my business?"

"In the small community, everybody's business is everybody s business," Larry began, when a woman entered. "Hi, dear" Larry said. "Meet my new drinking buddy, Solomon D. Wise. Sol, my wife, Helen."

Sol rose to greet the new arrival, an attractive, slender blonde with a youthful figure.

"Oh, yes. You're Harry's new assistant," Helen said, grasping Sol's extended hand and flashing a warm smile. "Solomon The Wise, that's cute. Your wife's name is Shirley, isn't it?"

Sol couldn't mask his surprise. "Why yes, how did you know?"

"I've heard it around from Larry, I think."

"Never mentioned it to you dear. I told you Solly. In a small town there are no secrets." Larry chuckled and lowered himself into the chair opposite Sol, took a deep swallow of his drink, put the glass on the coaster on the end table and filled his pipe.

Helen shook her head. "Now Larry, don't be so bitter. Sol, it's not so bad, but more important: We'd like to have you and your family over for dinner, say next Friday."

"That would be great," Sol replied, feeling the warmth of his drink and the hospitality of his hosts and newfound friends.

"Good. Now please excuse me while I get comfortable," Helen said retreating into the bedroom to change her clothing.

Sol rose from his chair saying: "Well, maybe I better be going."

"Relax. I said I'd drive you home. Here, let me freshen your drink."

"I've still got some," Sol protested as Larry refilled both glasses. But bowing to his host's persistence, he resumed his seat and asked: "So, what were we talking about? Oh yes, ulcer factories."

Larry placidly puffed his pipe, peered at his guest and proceeded: "You asked me about my problem. Well, my problem is Harry Lazar."

Sol sipped his drink, feeling a touch uneasy. "How is my boss your problem? I mean, you each head up your own agency."

"They're supposed to be completely separated by now. Lazar created the Council as an offshoot of the "Y" about ten years ago, and ran both, each as an autonomous entity till about two years ago. You see Lazar's health was deteriorating while the job load of both agencies was increasing. So, the community big shots separated the two completely; separate bylaws, boards of directors, staff, the works, overriding all of Harry's objections. They gave him his choice and he chose the "Y". That's when I came in to become the Council Exec."

"Considering the background you just described, didn't you realize what you were getting into?"

Larry hesitated, adjusted his glasses took another swallow of his drink and then shook his head: "Nope! I was pretty stupid not to have demanded a fuller description of the situation from the big shots. But I was very eager to get the job. I wanted to talk with Harry during the negotiations, but he was in the hospital recuperating from his second heart attack. I was assured though that everything had been worked out. Like a jerk, I believed 'em. I should have known a guy like Lazar doesn't give up so easily. Oh well—'ef em all! Hey—how're you doing with your drink?"

"Finished. And, I really must be going. Can I use your phone to call a cab?"

"Cab? Don't be silly—I'll drive you home."

"After two martinis?" Sol challenged.

Helen, who had come back into the living room, seated

herself and was listening intently to the conversation, now intervened. "I'll drive you. It'll give me a chance to meet Shirley."

Sol thanked Larry for "an interesting beginning of a promising relationship" and accompanied Helen into the car. En route, she explained: "Larry is under a lot of pressure and mostly because Harry won't let go of the Council. He keeps second-guessing Larry and undermines him with the Council lay leaders at every opportunity."

"Gee, that's for the birds, Helen. Well here we are at my place. Please come in and meet Shirley and my kids."

The two wives also discovered an immediate rapport and the dinner date was quickly confirmed. After Helen left and the family was at dinner, Sol Wise addressed his wife, a pretty and dark-complexioned woman with sympathetic hazel eyes. "Larry's a great guy. Sharp, irreverent and funny. But, frustrated and cynical about everything."

"Then maybe it's not such a good idea to get too close to him," Shirley said.

"I like him. What goes on between him and Harry is their problem."

"What's 'irevererer...' mean?" son Norman asked.

The friendship between the two couples flourished, as they dined, attended films, concerts and other social events together. All of which did not go unnoticed by Harry Lazar.

"Sol, who you have as friends is, of course, none of my business, but you ought to know that there are problems regarding Kagan and the Council" Harry said during one of their weekly conferences.

Sol gulped. He couldn't believe his ears and thought carefully before replying. "What has my personal life to do with Council problems? I believe I'm disciplined enough to separate my professional and social activities."

Harry Lazar leaned back in his high-back, vinyl-covered, black swivel desk chair, his hands clasped behind his head, smiled condescendingly and purred: "Well, I guess that's what they taught you in Social Work School. I never went to Social Work School; learned my lessons the hard way. What you said might be true in New York, or Chicago where you could enjoy the luxury of anonymity after work. But in smaller communities one can't compartmentalize the 'social' and the 'professional'. They're two sides of the same coin."

Sol sat stunned! "Are you telling me that my wife and I have to stop seeing the Kagans?"

"I can't tell you who to mix with. But you ought to think about what you're getting into," Harry warned, peering over the top of his half-moon reading spectacles and tugging on some hairs of his graying, stubby mustache.

Sol clenched his fists and struggled to stifle his anger. "Seems like you *are* telling me with whom I can or cannot socialize. As I said before..."

"Look," Harry interrupted, wiping perspiration from his baldpate, "for your own good, I'm trying to educate you about small town folkways and philosophy."

"I understand. And I appreciate your being direct with me, but I don't like this lumping everything together. I guess I'll have to think about what you said."

But the more Sol thought about it, and the more he discussed it with Shirley, the angrier he became. "I'm trying to understand it. But I still think he has a helluva nerve trying to tell us who we should have as friends."

"I know what you're saying. But what can you do?"

"I can stand up for my rights," said Sol rising from his chair.

"And maybe lose your job? We just got here."

Sol put his arm around his wife. "Hey, c'mon, honey. Let's not panic. Look, I'll talk to Larry tomorrow and see what he says."

"Do you think you should? After what Harry Lazar, your boss, just told you?"

"I'm not prohibited from talking to the guy. After all, there's still free speech in this country, isn't there?"

The next morning Sol went upstairs to the Council office where he was, as usual, greeted expansively by Larry. "Squeeze yourself into the other chair," Larry said as he sat down on his rickety lowback, swivel chair. "Now, what can I do for you, my friend?"

"That's it" was Sol's cryptic reply.

"That's what?"

"Whether you and I can continue to be friends."

"What the hell are you talking about? We're not only friends—we're drinking buddies! Can't get any closer than that!"

Sol sighed and said: "Seriously Larry . . . " and he proceeded to share his recent conference with Lazar and the dilemma deriving therefrom.

Larry nodded his understanding and said: "So Solly, you're being initiated. Harry didn't waste any time. So, what are you going to do?"

"I thought you might have some suggestions. I want to do the right thing."

"Right? By whom—Harry, me, or most important, by yourself?"

"All three, if possible."

"It's not possible" Larry groaned.

"Why not?"

Larry grimaced. "Well, you're on the firing line. Lazar regards you as a member of his team. It's good politics if you acted as one."

"Good politics, maybe. But it could also be unethical, unprincipled and expedient."

Larry raised an eyebrow. "Probably. But that's the way

the game is played, especially if you want to survive in this community jungle."

Sol had not anticipated this trend of conversation. He had assumed Larry would be more supportive—by being outraged and by declaring for free speech and individual rights. Instead, here he was being coldly cynical, and accepting the developments. Sol found it difficult to suppress his mounting anger: "Well, dammit, if more people would stand on principle, maybe the community wouldn't be such a jungle."

"Solly, Solly... I know the first awakening is the rudest. Your problem is that you're a graduate MSW—a starry-eyed, professionally trained social worker with lofty principles, ethics, and integrity, trying to live in a jungle of few ethics, little integrity and not much principle."

"Seems like everyone needs to knock my social work training," Sol hissed at Larry.

"Training is great. But you must adapt to local realities. Look: the tree that doesn't bend with the wind is likely to break. And I don't mean bending to every little breeze. Y'know, principles come in all sizes. You simply have got to learn to differentiate between important issues and daily trivia. Choosing your battles, in plain words."

Sol's body stiffened and his jaw jutted and he formed his words carefully: "Decisions based on expediency usually come back to haunt you."

"Words, words, words! You remind me of the guy who has the green light and starts to cross the street without bothering to check the traffic and this truck runs its red light and runs him down; and with his dying breath he says: 'But I had the green light!'"

Sol thought carefully about Sol's latest utterance. He lit a cigarette and asked: "Are you saying I should give in to Harry and let him choose my friends?"

"Well, since it's Friday I suggest we continue this fascinating dialogue at our Happy Hour at my place," Larry said.

"Now, that's the first thing you've said that I agree with. What time?

"Meet me at my car at 5:00 PM."

"Okay, but I'll have to be home by 6:00, the latest."

The two were feeling the warm, relaxing effect of Larry's latest batch of martinis, Sol smoking his inevitable cigarette, Larry his pungent pipe. Replying to Sol's question he said:

"I was in advertising and public relations. And if you think we're in a rat-race now . . . " his voice trailed off.

"Worse than community service?" Sol teased.

"Better believe it! That's the original 'Catch 22' situation. You know what 'Catch 22' is, don't you?"

"Sure. What do you take me for? That's the 'No Win' situation...."

"Well, you tend to be a little naive," Larry interrupted. "And maybe a little pollyannaish. But, I'm sorry, you were saying."

"Naive? Pollyannaish? Because I try to be principled and ethical?" Sol brushed aside his hurt. "Anyway, in school we were subjected to some 'Catch 22's'. For example, if we were late, we were 'resistant'; if we came early, we were 'anxious'; and if we came on time, we were 'compulsive'."

"That's about it—except in the outside, real world the stakes are higher and harsher. Like, Harry putting the pressure on you to act as a member of his team."

"I may be a member of the 'Y' staff, but I'm still entitled to a private social life," Sol persisted, the martini having reinforced his convictions.

"Not in the smaller community. That's what everybody's been trying to tell you—except you're not listening."

"Okay. What did I miss?"

Larry refilled his pipe, tamped down the tobacco and lit it: "At the office and again just a minute ago here, I said, 'to

ACT as a member of his team.' One must do a certain amount of manipulating," Larry blew some perfect smoke rings.

"Act? Manipulate?" Sol heard correctly. Yet, he felt compelled to repeat the words.

"Yes! Act! You play poker? Na! You're probably a chess player, right? Well, whatever you're into—you've got to **appear** to play the game and still not surrender to the pressures, or demands, whatever. I know! I'm an old manipulator from way back."

Sol puffed out his chest. "I'm not a manipulator."

"You just don't like the word. No. Social workers use psychobabble words like 'enabler' or 'indirection' or 'motivate'—right?" Larry chuckled.

"You're distorting the concepts. But there's a germ of truth to what you're saying. Uh, how about refilling my glass?" Sol was feeling relaxed—and reckless.

"We agree on something," Larry said refilling both glasses. Sol sipped the nectar: "So? How do I do what you're suggesting?"

"Shit man I've given you the major concepts—you fill in the details"

Sol sipped his drink again, and peered at his friend. "Okay, you phony philosopher. You convinced me. I've made my decision—details and all."

"Yeah? You're going to play on Lazar's team?"

Sol shook his head. "Nope. I like your four-to-one martinis too much."

"You mean you're going to stand on your 'principles'? I think you're naive and nuts!"

"My mind is made up so don't confuse me with your facts. Besides, I have to shave myself every morning, Larry."

"You'll get hurt," Larry warned.

"So? Then maybe I'll learn what you're trying to teach me. Besides, what alternative do I have?"

"Cooling our relationship for awhile."

Sol shook his head. "But then I'm surrendering my right to a private personal life. Say, aren't you the guy who's always telling me, quote: 'Don't let 'em shit all over you—open your mouth sometimes'... end quote."

"Geez, don't take me so literally all the time. Obviously, if you followed that advice, the results wouldn't be particularly gratifying either," Larry chuckled.

"Okay. Either way—Catch 22—right? So, now explain why Harry Lazar creates such conflicts dragging everyone—including me—into these battles?"

Larry took a deep breath. "Look, I don't like the man. But, I understand him. He worked hard for a long time, for little money, and even less appreciation. He took crap from a lot of pygmies over the years. Most of them have the attitude, they could run the place, but since they have their own business to run—they'll hire some schnook to be the 'Secretary' or later even 'Executive Director'. Finally, after all the years building the agencies—Lazar thinks he's finally sitting on top—and whammo they cut out half his job!"

"But, they didn't cut his salary in half," Sol interrupted. "The same money, for half the responsibility. Not bad."

"And half the authority and power. Frequently, power means more to some people than money. Especially for someone who has been crapped on for so long," Larry explained.

"You're making a big deal out of POWER," Sol challenged, crushing his cigarette in the ashtray.

"You don't want to buy the concept of POWER? Then, at least, if you're gonna continue in this rat-race, learn the professional's motto: 'Non Illigitimi Carburundum'."

"Which means?"

"Which means: 'Don't let the bastards grind you down'."

Sol laughed. "Okay, professor, call me a cab."

"So, you're a Cab."

Sol was eager for his next conference and possible confrontation with Harry Lazar.

"I see you and Kagan are chummier than ever."

Sol nodded and spoke slowly. "Harry, I thought about it. Seems to me that as long as I do my job, and am loyal to the agency . . . "

"In smaller communities the Executive Director is the agency," Harry interrupted. "I like you Sol. You're diligent, dedicated and honest, but not as smart as I thought. As I told you, I don't want to see you hurt."

Sol bit his lip. "Harry, I'm sorry to upset you. I assure you my loyalty to this agency is sincere, but I can't surrender my personal life. Neither do I want to get hurt. But allowing you to determine my social life would be hurting me-and my wife- even more." There! It was out now. The die was cast.

Harry, his chin resting on his fist, stared impassively at Sol. Then he said: "Okay. Let it go. What else is on your agenda?"

Sol was surprised and relieved at Harry's sudden relenting. He was pleased that he had succeeded in standing on principle. He sat back, sighed and said: "Well, there's a problem in the use of the Youth Lounge. Lenny White, the Youth Chairman y'know, has been pressing me for some time about displacing the kids every time there's an adult function."

"I don't see that's such a problem. All of our facilities are multipurpose regardless what they're called."

Sensing Harry's impatience with the issue, Sol decided to back off, and stated that he would discuss the matter further with White. But at Sol's next meeting with the Chairman, Leonard White expressed his unhappiness with Sol's report and stated that he would have to bring it up again at the next Youth Committee meeting.

At the committee meeting, Sol stressed the official agency position—as spelled out by Henry Lazar, the Executive Director—regarding the multi-purpose use of all its facilities.

But the committee members, aggressively led by Chairman White, insisted that if the Youth Lounge was to be, in fact, a Youth Lounge it had to be reserved for youth activities.

At his next Happy Hour with Larry, Sol shared his increasing frustration regarding the Youth Lounge. "The committee certainly has a point. And I can see some important principles at stake."

"Oh boy, again with principles! But, back up, buddy. I still don't understand Harry's giving in so easily in your first battle. That's not like him. Something's fishy."

"Larry, you've been in the jungle too long!" Sol replied. He was feeling confidant and suspected Larry was probably also a little jealous about Sol's clinging to his principles.

"No doubt about that," Helen concurred from the kitchen.

"Okay, I can't battle both of you. Tell me, Solly, what principles have you found in the 'Case of the Youth Lounge'?"

"For one thing, who determines policy; the professional staff or the lay leadership? And two; the right of the kids to have priority in the use of their own lounge."

Larry sipped his drink, peering incredulously at his friend over the rim of his glass. "If I were you, I'd forget the whole thing."

"What do you mean 'forget it'? How do I 'forget it'?"

"I mean, do it Harry's way. Don't you see, you're in another 'Catch 22', 'ol buddy!"

"Hm. Good drink, Larry." Sol paused. "So how do I get outta this '22'?"

"Ask your boss."

"You're an S.O.B., Larry Kagan. Now, next question; how do I get home today?"

Sol took Larry's advice, about asking his boss, and put the problem squarely before Harry at their next conference. But, Harry's counseling was not clear. On the one hand, he stressed the responsibilities to the committee. On the other hand, he stressed the responsibilities to the youth. And on the third hand, he recited the realities of the space limitations.

"Well Harry, to be honest, it's all rather confusing—especially with three hands."

"I know. Perhaps it would be best to bring it to the Board of Directors."

No agenda item was more important to Sol than "Usage of Youth Lounge." Leonard White stressed the purpose of the Youth Lounge and presented his committee's recommendation: that the lounge be reserved for youth activities. Sol took a very active role in the discussions. But then he became aware that he was the major torchbearer. He felt he was out on a very shaky limb. And it was precisely at this moment that Harry Lazar was recognized by the president.

Henry Lazar rose slowly, majestically. He peered at each face, speaking softly, and very deliberately. He commended Leonard White and the entire committee for their commitment and conscientiousness, but then reminded everyone of the realities of the space limitations. He was dramatic, convincing, entertaining and clearly in control of people and events—effectively manipulative, Sol thought.

"And as for my fine, young, new assistant," Harry intoned (and Sol felt his shaky limb quiver): "He is a dedicated, principled professional, just a few years out of school, who will, with more experience, and the proper guidance, learn to temper his eagerness with better judgment, and to understand priorities."

Although his anger and frustration were mounting, Sol found himself admiring the skill with which Harry Lazar twisted the knife while simultaneously sawing off the lonely limb. "So, ladies and gentlemen," Henry concluded, "as you deliberate your decision, remember that the committee and staff are to be commended for their diligence and concern. But, it would be impossible for me, as the administrator, to implement their recommendation." As Harry sat down, he flashed a condescending smile in Sol's direction.

The guy should have been a lawyer, Sol thought as he smiled wanly in return.

And then the board voted unanimously to reject the Youth Committee recommendation. Sol had expected a rejection, but was astonished that White and other committee members had voted against their own proposal! "Larry, you wouldn't believe your own eyes and ears had you been there."

"Have you talked to White?"

"No. The bastard dashed out right after the meeting."

"What did Lazar say?" Larry asked.

"Not much. He's smug and pompous. Said we could discuss the matter at our conference next week. Not the next day—next week."

"He's letting you sweat and stew. But the delay could be a blessing. Gives you a chance to talk with White."

"You have any ideas of what he might say?"

"Yep. I understand the whole episode," Larry said.

"So, give"

"It's better if you talk to White—and Lazar."

After ducking Sol's calls for several days, Leonard White agreed to meet. He picked Sol up outside Sol's garden apartment and drove to the outskirts of Essex. They sat in the car and discussed the meeting. White listened to Sol's complaints of feeling "deserted, left out on a limb, and holding the bag."

"I understand, Sol, and I'd probably feel the same way about it if I were you-a paid staff member. But Sol, you've got to understand that we lay people are involved as...well...as kind of volunteers. We don't get paid for our participation like you professionals. And besides, most professionals come and go, whereas this is my home. I have to live here despite disagreements and conflicts."

Sol couldn't believe his ears: "Precisely because this is your home, and the agency is your agency, it seems to me that you have more at stake than professionals who 'come and go'. I don't understand you."

"Well, look! You really can't expect me to fight with my friends, neighbors, and even my brother, can you really?"

Sol had forgotten that Donald White was the current 'Y' President so the last remark finally struck home. After a momentary silence, he could only mutter, "I guess not. Please drive me home."

And now Sol couldn't wait to talk with Larry. "It was unbelievable. With a straight face I swear he wanted my sympathies. And why have our conference in his car? Geez—we could have talked over a cup of coffee somewhere—my place or his—or any old coffee shop."

"He didn't want to be seen with you. Not until this thing finally simmers down."

"What kind of people are these?" Sol exclaimed as he ran his hand through his hair.

"Hey, Solly! These are normal people. Like any place else. I told you before—you're too Pollyannaish. You've got to learn to temper your idealism with realities. Anyway, Sol, you were set-up for this."

"By Harry?" Sol guessed.

"Who else? I can smell his technique a mile away."

"You're right! Say Larry, teach me how to 'manipulate' and I'll teach you how to be an 'enabler'."

"It's a deal. Skoll" Larry raised his glass.

"Down the hatch and to hell with Harry Lazar and 'ef 'em all!" Sol said draining his glass.

"Yeah. And, 'Non Illigitimi Carburundum'" Larry reminded him.

THE END

XIII. THE JAYWALKER

The car had been polished to a high luster, using a good grade of wax, lots of elbow grease, and much pride. For, although it was a "used car" it was, after all, our first automobile and therefore very new for us. The high noon Texas sun was also shining—bright and broiling. I had an appointment in downtown Houston and, with considerable care, guided our new acquisition to the Fannin Street address. I spotted an empty space at the curb, guarded by an unexpired meter, and pulled into it with a skill and dexterity far beyond that normally possessed by one who had only recently received his driver's license. My satisfaction, however, was short-lived, for upon exiting the car, the red "VIOLATION" sign popped up. I read the instructions: **"Dimes only! No Substitutes!"**

My pockets yielded pennies, nickels, some quarters and even a half dollar, but no dimes.

Assuming it to be a reasonable world, and being a novice in relating to parking guardians, I muttered to the meter: "Two nickels make a dime." **"No Substitutes! Violators will be prosecuted!"** kept blinking back at me as if taunting and daring. In any event, the coin slot was too small for anything but a dime.

"Sheesh I've got no dimes," I muttered to the meter, as an incipient panic possessed me. I spotted a pedestrian and walked up to him, saying: "Excuse me, sir, could you please uh, spare a dime?" And his startled and annoyed look prompted me to quickly add: "No, no! I'm not a panhandler?"

But he quickly walked passed me as I protested my innocence in that regard. I had not felt so embarrassed in a long time! And my panic mounted as I looked around and saw several other pedestrians making detours to avoid passing me. Fortunately I spotted a drug store across the street. Ah, a place to get change! I sure didn't want to get a ticket for over-parking a meter. A perfect record ought not to be marred so soon after getting one's very own car and driver's license, I thought.

I estimated it would take no more than a few minutes to dash across Fannin Street, get change at the drug store, and dart back to feed the threatening monster its dime. I stepped off the curb, after remembering to look to the right, and then to the left; and again to the right, and again left. The way was clear! I made a diagonal beeline across Fannin Street, straight to the drug store. But before I could complete my journey, a shrill whistle pierced the air: "Bleep! Bleep!"

"For whom does the whistle blow?" I wondered as I hopped to the safety of the curb. The bleeping became more insistent and I looked in its direction.

A picture-postcard policeman at the Fannin Street intersection was the whistle-blower. His navy-blue tunic, with gold buttons, was perfectly tailored and matched with his gray, flared pants with red stripes at the sides; the pants legs disappearing into highly-polished black boots. And topping off this dizzying display of the well-dressed trooper was a white plastic helmet with goggles. The officer had stopped all traffic with the blowing of his whistle. Now that he had caught my attention, he extended his right arm and hand to full length and pointed his index finger at me—as if beaming a laser in my direction.

I pointed to myself: "Who, me?"

His laser-finger, accompanied by a slight nod of the helmeted-head, indicated, "Yes, you." And then he crooked his finger in the traditional "come hither" sign.

I looked to my right and then to my left to make certain that he was, in fact, beckoning only me. His continuing charade-signs made it perfectly clear that it was, indeed only me that he desired to meet. I left the safety of my curb and walked towards him into the very dangerous, busy intersection.

With me at his side, he now resumed directing the traffic into a rhythmic flow and then focused his full attention upon me.

"Where y'all from, sir? He drawled.

My mind raced. I'd heard about the treatment afforded Yankees from New York. Even though I was only in Houston about two months, I wasn't going to give myself away so easily.

"Sir," he prodded, "where y'all from?"

Ahem, I cleared my throat. "Why, from Houston," in a tone which implied, "where else?"

He eyed me suspiciously, sighed and replied: "Well then, y'all surely know it's against the law to Jaywa'k, don't you?"

"Jaywalk?" I asked.

"Yes sir. Jaywa'k. See those lines?" And he pointed to the four sets of double white lines connecting all four crosswalks. "That's where pedestrians are s'posed to wa'k to git across the street. "S'cuse me, sir." And he turned to direct some more traffic.

I was confused, hot and anxious.

After what seemed an interminable period of time he returned to me. "Now, you sir, wa'ked diagonally across from that there parkin' meter to t'other side—and that's what we residents of Houston—of which y'all say y'ar one—call jaywa'kin."

"Ahuh," I sighed, unable to deny the allegation. "Now what?"

"Scuse me, sir," and he directed some more traffic. "Well, sir, Ah'm sorry but I must give you this citation for jaywa'kin." And, after taking my name, he proceeded to write out what looked like—of all things—a traffic ticket!

"Citation?" I gulped. "Which means... ?"

"Which means five dollars fine, sir."

"Five dollars! Tell me, officer, what's the fine for over parking a meter?"

"Over-parkin' a meter?" he repeated with a twinkle in his blue eyes-"Well sir, the fine for over-parkin' a meter is two dollars."

"Two dollars" I echoed. "Now there's a double irony for you!"

"How's that sir?" he asked while again directing traffic.

"Well, I've been walking for nearly 30 years—in many cities all over the good old U.S.A. Never owned a car until now. And in trying to avoid breaking the law with my new car, I get a ticket, but not for using the car. Nope—for walking!"

He looked at me with genuine sympathy. "For jaywa'kin, sir, not wa'kin. What's irony number two?"

"Huh? Oh, irony number two; if I'd known it was cheaper to get a ticket for over-parking a meter, as against $5 for walking, I'd have taken the meter rap.

"For jaywa'kin', sir not wa'kin'," he repeated. "There's a mite of a difference."

"What's the difference?"

"Well, at least three dollars sir. But more impo'tant, I suspect that y'all never again git a ticket for jaywa'kin, right sir?" And he smiled an all-knowing smile as he gave me a dime for the meter.

His words were prophetic.

THE END

XIV. FAILED JOURNEY

("EVERYBODY HAS THEIR OWN AGENDA!" Anonymous)

CAST OF CHARACTERS AND AGENDAS
Sol Wise: Aspires to become the Executive Director of his own Jewish Community Center (JCC).
Fred Furman: Field Secretary of the National Association of JCCs; eager to add a new agency.
Itz Steinberg: Past President of the Jewish Social Club. Wants it to be an affiliate of the NAJCC.
Al Shonen: Prefers to maintain the status quo. Sees the new Executive only as a Social Director.
Harry Kravitz: Treasurer of the Jewish Community Alliance and keeper of its books. Silent one.
Seymour Schulster: Current President of the evolving organization. Former NAJCC staffer.
Herbert Mailman: Head of the NAJCC's Bureau of Personnel. Recognizes call for "Help!"

ATLANTA, GEORGIA: JUNE 1956

Solomon David Wise really liked Fred Furman, the Field Secretary of the Southern Region of the National Association of Jewish Community Centers with headquarters in Atlanta, Georgia. He knew Fred before Fred took over the field secretary position—when he was still the Assistant Director of the Philadelphia JCC and they met at the various conferences. As Field Secretary Fred visited all the JCCs in the Southern Region and thus was familiar with all the latest developments in those communities. The NAJCC was the national organization representing the interests of the YM-YWHAs and Jewish Community Centers all around the country with its main office in New York City.

Fred was a short, rotund, dark complexioned fellow with a marvelous sense of humor and with a deep commitment to the Jewish Center field and a well-recognized professional with integrity. At one of the Southern Region's biennial conferences, which this time was held in Atlanta, Georgia, he sought out Sol and told him there was something he wanted to discuss.

Sol was in his fourth year as the Program Director of the Jewish Community Center in Houston, Texas and felt ready, after a grand total of twelve years in various part-time and full-time positions with "Y"s and JCCs in New York, New Jersey and Texas, to move up to his first executive director's position. So, he was more than ready to discuss whatever Fred had in mind. They met for lunch one day at the conference.

"Sol, I know you're a pioneering kind of guy and now ready to move up to an executive job. There's this Jewish organization in Jacksonville, Florida that started out as a sort of Jewish Social Club but is now interested in becoming a full-fledged Jewish Community Center. We've been working with them for the past couple of years regarding their achieving that goal. They know that a prerequisite is for them to be accredited and affiliated with our NAJCC and that at least two thirds of their current membership had to agree to the change. I was at their last membership meeting at which two-thirds approved their going in that direction. We've brought it to the point where it can now use a professional worker, on site so-to-speak, to complete the final stages. And they've expressed a willingness to employ such a person."

Sol expressed his interest, particularly about pioneering a new agency and starting with it from scratch and building it from the ground up. But he wanted to know more about the community in general and the Jewish community in particular.

Fred said that Jacksonville was the second largest city in Florida and was the county seat as well as the port of entry for Duval County located on a bluff overlooking the St. Johns River 25 miles west of the river's mouth on the Atlantic Ocean, about 135 miles south of Savannah, Georgia. He added that five railroad lines intersected there and many coastwise and overseas shipping lines originated there. Also, the Port of Jacksonville was a major shipbuilding center as well as home for a US Naval Station. In short, it was the chief commercial and industrial center, certainly in northern Florida. Although its 1950 census showed it to have a population of only 204,517 people, it was the center of a trading area of over 150 miles wide with a population of more than a million people!

Although Houston, in 1956, had a general population exceeding 500,000 and a Jewish population of over 15,000, Solomon Wise was impressed with the figures Fred was throwing at him, noting that obviously Jacksonville was a growing community. However he again pressed Fred for information about the Jewish community.

And Fred reported that the current Jewish population of Jacksonville was about half that of Houston, namely, 7000 to 8000 spread throughout the general community with no one concentration. As with most such "small to intermediate-size communities" it did have the three denominations of an orthodox, a conservative and one reform congregation. The conservative congregation called itself The Jewish Center—but that, Fred hastened to add—was not atypical all along the Atlantic seaboard.

"But wont that complicate the picture—having two organizations with almost identical names, like The Jewish Center and then the Jewish Community Center?" Sol asked.

Fred smiled and replied: "Not to worry. There won't be two 'Jewish Centers'. Our group has now officially changed its name to The Jewish Community Alliance." And then he went on to inform Sol that the JCA owned a beautiful ten acre site overlooking the St. Johns River containing many orange groves and an outdoor swimming pool with two bath houses, two tennis courts, a handball court and a small recreation hall. A small, prior existing building had been converted to an office.

"Well it does sound promising and enticing. But what about a central planning and fund-raising agency—does Jacksonville have a Jewish Federation or at least Jewish Community Council? And if so, what is its position on the creation of a new JCC, or in this case JCA, and what are the chances of the JCA receiving an allocation from them?" Sol asked.

Fred smiled again. "You know all the questions to ask, don't you? Well, they do have a Jewish Community Council and during the annual fund-raising campaign it's combined with the United Jewish Appeal, the one responsible for Jewish overseas and Israel needs, as you know, into a UJA/JCC Drive. The JCA has applied to become a constituent member of the Jewish Community Council, actually taking over the seat held by the former Jewish Social Club, and it will be invited to apply for allocations. So, any other questions, or can I tell them that you are interested and we could send them your profile, along with two others?" Fred concluded, still smiling.

Frank had pegged Sol right about his being a pioneering guy eager for his first executive director position, but he did not anticipate a continuing barrage of questions. Now it was Sol's turn to smile and say: "Just a few more questions. And I know the right questions to ask because Jack Dauber, the

JCC executive director back in Houston, has been priming me. You know Jack, right? So, what kind of budget will it have and what about personnel in addition to the executive director? And what kind of back-up is there in case things go wrong?"

"Of course I know Jack. You worked with him in Albany, NY, before coming to Houston, if I remember my facts. He's an excellent professional who trains his staff well—which is why I'm now discussing this prospect with you."

"Yes, I worked with him in Albany for two years and from there went to Essex in New Jersey. Jack then went to Houston as its executive director and when things didn't work out for me in Essex I went to Houston. But what about my questions about the budget, personnel and the backup in case things went wrong?"

Fred smiled his perpetual smile and replied: "The budget would, of course, be a slim one to begin with, and would include provision for an executive director, part-time secretary and a full-time maintenance person. But once the JCA begins receiving allocations from the Jewish Council/UJA and the local United Way a more substantial budget could be developed.

Fred then addressed Sol's question about "back-up in the event of problems" stressing that the JCA had agreed to set aside a sum of $20,000, in addition to the annual budget, as a guarantee for at least one-year's minimal operation. And finally, he assured Sol that he had the total backing and support of the National Association of Jewish Community Centers, especially himself as the Secretary of the Southern Region.

"Well, that seems to cover all the bases. Yes, I'm interested in applying so you can send them my profile," Sol said.

AUGUST 1956

By the end of July, Sol received a call from Itz Steinberg, a former president of the Jewish Social Club, and now the Chairman of the Search Committee of the Jewish Community Alliance of Jacksonville, Florida expressing interest in Sol and inviting him for an interview. Sol explained that he was going on vacation for the month of August, planning to motor back with his wife, Shirley and their two children, Louis and Shelly, to New York to visit his and Shirley's families there, but offered to alter his route so that he would pass through Jacksonville and stay overnight for the interview.

Which is what he did. They drove along the Gulf route passing through Louisiana, Mississippi, Alabama, and stopped off in Atlanta to visit briefly with Fred Furman and then on down to Jacksonville. They checked into a Holiday Inn and went over to Itz Steinberg's home for dinner. Itz was a tall, gray-haired fellow in his early fifties who dabbled in a number of business enterprises, some successful and some not yet successful. He and his wife were most gracious hosts and after dinner Itz's wife, Sally entertained Shirley and the kids while Itz took Sol into the den to talk about the next day's interview. He explained that they had already interviewed two others and that Sol would be the final interviewee, but from what he and his Search Committee already had learned by reading his resume and talking with Jack Dauber and other people in Houston as well as other communities where Sol had worked, Sol would probably be offered the position—provided he didn't run afoul of a few people—such as Al Shonen, for example—who was on the Search Committee which would be interviewing Sol the next day. And then Mr. Steinberg explained that a minority, led by Shonen had been opposed to changing the Jewish Social Club from its Country Club philosophy and structure to a Jewish Community Center and was still trying all kinds of maneuvers to block, or at least slow down the change. "But that wont happen, so don't be concerned," Itz Steinberg concluded.

Despite his host's assurance, Sol couldn't help feel a pang of anxiety.

To Sol's (and everyone's) relief the interview went well. Al Shonen, to everyone's surprise was not combative; in fact he presented himself as cordial and cooperative, interested in Sol's program skills because in his opinion Sol's major responsibility would be "the equivalent of the Social Director of a Country Club." Fred Furman—who had driven down from Atlanta to be present at the meeting—demurred at that point and read a typical "Job Description for Executive Directors of Jewish Community Centers." To which Shonen replied: "Same difference." The Search Committee thanked Sol for coming for the interview, told him that they would notify him within a few weeks and wished him a bon voyage and happy vacation.

The next day Sol and his family resumed their auto journey up along the Atlantic coast highway system using for the most part U.S. # 1 to visit their families in New York. The Burma Shave poem-ads amused them, particularly one which they kept zipping past: "A mile a minute; there's no future in it!"

"What does that mean, Dad?" Louis asked as they sped past another one.

"Well a mile a minute means 60 miles an hour, and they evidently think that's too fast," Sol explained as he slowed from 65 mph to 58 mph.

They spent a pleasurable few weeks in New York and returned to Houston, Texas to await the decision from the JCA. By September 1st Itz Steinberg called Sol to congratulate him on being selected for the job. After giving the mandatory month's notice Sol left Houston with his family to assume his new responsibilities as the first Executive Director of the new Jewish Community Alliance of Jacksonville, Florida. They stopped in New Orleans to spend a weekend with their dear friends, the Sturms, Manny Sturm having been one of Sol's program assistants in Houston until taking a job with the JCC in New Orleans. Sol officially assumed his duties on October 19, 1956 when he turned 35, a significant birthday present, Shirley observed.

"CONCENTRATE ON THE PROGRAM"

As agreed, the JCA membership—despite the opposition of a vocal minority lead by Al Shonen—had amended its constitution and bylaws establishing it as a non-profit community service agency devoted to the recreational and cultural needs of the Jewish community. They had agreed to change their membership fees structure, "at the appropriate time" so that instead of an annual $1000 Family Membership fee, plus periodic assessments which could cost a family thousands of dollars, the JCA would institute a schedule of membership dues typical of Jewish Community Centers. To offset the anticipated losses from such a change, application would be made to the UJA/Federation and the United Way to provide allocations to help with the operations.

At his first executive committee session, followed by a board meeting the next week, (both chaired by president Seymour Schulster, whom Sol met for the first time since Sy was a traveling salesman on the road most of the week) Sol agreed to the basic strategy of his concentrating on programs, public relations and the structuring of the new agency leaving financial matters and budget to the finance committee, with its chairman, Harry Kravitz, the treasurer, who would continue to serve as the bookkeeper for the agency.

Sol liked both men. Sy Schulster, a curly-red-head fellow of medium height and slender weight had worked for the NAJCC as its Southern Region Armed Services Division with his headquarters in Jacksonville because of its naval base. When he left them to work as a salesman of educational supplies canvassing school districts throughout the southeast, he decided to stay in Jacksonville with his family even though he himself would be on the road most of the week. He was an effective ally to Itz Steinberg in moving the Jewish Social Club to affiliate with the NAJCC and to change to the Jewish Community Alliance. Sy was a very charming and persuasive guy who had positive relations with everybody including Al Shonen. Yet even Sy's charms and arguments failed to totally convince Shonen and win him to their side. But, when in town, Sy was able to round out some of Al's sharp edges. The trouble was, that he was out of town so often that Sol, had to compensate for his absence by relying more on others such as Itz and Sully.

"What I'm trying to say is that if Sy were available more fully he might have made more of a difference in the balance of things," Sol said to Fred Furman in one of his many phone conversations with him.

And Sol liked Harry Kravitz, the treasurer and chairman of the finance committee, because, even though he and his two brothers operated a growing chain of discount stores called THE LAST DOLLAR catering mostly to black ghettos, he and his brothers were diligent, hard-working, and personally honest and direct. Harry was the oldest of the three brothers and apparently the brains of the business. Sol lunched with him periodically for updates on the financial condition of the JCA. Although a young man in his late thirties he was already balding and very conscious of the fact. He told Sol that in many ways, the effort to create the JCA was like building his business with all the uncertainty and challenges. But the rewards to be reaped were great. "The greater the uncertainty and the challenge, the greater the reward, and one should not be unduly concerned with minor blips and glitches," he kept telling Sol.

So, with the basic strategy agreed upon and the principles as well as principals in place, the program season was ushered in with a gala ball at a downtown hotel (since the JCA's small recreation hall was inadequate for the event), which simultaneously celebrated the arrival of the new executive director and the new direction of the new agency. And the honeymoon was happily launched. But it would prove to be a short one.

Sol functioned as a veritable whirlwind, launching a Membership Campaign, recruiting volunteers from the small, but now growing membership to staff several programs including arts and crafts, sports and athletics as well as cultural and social events for adults and teens. Even his wife Shirley was drafted to run a Story Reading Program for the younger children on Sundays while their parents lolled on the outside pool deck.

Sol also concentrated on meeting with community leaders, educators, each of the rabbis of the three congregations, most of the ministers and/or priests of the many churches, directors of the social agencies, especially the Jewish Community Council and the United Way with whom he discussed JCA's affiliation and its ultimately becoming a beneficiary agency to receive annual allocations. And it was in some of those meetings that the first drops of rain began to fall.

The priests and ministers were unanimously friendly and ready to cooperate. The rabbis presented a mixed bag of ambivalent emotions and rationalizations. They were overtly cordial and friendly, although each had questions about "the necessity for another Jewish organization." And the rabbi of the conservative Jewish Center was even more direct, claiming that his congregation already fulfilled the need for such an organization. Sol asked this rabbi if Fred Furman hadn't discussed the issue with him and the rabbi replied that he had although he also stressed that he told Fred that Judaism "has room for many houses in its heart" and Sol came away feeling that "this guy is a phony."

Nevertheless Sol called Fred to share with him his various sessions but especially the one with the conservative rabbi and Fred confirmed Sol's suspicions that the guy tended to play both ends against the middle. But Fred also emphasized something that Sol had already learned in his many years in communal service; that congregations, by their differing religious emphases, tend to divide communities whereas Y's and centers tend to unite and unify. So, Fred suggested that one had to take religious leaders with that factor in mind.

Sol next shared with Fred his concerns arising from his meetings with the directors of the two campaigns that JCA sought to become affiliated with and derive allocations from, namely the UJA/JCC and the United Way. The UJA/JCC director was confident that the JCA would be approved to become an affiliate but was a bit pessimistic about how much could be expected in the first allocation. And the United Way executive explained that there was a three-year waiting period for new agencies to be admitted. That regulation was put into effect this past September.

Fred expressed his disappointment with such news, but suggested that Sol should insist that the three-year time period be counted from when he, Fred and the JCCA first approached the United Way two years ago. Fred acknowledged Sol's concerns but assured him that the issues could and would be resolved to the benefit of the agency and then he complimented Sol for his very active and aggressive beginning of his tour of duty stressing that he was hearing very positive things.

Which provided Sol with some measure of reassurance, but still left him with a residue of anxiety. Sol thanked Fred and asked when he would next see him. But Fred was noncommittal.

DO WE HAVE AN ANGEL?

Sol also met with community business leaders including P.N. Golman, President and CEO of the American Utility Pole Corporation whose young-adult nephew joined the JCA as a result of the ongoing Membership Campaign. Sol had organized a Young Adult Singles Club (YASC) when his attention was brought to the fact that there were a surprising number of such people in the Jewish community and none of the congregations were addressing the problem. David Golman came in to see Sol and shared with him the problem.

David was a short, slim, black haired and dark complexioned young man of 19 with thick horn-rimmed glasses and an infectious smile. He was attending Tufts University in the Boston area, studying Business Administration in preparation for entering the family business in Jacksonville, now operated by his uncle P.N. Golman. He described the business as a rather unique one; curing poles and chemically treating them so that they would be insect and termite-free so that they could be used for the utility poles and cross-bars on the poles all across the country. The practice of burying utility lines rather than stringing them on rows of poles along roads and highways, was just getting under way in the United States, so that there was still a tremendous demand for the cured and treated utility poles and their cross bars.

While attending school in Boston David also participated in the activities of the several YM-YWHAs in the area, including Hecht House and the Boston YMHA and he loved it. And when he heard of the creation of the JCA in his hometown of Jacksonville, he couldn't wait to get home and become a part of it. Although he still had two years of schooling in Boston, he felt he could contribute when he was home on holidays or during the summer. And when Sol organized the Young Adult Singles Club, he joined that too along with the JCA.

David said that he had talked to his uncle about the JCA and the YASC and his uncle said that he would be interested in talking with Sol at Sol's convenience and if Sol would call P.N. he could arrange for an appointment.

Sol called and within a week he was in P.N.'s office explaining to him the goals and ambitions of the JCA and of the entire Jewish Community Center movement nationally. Paul Nathan Golman was an older copy of his nephew, short, thin dark-complexioned, as Sephardic Jews were wont to be, also with horn-rimmed glasses. He listened politely, if not attentively nodding now and then but saying little. And when Sol handed him some brochures explaining the goals and objectives of the JCA, he murmured that they were very well done and said that he would try to get out to the site soon to see for himself what was underway. He thanked Sol for taking the time to come see him and walked him to the door giving a firm handshake and a pat on the shoulder.

Another week later P.N. called to ask Sol if it was convenient for him to come over and see the site and grounds and Sol struggled to control his excitement and eagerness. P.N. arrived within the hour driving up in an old Chevy Bel Air. In Sol's office he looked at an architect's schematics of what the future buildings and facilities might look like once the agency undertook its Capital Funds Campaign, estimated to cost close to one million dollars. He smiled as he looked at the attractive drawings and murmured: "Yes, that's right, make no little plans." And then Sol walked him all over the beautiful ten acres overlooking the St. Johns River and heard P.N. grunting approval although wondering why they had to get rid of so many trees.

On their return to Sol's office, P.N. spoke bluntly: "Sol, I like what I've heard and most of what I've seen. But I have to tell you that I firmly believe in helping people to help them-selves and that includes organizations and agencies. I know most of the people on the board of the JCA and many of them are good, hard-working, honest people. But I know some, whom I will not name, who I believe to be merely promoters—always looking for short cuts. I'm giving the JCA a check from the Golman Family Foundation, which should help you get the ball rolling, and as for the future—well, we'll just have to wait and see."

Sol thanked him for coming and for his donation and walked him to his ancient car and after his departure opened the envelope and removed a check for one thousand dollars payable to the Jewish Community Alliance! He was so excited and ecstatic that he called first his former supervisor and mentor, Jack Dauber in Houston and then Fred Furman, to share with them the recent event. And both professionals congratulated him with Fred noting that Sol had "planted an important seedling."

"INTO EVERY LIFE A LITTLE RAIN MUST FALL"

Although the Membership Campaign was yielding encouraging results, some additional raindrops now fell. In revising the membership dues structure the biggest problem was what to do about people who were original members of the old Jewish Social Club and who had paid their $1000 fee plus assessments. Sol had suggested that such people be designated Charter Members of the Jewish Community Alliance and be given credit towards one or two years membership in the new agency under the new membership fee structure. And despite some hassling by Shonen this recommendation was approved albeit limited to one year's credit. Still there were some grumblings by some "Charters" about the "newcomers getting in so cheaply."

By the end of December the UJA/JCC allocations were announced and the JCA was granted a mere $5000 as its first year's allocation instead of the ten thousand requested with the explanation that the campaign had not raised as much as it desired (although its official goal had been reached) and the new agency had not yet demonstrated its staying power.

But more important than the developing financial pressures and concerns were the problems of erosion and loss of not only topsoil but substrata as well. Tom McCall, the maintenance supervisor hired by Sol right after his arrival, called Sol's attention to the problem. He pointed out the three small chunks of concrete that had broken off from the handball court, which was nearest to the edge of the bluff overlooking the St. Johns River on which the ten-acre property was located.

"Ya see, Sol, this property was an orange grove with hundreds of trees which kept the topsoil and the substrata in place. But once they bulldozed all the trees to make way for the pool and bathhouses, there was nothing left to hold the soil and substrata. Either a good number of trees should have been left intact, or they should have bulwarked the sides of the bluff to prevent the erosion and soil-runoff after each of the heavy rains." Tom explained.

Sol asked Tom whether he could repair the current damage himself or whether outside help would be required and Tom indicated that he could repair the handball court, but whatever repairs he made now would be only a stop-gap measure but that the problem would worsen if steps were not taken to remedy the basic condition.

Sol brought the problem to the attention of Sully Zeppa, chairman of the grounds and maintenance committee—who chuckled and smirked as he examined the spot that Tom had refilled with rocks and gravel and then re-cemented.

"What's so funny?" Sol asked.

"Well, I was on the development committee that was responsible for—they called it "improving the property" when we first bought it. Al Shonen was the chairman—and a more stubborn sonovabitch you don't want to meet—and I objected to the massive bulldozing of the orange grove because I suspected that we could end up with a problem like this. But he insisted that 'dozing was the least expensive and the quickest way to clear the property so that we could go ahead with the pool and bathhouses. He said we could plant some other trees later if that was needed."

At the subsequent meeting of the total G & M committee it was agreed to bring in some experts to advise on short-term and long-term solutions to the problem. And when these were provided the proposals were submitted to the JCA Board of Directors at its January 1957 meeting.

At that meeting, Al Shonen dismissed the proposals out of hand and tended to minimize the problem, criticizing Sol for "making a mountain out of a molehill" and spending scarce money unnecessarily on so-called "experts." As a builder of homes and as a "developer" he knew that the problem was manageable and all that was needed was the planting of some trees along the rim of the bluff and the prudent use of sandbags in appropriate locations.

The board decided to keep the proposals on file—for future references if necessary—but to accept Shonen's motion—seconded by Sully Zeppa—to proceed with the trees and sandbags.

FRED FURMAN'S FEBRUARY FIELD VISIT

Sol was in regular telephone contact with Fred Furman, keeping him apprized of the developments of the new agency. He reported that while there were encouraging gains in the continuing membership campaign he was becoming increasingly concerned about the unplanned expenses they were incurring. He wasn't getting many details about their financial situation from Harry Kravitz, the treasurer and bookkeeper. Also, while he presented the United Way with the scheme that Fred had proposed, they came back with a compromise of "crediting" the JCA with just a one-year of "prior existence" which meant they would not be considered for an allocation until the 1958 fiscal year.

"Okay buddy, I'll be visiting you guys in February, so just hang on and keep smiling," Fred said.

At the Executive Committee meeting in February 1957, with Fred present, Itz Steinberg chaired the meeting because Sy Schulster was again out of town on the road. Itz was his usual charming self and full of compliments for the job that Sol was doing and expressing optimism about the progress they were making.

Al Shonen, on the other hand, expressed his disappointment with Sol, saying that as far as he was concerned, Sol should be focusing solely on the programs, like a Social Director should be doing, and not be involved in things not of his concern.

There was lively discussion about the two points of view with Sully and most other committee members backing Sol, but a handful credited Shonen with having some points.

Both Itz and Fred attempted to bridge the developing chasm and the meeting ended with a papering over of the differences and concerns.

After the meeting Sol met privately with Fred expressing his unhappiness with the failure to face up to the realities that Sol had uncovered. Fred was duly sympathetic but said that Sol needed to be more aggressive with regards to people like Shonen. He said: "Sometimes, Sol it's necessary to get into the gutter, with people like Shonen, and wrestle with him there."

Sol was momentarily speechless because he couldn't believe what he was hearing from Fred. This was not the Fred that he had known over the years. But then he marshaled his nerve and said; "I'm not getting into any gutter with any people."

And now Fred faced with such determination sought to modify his comment: "Well I don't mean that you actually get into the gutter with people. I mean you need to take a firmer stand and lock horns with the likes of Al Shonen." And then Fred suddenly shifted his stance and asked whether Sol had ever tried to have a sustained one-on-one conversation with Al Shonen and Sol admitted that he had not tried that. He had always been engaged with Shonen on some controversial issue and always in the presence of other people.

Sol mulled the thought over in his mind and then told Fred that unless he gave that a try he would never really feel that he had tried every angle.

Sol called Al Shonen to try to arrange for a one-on-one meeting with him, indicating that it could be lunch or whatever was convenient for him.

Shonen was cordial enough over the phone but cited business pressures, which made it difficult for him to make any definite appointments, and Sol was definitely getting the impression that the guy was merely stalling. Yet he persisted and Shonen finally agreed to a luncheon date after he returned from some out of town business. And so it was late March when they met for lunch at a downtown restaurant.

At lunch Sol made an effort to take another look at this man who appeared to be his major adversary. After a round of martinis, while they made some small talk and partaking of the lunch Sol perceived a short, balding man with bushy eyebrows and a tense manner. Even his cutting of his meat was done with short, precise and deliberate strokes. Yet, after a second martini, Al Shonen showed himself capable of a smile now and then.

Shonen asked Sol how he liked Jacksonville and what kind of living quarters he had.

Sol thought it a little odd that he and his family had been in town for six months and the guy was only now asking him about his living arrangements. But he caught himself, remembering that this was a session to try to find some middle ground, and—what the hell, better late than never. And so he explained that they had bought a house one month after moving to town because they liked Jacksonville and felt they wanted to sink roots there.

Al Shonen was genuinely surprised to hear that and—because he was a builder/developer he wanted to know all about the house they had bought, the part of town it was in, the neighbors, whether there were many Jewish families. And then he surprised Sol by saying; "You should have come to me before deciding on anything. I might have been in a position of getting you a good deal. But no matter, I think the fact that you bought a house is an indication of your making a commitment."

"I'm glad you see it that way. But I hope you can see other aspects of my commitment. And my professional skills and experience." Sol added, eyeing his antagonist.

Shonen cleared his throat and said: "Sol, don't misunderstand me. I have no doubts about your professional skills—in fact I admire what I've seen you do so far. In fact, as I think I've indicated, I would have loved to hire you as the Social Director of our Jewish Social Club. But it's not about you but rather a difference of philosophies. I was never in favor of our giving up our Country Club in favor of a Jewish Community Center. Call me what you will, selfish or calloused, I prefer one kind of organization and others prefer another. And while I may have lost a few rounds, I don't believe I've lost the entire fight. Not yet anyway."

The frankness caught Sol unprepared. On the one hand he was unhappy to still hear the remarks spewing forth from Shonen. On the other hand he had to admire the man for his honesty and straight-forwardness. And he said so and then added: "But Al, when the organization voted by two-thirds to go the route of the community center, weren't you bound to go along with that majority?"

"I am going along, but in my own way. I feel that when this experiment fails, I have to be in a position to pick up the pieces and put our organization back together again."

Sol further tried to persuade the man of the benefits and advantages of the community center concept.

Shonen retorted with some arguments that Sol had not heard before and that on the face of them could be seen to have some merit. "Look Sol, I also happen to believe that Judaism is primarily a religion and that religion should be left to churches, synagogues and the like. We have three Jewish congregations here in town. Each of them offers programs for their membership in addition to their liturgy. And if Jewish members of the congregations want more activities from their congregations, the congregations should provide that."

Sol then tried the argument that churches and congregations tend to divide communities while centers tend to unite.

"Well I think the uniting part is done by the Jewish Community Council and the United Jewish Appeal. We don't need another community-sponsored and funded organization to do the same things.

And all through the lunch the "discussion" continued and it became obvious to Sol that each man had his mind made up and would not be confused with facts. And he voiced that opinion.

Al Shonen smiled a rare smile and said: "Well, now I believe we begin to understand each other. And again I want to stress, Sol, nothing personal. I'm glad we had this lunch. You strike me as a very nice, intelligent and dedicated individual. And I admire your commitment and convictions and I hope you will do the same for my convictions." He reached to pick up the check but Sol insisted on paying for his own lunch.

Ever since his arrival in Jacksonville, Sol maintained a regular correspondence and had occasional telephone calls with his former supervisor and mentor in Houston, Jack Dauber with whom he shared his experiences. And Jack, careful not to step on Field Secretary Fred Furman's toes, now and then raised a question, one point or other—which helped Sol to sharpen his focus.

JUNE-AUGUST 1957: "WITHOUT A PUMP THERE AIN'T NO POOL"

The spring of 1957 was hectic for Sol and his volunteers as well as the lay leaders. The Membership Campaign had slowed and it was agreed to postpone it until the fall for a fresh start because Sol needed to concentrate all his energies on planning for and implementing the agency's first day camp season. Enrollment was gratifying despite some compromises which Sol agreed to but wasn't happy with.

Sol urged that Family Membership (which at the time was pegged at $200 per family for the year regardless of how many members in the family) be a prerequisite for enrollment of any child in the Day Camp program but the committee members, supported by the board of directors, were anxious about achieving a full camp enrollment of 100 children and offered members a 25% discount on the camp fees instead. Thus, about 50% of camp enrollees were non-members. But an even greater resultant problem was the throwing off of the projected membership figures-because if people could derive benefits of membership without becoming members, they could defer membership. However, the camp enrollment went over the 100 mark, in fact to 125 kids.

The happiness with these figures however was diminished with Tom McCall's announcement the Thursday before the Monday of the beginning of Day Camp that the pool pump had completely broken down and a new one was required. There was some argument whether that was a Capital expense item or one for the normal maintenance budget. Not that it really mattered, because the Capital Campaign had not yet been launched and the funds therein were minimal, and the operating budget was already strained. Sol was made aware of that fact when he put in orders for almost any item, be it office supplies, maintenance, or program equipment and he was asked by suppliers when the JCA was going to pay its bills which were piling up.

But the pool pump had to be replaced and Sol went with Sully Zeppa and Tom to select the appropriate one, which of course had to be a heavy-duty commercial type and not just one for the backyard pool of residence. Knowing full well the strained condition of the operating budget Sol nevertheless signed an agreement for full payment within 90 days for a commercial pump costing almost $2000.

Having purchased the pump, the next challenge was its installation. Tom volunteered to do the job since he was quite expert in the matter and was willing to accept straight time even though it meant working straight through the weekend. And in order to save labor costs, both Sully and Sol worked alongside Tom in the installation of the pump.

Shirley, who had been very patient and cooperative through all of the stresses and strains now began to express some of her exasperation: "Sol, you know that I support you 100 per cent in this undertaking, but I'm beginning to wonder whether they told you the whole truth about this place. I mean, I didn't complain when the first week on the job I came to bring you some lunch on the site and couldn't find you in the office or anywhere because you were up a tree with Tom doing God knows what. I mean, what executive director does that kind of thing? And now you'll be spending the entire weekend, day and night working to install a new pump for the swimming pool."

Sol put his arm around his wife: "I know honey, I know this thing is kind of unraveling and it's not what we pictured it would be. But without a pump there ain't no pool and without a pool there ain't no camp, and without a camp for this summer we might just as well throw in the towel on the whole undertaking."

"I know. And I don't think we should do that—at least not just yet anyway. How long do you think it will take to have the thing installed and operating?" she asked.

"Tom thinks it could be done by Saturday, but certainly Sunday the latest."

In fact, it took them all of Friday, Saturday and Sunday to have the pump installed and the filtration system working the way it should. In fact, they were not finished until Sunday night 9 pm!

WHEN IT RAINS, IT POURS

While the repair of the pool pump and filtration system allowed the camp season to begin on time and for the general membership to use the pool after camp hours, the erosion/soil depletion problem again surfaced following some torrential downpours. This time larger blocks of cement broke off the handball court and cascaded down the slope into the St. Johns River along with a dozen of the seedlings planted to hold the soil. And this time Tom felt that he could not do the necessary repairs himself but was required to call in a professional contractor—who made the necessary immediate repairs at a cost of several thousand dollars billed to the agency—and who warned that a major shoring up job was required to avoid future such happenings.

When he next spoke with Jack Dauber in Houston to share with him the latest developments, Jack suggested that it might well be time to consider dipping into the reserve funds that had been set aside. Jack also suggested that it might also be a good idea for Sol to write a detailed letter to Fred including all the developments since Sol's arrivals so that Fred and the NAJCC could reappraise the situation.

Sol called Fred to discuss Jack's suggestion about considering the use of the reserve funds and Fred replied that that would be a drastic action-implying crisis.

"Well Fred, I think we are rapidly approaching what could be a crisis, if we are not in fact in the middle of it now!" Sol retorted. And again he shared with Fred the many dunning letters and billings that were deluging his office and which he turned over to Harry Kravitz. And while Harry seemed not to be unduly concerned by them, telling Sol that's what he gets in his own business all the time, Sol was not convinced.

Fred listened patiently and then promised Sol that he would *try to revise* his schedule so that he could visit Jacksonville earlier than scheduled.

That response was all the incentive that Sol needed to sit down and write the detailed letter that Jack had suggested. It listed his experiences from his arrival through the recent episodes involving the pool pump and the soil erosion. It cited Shonen's disruptions, Sol's effort to reach out on a one-on-basis with Shonen, the tepid reactions of the congregation's rabbis, the erosion and soil run-off problem resulting from mass bulldozing of the property, the increasing financial stresses with vendors crying for payment, the paltry allocation by the Jewish Community Council/UJA and the postponement by the United Fund in considering allocation to the JCA further jeopardizing the financial stability of the agency. All of which was causing Sol to wonder whether the situation was as viable as had been portrayed by the lay leadership of the JCA.

In late July, Herb Mailman, the Director of the JCCA's Personnel Bureau, called Sol to tell him that Fred had shared his letter with him and that he, Herb thought he saw in it what Fred had perhaps tended to overlook. "I told Fred; 'this man is calling for help' and we've got to get down there and help him because the situation down there may not be as rosy as we all thought it to be," Herb Mailman told Sol.

In early August 1957 Fred Furman visited the Jewish Community Alliance, meeting with the executive committee, this time chaired by Sy Schulster, the president, who took time from his work traveling throughout the state to be present at the crucial meeting. Although not an officer and hence authorized to sit in on the executive committee meetings, Al Shonen's request to sit in on this meeting was approved by the committee.

None of the incidents, or events cited as causing concern was disputed by anyone altho' Mr. Shonen alleged that the original situations were exacerbated by the manner in which Sol and his staff handled it. In other words; "he didn't do what he should have, or he didn't do it right!"

Sol maintained his calm and patiently outlined the current situation, which, to him at least, warranted consideration of using at least some of the $20,000 reserve funds. As he understood it this was a "Rainy Day Fund" and boy it had been raining rather heavily in recent weeks, he pointed out.

Fred Furman agreed with Sol and asked what was the problem in at least borrowing some monies from the $20,000 reserve to tide the agency over until the allocation from the United Way kicked in. He knew that the $20,000 was there because it was part of the agreement for the agency to be an affiliate of the NAJCC.

There was a long silence as various members of the executive committee looked at one another as if trying to determine who would be the one to respond. Sy Schulster nodded towards Harry Kravitz who cleared his throat and explained: "Well yes we have the $20,000 as you know but actually we can't touch any of it because it's been used as additional collateral against all of our loans from the bank resulting from our purchase of the property and its subsequent improvements. I thought you knew that, Fred."

Momentarily stunned, Fred remained silent. Then he spoke: "No, I did not know that! When the NAJCC talked about having a reserve fund, we meant funds that were unencumbered. And I'm sure that's what Itz Steinberg and you—Sy understood! As I understand what you're now telling me, in fact the JCA does NOT have a reserve fund. And if that is the case, then our entire collaboration is based on false information and the JCA *has not* fulfilled its agreement."

And Fred Furman sat back in his chair deeply annoyed and disappointed.

Itz Steinberg hastened to fill the silent void: "Now Fred, I wouldn't characterize it the way you just did. I admit examining it now, from this perspective, it looks suspicious. But at the time we were so eager to get the project underway we may have unintentionally cut some corners never dreaming that we would be facing what we're now facing. And as a matter of fact, I don't believe that what we're now facing is unsolvable. It's only a matter of money. And that is not an impossible hurdle to overcome."

"That may be so," Fred responded, "but that is not what we presented to applicants for the position. And I don't think it's fair to have a professional come to this community and then have him find out, via harrowing experiences, what the real situation is like."

"Shouldn't that be up to Sol to decide—I mean whether he would be willing to struggle with us to resolve the situation and move on with the dream," Itz retorted.

"In one sense, yes. But I don't know what the NAJCC's reactions will be to my report," Fred countered. "I'll be happy to discuss it further with Sol," he added, nodding to Sol, who ret-turned his nod.

Following the meeting, Sol and Fred met to discuss the implications for Sol and what his preferences might be. They agreed that the entire scheme, despite the best of intentions, seemed to be failing because it was premature in many respects and because of all the different agendas of the different principals, which weren't recognized and addressed, and because the NAJCC had failed to develope a consensus, which could be used to build the new agency.

Fred said that the NAJCC was ready to find another position, of equal status or better, for Sol if that's what Sol desired and Sol replied that he wanted to discuss the matter with Shirley.

OCTOBER 1957

The NAJCC Personnel Bureau helped Sol obtain a new job with the JCCs of Chicago as Area Director of the Niles Township JCCs, thus allowing him to fulfill his aspirations of an executive position and of being a pioneer in establishing a totally new agency. And ultimately Sol discovered that, although his effort in Jacksonville was a failed journey, he learned more from such a failure than from success!

THE END

XV. ZWEITACK'S BOIL

HIS FIRST JEW

"Yes, I grow the vegetables myself," Paul Zweitack replied from behind his roadside produce stand. He examined his questioner who was about five foot-six, with graying temples, wearing black-rimmed glasses, and probably in his mid-thirties. "You passing through?" he asked.

"No, no. We just bought a home in Elkville. Y'know, the development being put up by Hometex."

"I know. They're still trying to buy my farm but I still refuse to sell. Me and another guy are the last holdouts. So, how do you like living there?" Paul asked.

The stranger selected some tomatoes and then looked up at Paul with a thin smile. "Oh, it's fine although somewhat isolated right now."

Paul raised his eyebrows. "Isolated? In what way?" For him, the description was strange because he was feeling increasingly hemmed in by the rapidly expanding development, which had now completely encircled the two remaining farms. He stared at the man perplexed.

"Don't get me wrong," the man said. "We like it. But I mean, until Hometex puts in the shopping center—well we have to go ten miles to Arlington. As for religious schooling—well that's a real problem." The man hesitated, and cast an anxious glance at Paul.

Paul's perplexity increased as he eyed the stranger.

"How's that a problem? There are plenty of churches around here."

The man shifted uneasily from one foot to the other. "Well, churches don't do me much good. He hesitated, and plunged. "You see, my name's Arons. Selwyn Arons."

"Arons? Well hello Mr. Arons, my name's Paul Zweitack." He wiped his right hand on his corduroy trousers and extended it. This guy's kinda nervous he thought.

"Glad to know you Paul," Selwyn said, extending his own hand which Paul grasped just a little too firmly. Arons winced. "Hey Paul that's not a tree limb you're squeezing there!"

"Oh, sorry. Please excuse me." And he relinquished the limp hand. "But, you were saying?"

"I was saying that since I'm Jewish the fact that there are lots of churches doesn't do me much good."

Now Paul felt Arons's eyes piercing him—seeking a telltale reaction. "Jewish, eh?" Paul asked, trying to mask his surprise. "Are there many Jewish families moving into Elkville?" But before Selwyn Arons could reply, another customer signaled for Paul 's attention. "Excuse me a minute, Mr. Arons. Don't go away," Paul said as he turned to wait on the other customer. Out of the corner of his eye he could see Arons was restless. He wanted him to stick around because he felt that the conversation was becoming interesting. "Thank you, ma'm," he said ringing up the sale and hurried back to Selwyn Arons. "So, I was asking whether there were other Jewish families moving into Elkville, the Hometex development?"

"Not many, yet," Arons replied, adjusting his dark-rimmed glasses. "But I'm sure more will come. Some Jewish families have also moved into other nearby developments like Green Meadows and Hartman Estates and we're thinking of forming a Jewish congregation." And now Selwyn Arons was speaking more comfortably.

"Is that so? A Jewish congregation, eh? You know, Mr. Arons..." Paul began, his interest aroused.

"The name is Selwyn," Arons interrupted.

"Okay, Selwyn. I've done a lot of reading about Judaism, and..." but another customer solicited his attention. "Excuse me again, please," Paul apologized. He was feeling impatient. Here was a Jew. His first real, live Jew, and, oh, well, business must come first. He waited on his other customer and again returned to Selwyn Arons.

"Well, Selwyn—as I was saying. I've read a lot about Judaism—about all the religions as a matter of fact, and..."

"Excuse me, Paul," Selwyn interrupted, barely concealing his discomfort. "This is very interesting. But, it's getting late and I've got to go. What do I owe you?"

Paul Zweitack was puzzled and annoyed. "Er, nothing. Be my guest."

"No, no! I couldn't do that. Please, what do I owe you?"

And finally they compromised, with Arons paying for the tomatoes and cucumbers, and accepting the corn as a gift. "I sure do thank you," he said.

"It's nothing. But Selwyn, I really want to talk with you about Judaism. Y'know, I've read the entire Pentateuch" Paul said, watching for Selwyn's reaction.

"The Five Books of Moses? Really? I don't recall if even I've done that!" And then he caught himself. "Paul, I would like to talk more with you, but I really have to go." And Selwyn Arons left.

At supper that evening, Paul Zweitack reported his meeting Selwyn Arons to his family: "I met my first Jew today."

"Really? What does he look like?" asked Mary.

Paul peered at his plump, blonde wife not sure how to take her question. "What do you mean 'what does he look like?' He looks like ... well, must be about my age, gray hair, blue eyes. Wears glasses. He does seem to be a decent fellow. He told me there are other Jews moving into Elkville and Green Meadows and Hartman Estates and said they are trying to form a Jewish congregation." And then he proceeded to cut and chew his lamb chop.

"A Jewish church?" blonde, ten-year old daughter Helen asked.

"No. Jews don't have churches. It's either a synagogue or a temple," her father replied.

"How come you know so much about them?" Tommy asked, poking at his string beans.

Paul studied his eight-year old son's freckled face. "I read a lot, especially about the world's religions."

"We're Catholic so why do you want to read about other religions?" Helen asked.

Paul swallowed. "Because I'm having lots of questions about our religion. Especially since we found out about all those horrible things that were done to people during the war. Not just to Jews—other people too—Russians and Poles. I had three uncles, an aunt, and who knows how many cousins murdered by the Nazis. And we Christians allowed such things to happen!" Paul Zweitack's voice rose, his face reddened, and his fist clenched until his knuckles whitened.

Mary put her hand on his. "Calm down. I know. I know. You've talked about it before. Sometimes you talk too much...especially in church. Father Gregory says you really shouldn't raise so many questions."

"Yeah, I know. Even though we don't go too often now, our so-called friends are more than suspicious—they're angry now," Paul said.

"Aw, what's this all about anyway?" Tommy asked, pushing his half-filled plate away.

"Eat your vegetables!" his mother ordered. "And let's all finish our supper in peace."

Paul stared vacantly into space and mumbled: "Hope I see Arons again soon."

THE LAWN, LOX AND BAGELS

It was three weeks before Paul Zweitack again met Selwyn Arons on a Saturday, when Selwyn stopped at Zweitack's "Farm-Fresh Produce" stand.

"Hello Paul. How are you?"

"Fine. Where've you been keeping yourself? I thought you moved out of Elkville."

Selwyn laughed. "Oh no. It's been a pretty hectic few weeks. I was out of town at a Social Work Conference. And I've been trying to plant grass in our front lawn and back yard. Gad, what frustration! I seeded three times, and each time the damn rain washed most of the seed down the sewers."

Paul eyed the amateur. "Too bad. You should cover the seeded area with burlap. That keeps the seed damp and prevents washout."

"Hey, that's a great idea!" Selwyn exclaimed. "Where does one get burlap?"

"I've got plenty. What's your address? I'll bring some over tomorrow." Paul picked up a pad and pencil.

"You don't have to bring it over. I'll pick it up. How much would it be?"

"Don't worry about that. I told you, I'd bring it over. I'd like to see one of the Hometex development homes. And while there, I could give you some more pointers about grass."

"I'd sure appreciate all the help I can get with my landscaping. Here's my address. I'll see you tomorrow then," Selwyn said, picking up his purchases.

Early Sunday morning Paul pushed Arons's doorbell button, shifting nervously from one heavy-booted foot to the other. After a few moments, a short, attractive woman in her early thirties, with dark hair offsetting a dark complexion, opened the door,

"Yes? What can I do for you?" she asked, squinting through only partially opened hazel eyes.

"Hello, my name's Zweitack, Paul Zweitack. I've brought the burlap that . . . "

"Oh yes," she interrupted with a smile. "Selwyn told me about you. I'm Shirley. Please come in. I'll tell Selly you're here."

Paul wiped his farm boots on the welcome mat and entered the modest, ranch-style home, stepping into the sparsely furnished living room. Gingerly he settled himself on the edge of the sofa to avoid soiling it. As he sat and waited, some oil paintings signed "Arons" caught his eye. Which one is the artist, he wondered. Then, as he was gazing at the coffee table, featuring a handcrafted mosaic surface, Selwyn Arons appeared in his bathrobe.

"Hey man, you really get up early, even on Sunday. What time is it, anyway?"

"Must be almost 7:30 AM." Paul replied. "Is this too early? I'm used to getting up early."

"Yes, but you're a farmer, I'm a social worker! Well as long as we're all up, let's have some breakfast and you can show me how to grow grass."

"I've eaten, but I'll have a cup of coffee with you," Paul replied.

Shirley and the Arons children joined them and Selwyn introduced his family. "You've met Shirley. And this is Louis, big fella for a thirteen-year old, wouldn't you say? Now Shelly here is our baby."

"I'm nearly eight, dad. I'm not a baby!" Shelly snapped.

"Shelly's the same age as my boy, Tommy," Paul said.

"Hurry up kids," Shirley interrupted, "or you'll be late for Sunday School."

Louis and Shelly bolted their breakfast, and left through the kitchen into the attached garage, followed by Shirley. "I'll see you fellas later. I'm stopping at the Beckers after I drop the kids at Sunday School. Don't work too hard," she cautioned.

Selwyn finished his breakfast and donned his gardening clothes, while Paul fidgeted, impatient to begin. "Did I hear correctly, I mean about your children going to Sunday School?"

"Yes. I told you about the congregation. Well, aside from having a Friday evening and Saturday morning service, the first thing we organized and got going was the Sunday School. Okay, I'm ready, let's plant some grass."

The two worked diligently, raking, seeding and laying down burlap covering on both front lawn and back yard. They spoke occasionally, with Paul pointing out significant gardening tips and at 12:15 PM Shirley Arons returned with the children and prepared lunch.

"I hope you fellas are finished because lunch is ready."

"Honey, you couldn't have timed it any better." Selwyn said from the back yard. "C'mon Paul, join us for lunch."

Paul wiped his brow. "I really can't. I must get home." Mustn't overstay this first time, he thought.

"I won't take 'no' for an answer. Since you won't take money for anything, the least I can give you is lunch."

"Well, okay. Let me call Mary," Paul replied. He completed his call, informing his wife that he would be home a bit later, and joined the Arons family.

"Have you ever had lox, cream cheese and bagels?" Selwyn asked.

"No, but I've heard and read about it." He took a bite and added: "It's very tasty."

"It's actually smoked salmon," Shirley explained.

"Read about it?" Selwyn exclaimed. "That's right. I remember you said you read a lot about Judaism. I didn't realize that took in lox and bagels."

"You'd be surprised what's been written about religion," Paul managed to say through a mouthful of the delicacy.

"Dad says you read the whole 'Five Books of Moses'" Louis said challengingly.

Paul looked at his hosts deciding definitely that he liked them. "Yes. I've read the entire Pentateuch. And since meeting you Selwyn, I'm using every spare moment to read up on Jews and Judaism."

"Really? How come meeting me caused you to do that?" Selwyn stammered.

"Oh, you were probably just the...just the... " Paul searched for the right word.

"Catalyst?" Selwyn suggested.

"That's it. Catalyst. You were the first Jew I ever met face to face. And when you told me that a Jewish congregation was being organized, that interested me even more." Now Paul was beginning to feel uneasy as all eyes focused on him.

"But Paul, what's the point of all this?" Selwyn asked.

And before Paul could reply, Shelly interrupted: "I'm finished. May I be excused?"

"Yes, you may go," Shirley, answered. "You too, Louis. We should leave your father and Mr. Zweitack alone."

"Aw, do I hafta?" Louis asked. "Just when things were getting interesting."

"Listen to your mother," Selwyn ordered and the children followed their mother out.

"I really should be going too," Paul said.

"Answer my question first, what's the point of all of your research?"

Paul Zweitack shifted in his chair. "I've...I've been searching for some time for a religion which is more satisfying."

"I thought you were Catholic. I mean, with a Polish name and all, I assumed you were Catholic," Selwyn stammered.

"I am. I mean I was. Oh, I'm not sure where I am now. Except I do know Catholicism—in fact, Christianity is no longer for me." Paul blinked his eyes rapidly, as if fighting back tears and bit his lower lip.

Selwyn whispered. "That was pretty hard to say, wasn't it?"

Paul nodded and sighed. "But I'm glad it's out. This thing's been bothering me for a long time. And my priest hasn't really been helpful. He's a nice man, but I am afraid he takes my questioning—and doubting—as his personal failure." Paul could see that Selwyn understood.

"But why at this stage in your life—you're in your thirties, right? Why change your religion now?" Selwyn asked.

"I'm thirty-four, and why not now? Isn't it one of your sayings; 'If I am not for myself, who will be for me; but if I am only for myself, what am I; and if not now, when?' Paul rose from the table and paced the floor. "Look, this is not an overnight thing. The war started me thinking and that's when I started reading everything about religion that I could get my hands on. The Arlington Library has a surprisingly good collection. And as of now everything seems to point to Judaism," Paul Zweitack peered at his newfound confidante, workmate, neighbor and yes, he felt his newfound friend.

Selwyn shook his head. "From Catholicism to Judaism? I've heard about situations in the reverse. But..."

Suddenly everything seemed to come together for Paul. He stared at his companion and interrupted: "Selwyn, how does one become a Jew?"

The suddenness stunned Selwyn. He pondered the question, returned Paul's intense gaze and replied solemnly: "One is born a Jew."

"Is there no other way?"

"I'm not sure. Jews don't do much proselytizing."

"Proselytizing? That's conversion, isn't it?" Paul asked.

"Yes, it is."

"Well, is it possible for me to convert?" Paul asked with a touch of impatience.

"I'm not sure. I don't know the technicalities. But the Rabbi would know."

"You have a Rabbi?" Paul asked, his excitement barely restrained or concealed.

Selwyn shook his head. "Not a full-time one. Rabbi Horn—Robert Horn—comes on weekends to conduct Friday night and Saturday morning services. And to teach Sunday School."

"Do you think I could talk to him?" Paul bit his lower lip.

"I think so. I'll arrange for you to meet him. Is next Saturday good for you?"

"Perfect. Where should I meet him?" Paul leaned forward.

"Would you like him to come to your place? Say about 1:00 PM?"

"If he doesn't mind sitting in a farmer's house, I would be most honored."

THE RABBI AND THE FARMER

Through the kitchen window Paul could see the chickens scurrying out of the way of the old Plymouth as it crunched over the cinder and gravel drive and came to a halt. He hurried to the door, and was embarrassed to hear Tommy address the man: "You must be the Jewish priest, huh?"

"Yes, sonny. But I'm a Rabbi, not a Priest. Is your father home?"

Paul opened the screen door and stepped out onto the porch. "Rabbi, welcome I'm Paul Zweitack. Please forgive Tommy, he's not familiar with such things." He extended his hand.

Which Rabbi Horn grasped firmly. "Glad to meet you. Selwyn Arons told me a little about you. And, there's nothing to forgive Tommy for." His broad grin enhanced his entire visage, topped by a bushel of black curly hair.

I like this man, Paul thought as he invited him into his home.

Inside the modest farmhouse Paul introduced the Rabbi to his family. The Rabbi began by explaining that at this juncture he preferred to talk only with the parents, although later, the older children would have to be included in any final decisions. Paul told Helen and Tommy to look after two-year old Catherine, and he, the Rabbi and Mary went into the cozy kitchen where Mary served ice tea and cookies.

"You have a very comfortable place here," Rabbi Horn began, with a disarming, boyish grin. "How come you haven't sold out to Hometex yet?"

"Our family has farmed this place for a very long time. And besides, the longer I hold out, the higher the price. But Rabbi, you're not here to talk about land values."

"No, not land values. Other values. Seems like you've been doing a lot of thinking about 'more important' values," Rabbi Horn said.

Paul put his cup down. "Yes. Thinking. Reading. Arguing. And, more reading."

"And you, Mrs. Zweitack? What are your values? And your thoughts?"

"I'm a good wife. I'm still a little confused. But, I agree with Paul."

"I see. Well then Paul, what does she agree with you about?"

Paul appraised the man. "Rabbi, I'd like to come straight to the point: How can we become Jews?"

"Why do you want to become Jews?"

"Because Judaism most closely meets our own values."

"You are Catholic, aren't you?"

"We were," Paul replied sadly.

"Were?"

"Yes, were. We are now in-between," said Paul, clasping his wife's trembling hands in his own. His eyes met the Rabbi's brown orbs.

"I understand. But now understand me. It is not easy to be a Jew! The formal procedure of conversion is nothing compared to a lifetime of being a Jew"

"We are ready to hear of the formal procedure," Paul said.

"Well, simply put, one must undergo at least thirty-six hours of very intensive formal instruction, usually two hours per week for eighteen weeks, involving Hebrew language, customs, holiday rituals, and so on. Also, one must undergo a ritual immersion, as well as the ritual drop of blood; not to mention circumcision."

"Immersion? You mean 'baptism'?" Paul's eyes widened and his eyes popped open.

"Why are you surprised? Yes, baptism. So much in Christianity derives from Judaism and Judaic practices." Rabbi Horn began.

Paul interrupted. "I know—I know. That's why we wish to return to the source. When can we begin?"

"Whenever you are ready. But remember, I said the older children must have a say in the final decision."

"They will," Paul said, as Mary nodded.

THE PLUNGE

The next Friday Paul and his family, including two-year old Catherine, attended the evening services of the fledgling Beth Tikvah congregation conducted in the small auditorium of the Bell Public School in Elkville. Paul was surprised to see about 45 to 50 people, including children of many ages. But he was also nervous and self-conscious as he and his family settled into the first row seats, right in front of the lectern serving as a pulpit.

Rabbi Horn welcomed the family. "Our guests this evening are not really guests. They are special. Paul and Mary Zweitack, and their children, have expressed a desire to become Jews. Judaism does not make a practice of proselytizing. Our burdens as Jews are heavy: we do not seek to impose them on others. The fact that people, from time to time, express a desire—choose to become Jews—is a credit both to Judaism and to those seeking to join us. I have begun to study with them on how they can, in fact, become Jews. I believe Paul and Mary are sincere. We must all help them."

Paul looked at Mary and smiled.

At the Oneg Shabbat social hour following the services, everyone was formally polite, yet distant, except Selwyn and Shirley Arons. "Hello, Paul. You know Shirley, and my kids," Selwyn said.

Paul beamed and introduced his family. The amenities exchanged, Selwyn suggested that Mary take the children to partake of the refreshments. Shirley, Louis and Shelly volunteered to accompany them.

"So." Selwyn began: "Shabbat Shalom. I see you're taking the plunge after all."

"Yes, we've definitely decided to convert. Shabbat—what?" Paul asked.

"Shabbat Shalom. It means 'Good Sabbath' or 'Peaceful Sabbath' literally. So, how's it going so far?"

Paul nodded. "Good, very good; And Shabbat Shalom to you, too. Rabbi Horn is quite a man, intelligent, warm and understanding. But, there's quite a bit of studying to do"

"Is that all there is to the conversion process? Reading and studying?" Selwyn asked.

Paul smiled. "Don't minimize the studying. The Rabbi himself said, 'If those who are Jews had to do the same studying in order to remain Jews, the erosion rate would really be frightening!" Selwyn laughed as Paul continued. "Fortunately, I won't have to undergo surgery for—you know what. My parents had me circumcised. God bless 'em."

"How lucky can you get?" Selwyn smiled. "But you sound pleased."

"I am. I'm now really convinced that Judaism is for me and my family."

"May I ask why you feel so?"

Paul evidently gathered his thoughts and after a momentary pause replied: "Well, aside from the fact that my grandmother was Jewish," (he enjoyed Selwyn's surprise) "the entire ethical system appeals to me. But mostly, I guess it's Judaism's refusal to acknowledge any man as God. I think Rabbi Horn called it apotheosis, or something."

"Yes, apotheosis or deification. It means elevating a person to the status of a god," Selwyn explained.

As he continued, Paul was becoming exhilarated. "Another thing I like is the Jewish idea that every man can have a direct relationship with God—that an intermediary isn't required."

"Yes, I guess we Jews have always been pretty independent and individualistic, or maybe the word is 'personal' about our religion," Selwyn said.

The conversation had so engrossed them that they hadn't noticed that all the congregants had left, and Mary and Shirley and the children were shifting restlessly by the now empty refreshment table.

Finally, Shirley came towards them. "Sorry to break in on you but it's time to go home." The Arons said goodnight and "Shabbat Shalom" to the Zweitacks and to Rabbi Horn and the Zweitacks were finally alone with the Rabbi.

"I think you did quite well for your first Friday evening service," the Rabbi said with a sympathetic smile.

Paul peered at the Rabbi. "You really think so? But Rabbi, Selwyn and Shirley Arons were the only ones who related to us. The others felt even more uncomfortable than we did."

Rabbi Horn nodded. "It takes time," he said. "The academics and rituals are the easy part of any conversion."

NATURE AND THE BOIL

Paul liked Selwyn Arons and was pleased with the developing relationship between them. He enjoyed going to the Arons home (usually on a Sunday) always with some fruits or vegetables, cuttings of shrubs, bulbs or tubers and even young trees. He took pride in helping to make Selwyn's front lawn and back yard the envy of the neighborhood. And he liked the lox, cream cheese and bagel brunches.

"Selly, these silver maples will do very nicely along your back yard property line" Paul said as he tamped the soil around the little trees.

"Yes, they sure will, but Paul, c'mon, you can't keep bringing all this stuff without some payment."

"Oh don't be silly. I had to clean out my west meadow and these two seedlings would have been thrown away." Paul said with seeming sincerity.

"I don't believe you."

Paul stopped his digging additional holes for other plantings and looked at Selwyn with evident appreciation. He wiped his brow and began: "Well, let's say you do repay me, more than you realize. The talks we have are good. They really help me to understand the readings and my sessions with the Rabbi. And your friendship is priceless."

"Well I don't know who's getting the better of the bargain. You're getting to know more about Judaism than I do," Selwyn said with a wisp of envy.

Paul lit a cigarette, inhaled and blew smoke rings. "I doubt it, but Selwyn this learning alone is not enough." Paul sighed and bit his lip.

Lighting his cigarette Selwyn stared at Paul and said: "What d'ya mean? I thought you said that everything was going so well."

Paul shook his head. "The study part is going well. The social part is not so hot. The Rabbi is great. The studies are fascinating, but aside from you and Shirley—well, the congregation is just not accepting us. We're just not *really* being accepted. As a matter of fact, Bob Doberman—y'know one of the vice presidents—told me straight-out that he didn't believe in conversions. Said something like 'once a goy, always a goy'." Paul paused and scratched his head. "And, also—'scratch a goy and find an anti-Semite.' No, I wouldn't say we're being greeted with open arms," Paul concluded. He saw his friend getting red in the face.

"Shit! Doberman's a jerk. You shouldn't really pay any attention to him. He's the kind of Jew who takes our being the 'chosen people' literally. For him, Jews aren't born. Each one is individually molded by god himself."

Paul chuckled. "That means each one is 'touched' right? Oh hell I knew it wouldn't be easy. So why am I bitching. C'mon, let's get these shrubs into the ground before they die of old age." And Paul set to digging with renewed vigor and channeled anger.

Selwyn joined him in the digging, muttering: "You'd think we Jews would have learned something about prejudice and discrimination. Wait till the next board meeting."

"Why, what's happening at the next board meeting?" Paul asked.

"Nothing. Never mind," Selwyn replied.

Paul did not see Selwyn for a few weeks because each had become very busy with his own endeavors. Selwyn had to attend some social work conferences out of state and while Shirley and her children continued being friendly and hospitable to Paul and his family, it was evident that Paul missed his buddy Selwyn. When next Paul and Selwyn met they were each dropping off their children at Sunday School.

"Where've you been hiding?" Paul asked.

"Didn't Shirley tell you about my being at the social work

conferences? So what've you been doing these past few weeks?"

"Hell, between harvesting the crops and dealing with the Hometex realtors wanting to buy my place, and learning to become a Jew—I'm lucky to be with you now," Paul said.

"I think I know what you mean. But now that I've got you, Paul, remember those lilac bushes you put in for me some time ago? Well, they just don't seem to be doing well. Everyone else's is in full bloom, and mine seem—well almost wilting."

"I'm not surprised about the delayed blooming. But, okay I'll be over this afternoon and take a look."

That afternoon Paul examined the shrubs. He poked around the base, added some root fertilizer, then straightened up, lit a cigarette, furrowed his brow and squinted his eyes. He shook his head sadly.

"Hey, what's wrong?" a worried Selwyn asked.

Paul relaxed his stern expression and laughed: "The shrubs are okay—just needed some aeration and a little more fertilizer."

"And what about the no-blooming?" Selwyn asked.

"Frequently flowering shrubs won't flower the first year after being transplanted and after having been pruned sharply," Paul explained. "And my friend, let me explain something: Mother Nature won't be hurried. She runs her course in her own sweet time. We can help nature along by fertilizing, aerating, weeding, and so on," Paul paused. "You know, it's like a boil—it can't be hurried. It will come to a head in its own sweet time," he concluded.

Selwyn listened attentively. "I see what you mean," he said.

"But to change the subject; how goes the conversion battle?"

Paul sighed and leaned heavily on his hoe. "To tell you the truth, Selly, your use of the word 'battle' is pretty accurate. I'm really surprised; Jews are supposed to be accepting of 'the stranger in their midst'. Well, this 'stranger' finds himself and his family still not being accepted! And Bob Doberman—well, I'll say this much for him, he's above board—honest and direct. Keeps telling me I ought to give it up. 'Nothing personal,' he says."

Selwyn looked at Paul with a mixture of sympathy, embarrassment and plain puzzlement. "Gee, Paul. Isn't there any improvement at all? I thought there'd be some change—especially after our last congregation board meeting,"...and suddenly Selwyn caught himself.

"I was an issue at the board meeting?" Paul asked.

Selly slapped his mouth. "Me and my big mouth. I wouldn't say you were an 'issue,' but yes, the 'acceptance' of the Zweitack family was discussed. And you really would have been pleased with the Rabbi, especially."

Paul nodded. "And I am sure you went to bat for us. So that's why most everyone, lately has been more talkative with us. If that's the change you're talking about. But Selly, it's stiff, formal and forced. Don't you understand? There's still no—well no real emotional acceptance."

"I understand Paul. I really do. What else can I tell you?" Selwyn paused, absorbing a thought, then continued; "It takes time. Maybe like you were telling me about nature—and boils—neither can be hurried. Each must run its course."

Paul stared at his friend and reflected on Selwyn's last remarks and then he nodded knowingly. His grim expression dissipated, his eyes brightened: "Yes, of course—you're right. That's it. That's my boil—my being accepted by the people that I've accepted: O.K. Let's finish treating these lilacs—I've got a reputation to maintain." And Paul Zweitack hoed with renewed vigor.

GOD'S WONDERS

Paul Zweitack continued to be patient, but not with Bob Doberman. To Doberman, he gave better than he took, although Bob still truly believed there was "nothing personal" in his refusal to accept a convert.

The Zweitacks continued attending services even though Mary was now in her seventh month of pregnancy. Paul was particularly pleased with this pregnancy. "This child will be born a Jew," he proclaimed to Selwyn.

"You're giving it back to me, eh?" Selwyn recalled his first answer to Paul's question about how one became a Jew.

"You should know that I listen very carefully," Paul replied.

The flowers for the Shabbat services invariably came from Mary Zweitack's garden and were arranged so beautifully that other women of the congregation couldn't resist inquiring how she managed to grow such beautiful specimens, and where she learned her flower arranging. And more of the men began approaching Paul with their lawn and garden problems after seeing what he had accomplished with Selwyn's front lawn and back yard. It seemed that the thaw was beginning for the Zweitacks. And yet, there was still one more "mysterious way" in God's wonders regarding the conversion of the Zweitack family.

Driving home from the Friday evening services, Paul observed: "Y'know Mary, I think they're warming up. A lot of the men talked with me. About gardening mostly... but still... "

"Yes. I found the same thing with the women. They asked mostly about the flowers But. still..." Mary replied, keeping an ear tuned to the sounds of sleep from the children in the back seat.

"Yes, Rabbi Horn, and Selly have been saying that it takes time" Paul said.

"Yes...but Paul—watch out—those lights..."

"I see—dammit, no I can't see, the lights are blinding me...he's coming right at us!

"Paul! My God!"

"Mama, what's happening?"

"Mama! Mama!"

Paul ached all over. He forced his eyes open and focused on the hazy figure at the right side of his bed. "Who is it? Oh, Rabbi Horn? It's you?"

"Yes, Paul. It's Bob Horn. How do you feel?"

"How am I? Alive? I think. What happened?" Paul asked.

The Rabbi cleared his throat. "Head-on collision on Route 9. Some drunken driver slammed into you."

"My family? What's with my family?" Paul shouted, grasping Rabbi Horn's hand.

"They're Okay. Try to relax. Miraculously, Helen and Catherine had only minor injuries and Tommy just some bruises."

"And Mary? What happened to Mary?" Paul demanded.

"She's all right. Except..." Rabbi Horn's voice trailed off again.

"Except what?" Paul tried to raise himself but fell back again groaning with pain.

Rabbi Horn placed a comforting hand on Paul's shoulder. "Except that she lost the baby."

"Oh god. No, not the baby! No!"

The Rabbi patted Paul's shoulder. "Yes, Im afraid so. But Paul, it's really a miracle. A head-on crash. And no one killed. Truly a miracle."

Paul glared at the Rabbi. "No one? What about my baby?"

"Hello, Paul. Why aren't you at services? This is a helluva way to spend Saturday morning."

The voice was familiar and Paul peered through the peepholes of his totally bandaged head. And then he recognized his friend. "Selly? Hi. Rabbi Horn was in last night—or was it this morning—I don't know which."

"He was in this morning. It's two o'clock now. Shirley is visiting with Mary and the kids.

So, how are you doing?"

"Me? More important is how Mary and the kids are doing. So how are they?" Paul raised his head, and sank back.

"Take it easy. They're all okay. But, how are you?" Selwyn repeated.

Paul looked at his friend and sighed. "How am I? Look at me. How the hell should I be? My whole family almost wiped out.'"

"Almost, but not quite," Selwyn replied.

"Rabbi Horn told me that Mary lost the baby. Maybe, I'm being punished."

"Punished? Punished for what?"

"For deserting my religion. Going against my God. Who knows?" Paul complained.

Selwyn Arons hesitated. "That's right. Who knows how God works his wonders."

"His wonders?' Paul sneered.

"That's right. Look, no one was killed. Right?'

"Wrong My unborn child will never be born. And that was to be the first Zweitack born a Jew. At least this generation." Paul argued. The exertion caused him to wince with pain and he pressed the button for the nurse.

When she arrived she adjusted the pulleys and knobs and said to Arons: "You really shouldn't stay too long."

"I'm all right now. Thank you, nurse."

At which point, Shirley returned from visiting Mary and the children and reported that baby Catherine was comfortable in a crib next to Helen's bed; that Helen was concerned about who was going to milk the cows and Tommy was up and around. In fact, the doctor was recommending that Tommy be discharged. And Mary was being well taken care of and in fairly good spirits.

Paul became agitated. "Helen is right! Milking the cows is her chore and she's right to be concerned about it. And Tommy is to be discharged? Where the hell to? His whole family is here—in this goddamn hospital!'

"Paul, take it easy. I've talked with your neighbors and they agreed to look after the cows and the other animals and the farm generally. And Shirley and I discussed Tommy's discharge and we'd like to have Tommy stay with us."

Paul stared at them. "Oh no. It's nice of you. But it wouldn't work out."

"Why not?" Selwyn asked.

Paul waved his hand. "Too much trouble."

"What kind of trouble? Look, let's try it. If it's too much trouble, we'll work something else out."

Paul sighed and smiled feebly. "Well, Okay, let's try it. And thanks for talking to my farm neighbors. They really are very good people, even if they are Protestants."

A few days later the Aronses found Mary in Paul's room together with some new visitors.

"Hi, guys!" Paul chirped. "Look who's here."

"Oh, hello," said Bob Doberman. "Frances and I heard about the terrible accident and, since we were in the vicinity—well, here we are." He grinned sheepishly.

"Bob, it's great! You're great!" said Selwyn, as Shirley and Frances engaged in some chitchat.

Mary broke in to express her appreciation for everything that everyone was doing and announced that Tommy was ready to go home with the Aronses." And she looked to Selwyn and Shirley.

"Fine. We're ready to leave now," said Selwyn.

Tommy came in to say goodbye to his parents, who provided him with instructions on how to behave, and how to make himself all but invisible.

"Is he's staying with you?" Frances Doberman asked.

"Of course," said Shirley. "What's a congregation for?" And the Dobermans nodded.

A week later, Catherine and Helen were discharged to the care of the Dobermans leaving only Paul and his wife, Mary still in the hospital.

"So Paul, how's it going now? You're looking better," said Selwyn on his regular visit.

"I'm feeling better, Selly. Much better. Everything is looking up. And the doctor says Mary and I can be discharged soon."

"That's wonderful news. But can you and Mary really manage?" Selwyn asked.

"I'm sure we can. For one thing, we'll have a Visiting Nurse. And my sister (who hasn't talked to me for the past three months since I began my conversion) is coming from Detroit to help us out" Paul concluded with a smile.

"Wonderful again! See, 'God works his wonders in mysterious ways' after all, doesn't he?" Selwyn said.

"Yes, I guess he does. But I wish he didn't bring 'my boil' to such a painful bursting. There's no question now about the congregation accepting us. But, did it require such a terrible accident?" Paul asked looking up at the ceiling.

"You sound like Tevya in 'Fiddler on the Roof'," Selwyn said.

"Who's he?" Paul asked.

"Never mind. You'll come across it in your studies some day," Selwyn smiled.

THE END

XVI. "TURN OFF THE IGNITION!"

I leaned towards the driver; "Don, you've been driving since we left Dallas. You must be tired. How about my relieving you?"

He flashed an appreciative smile and said: "Well it's not much further to the Houston Astrodome. But I am a little tired so it's a good idea for you to take over." He pulled off the road and I slid over to the driver's seat, while Don's wife, Betty moved her heavy frame from the back to the front passenger seat allowing Don to join his friend, Bob and my 15-year-old son Norman, in the rear. As the new 1962 Chevrolet rejoined the stream of traffic approaching the outskirts of Houston, I heard loud snoring from the back. "What the hell is that?" I asked.

"It's Don. He's out like a light," Bob said. "He sure was tired. Good thing you took over the driving when you did."

I nodded. Don's a nice guy, I mused, but odd sometimes—as sports addicts are prone to be. He was one of our younger neighbors on our block in Dallas and proposed going to the Astrodome in Houston shortly after it had been completed, offering to use his new Chevrolet for the journey. I focused on the increasingly heavy traffic and became aware of the disappearing sun and the ominously darkening sky. A light rain began to fall, headlights snapped on and windshield wipers waved in metronomic cadence.

"The car handles real well" I said loudly, seeking to dispel the developing gloom.

"Yeah, smooth," Bob, agreed.

"It's like riding on air," Betty added.

"Almost too smooth" my son Norman observed and following a momentary pause, he added: "We probably are riding on air. I think we're hydroplaning."

"What's hydroplaning?" Betty asked with a touch of anxiety.

I ventured to explain; "Hydroplaning occurs when light rain fails to wash away roadway oil slicks and the car wheels ride on a thin sheet of water and oil instead of the road. And Norman, I think you're right; we're hydroplaning!"

"Then we better slow down," Bob observed.

"Will do,' I replied, and began gently pumping the brakes. The car, however, began to skid. "Hang on people!" I shouted as I steered in the direction of the skid, still lightly pumping the brakes. A heart-sized lump clogged my throat as the car began circling out of control, like a rudderless craft.

"We're going to crash!" Betty shrieked, clutching at me as her body slammed against mine. Obviously she had neglected to fasten her seat belt when she moved to the front seat.

"Let go!" I shouted. "We sure as hell will crash if you don't let go of me, Betty!" I jabbed my right elbow into her bulbous, quivering side to get her to release me.

Awakened by all the commotion, a still drowsy Don asked: "Hey what's goin' on?"

"We're hydroplaning and skidding out of control," Norman informed him matter-of-factly, as only a 15 year-old authority of cars could do.

"Oh shit! Damn it. I was afraid of sumthin' like that" Don muttered before fading back into the rear upholstery. I wanted to ask him what the hell he meant by THAT, but the car continued circling, clipping off a median post with each turn. For the moment the posts were serving their purpose of keeping our car out of the paths of oncoming traffic in the opposite lanes.

But for how long, I wondered. How long? My head and heart pounded. My hands were riveted to the steering wheel. I bit my lip and ground my teeth. "Above all, stay calm, stay calm" I advised myself. But it wasn't easy. Around and around the Chevy careened, snapping off six and seven more concrete posts

From in back, Bob asked: "How're you doing Sam?"

I grimaced. "I don't understand it. I'm doing everything I'm supposed to do: handling the brakes, steering in the direction of the skid. But nothing seems to help".

Betty bounced and sobbed uncontrollably. Only Norman was not heard from. I shouted: "Hey Norman, you okay?"

"Yeah Dad. I'm OK. Just handle the car and don't worry about anything else."

It was now clear to me however, that nothing I did had any effect as the car continued circling almost lazily in slow—motion, sheering off median posts. Finally, as if tiring of the repetition the car lifted itself and skidded on its two left wheels, hovering for an instant before crashing down on its left side. An unbelievable screeching rent the air as the car protested its sudden, unplanned meeting with the highway concrete. The car then continued sliding on its side for several more yards along the median strip, demolishing still more posts. When it did finally ground to a halt, a weird combination of sounds assailed us like the whirring of four spinning wheels, the wild racing of a motor, the popping and crackling of breaking glass, the pelting of rain drops—all accompanied by gasps, groans, sighs and whimpers.

Betty landed on top of me! Don, flung from the back seat against the front windshield caused it to pop out, and bouncing off the windshield, Don landed on top of Betty. Norman and Bob piled up sequentially in turn, all like so many dominos, all on top of me, the driver—the only one who had fastened his seat belt! I gasped for air and managed to whisper: "Betty, get off me, please."

"I can't," she wheezed. "Don's on top of me. He's not moving at all and he's so heavy. God, hope he's not...not."

I wasn't sure how long we remained in this state, probably only moments. But it seemed much longer. Then a voice from above and behind commanded: "Dad, turn off the ignition!"

It sounded like Norman. Oh yes, I thought. It makes sense. Turn off the ignition. Got to avoid fire or explosion. I was beginning to feel drowsy, and I gasped for air.

"Dad! You hear me? Turn off the ignition!" There it was again. Norman's voice.

Was the ignition off? No, it wasn't. Okay, I better turn it off. I stretched to reach for the ignition key. Ugh, can't reach it. This fat dame's got me pinned down good. "Betty, get off me. Got to turn off the ignition."

"I can't," she replied. "I told you, Don's on top of me. I can't move either."

Shit. This is crazy, I thought. Got to do something. "Don can you reach the ignition and shut it of f?" I asked.

"He's out cold," Bob groaned. "See if you can get to it, Sam. Try again."

"Betty, pull back as much as you can," I urged. And as she strained to do so, I reached for the key in the ignition. My fingers almost touched it that time. "A little more, Betty, please." I urged.

"I'm trying. God, Don is so heavy. Ugh"

I tried stretching further. My fingers touched the key rim, A little more...yeah...a good grip...twist. Ah! It was off! The engine died. Thank god, only the engine. How long had it been? Five minutes? Ten? Mere moments, but the ignition was off. No fire. No explosions. And then an eerie silence. Only the pelting of the rain drops and a siren wailing in the distance coming closer.

And then I heard: "Good Dad. That's good!" my son Norman said.

"Yeah, great!" I repeated. "But how do we get out?" I sensed outside eyes staring down at us—hands tugging at the right side up car doors. People were trying to help us. Trying to open the car doors. More sirens...wailing and lights flashing.

"How do we get out?" I wheezed. I felt my chest being pressed as in a vise by the weight of so many bodies. I was being slowly suffocated and crushed! As if in a dream, I heard voices: "Norman we've got to get Don away from the windshield opening. He's blocking it so help me pull his body over this way. That's it, just a little more. Good, good." And then I realized that Bob was directing the evacuation.

"Right Bob," said Norman. "I got him. Ugh, he's real heavy"

"Yeah," Bob said, "that's what's meant by 'dead weight'. Unconscious and dead people are very heavy. Ugh, good he's out of the way. Now Norman crawl out the empty windshield and I'll follow you."

"Good thing the windshield popped-out earlier" I heard Norman say.

The weight on my chest was much lightened and I managed to suck in some air. But Betty's hulk still smothered me. And suddenly it was gone. Still whimpering, Betty was literally hoisted out by Bob and Norman pulling her from the outside.

I gulped in air by the buckets and it never tasted so delicious. My chest heaved as my lungs breathed in the life-giving element. I was so relieved. Yet the tears streamed down my cheeks. And then I heard a groan. It was Don coming to.

With me pushing from the inside and Norm and Bob pulling from the outside, Don too finally made his exit.

And now it was my turn! I hesitated but a moment and then crawled out through the windowless windshield opening into the beautiful gray, beautiful wet, beautiful live world!

Two ambulances took us to the hospital emergency room. I had a black eye, bruised ribs and an aching back. Bob had several ribs broken, while Don had a slight concussion and a hairline skull fracture. Norman was black and bruised. Only Betty had no physical injuries. Can you beat that? She's sure well insulated, I thought.

I gave a full report to the State Highway patrolman—who kept telling us how lucky we all were to be alive—attributing that to the fact that I, at least, had my seat belt on. If it weren't for that, there was no way of knowing how many scrambled eggs they would have had to deal with.

I acknowledged this and then asked about the failure of the car to respond to my efforts. "I did all the right things; pumped the brakes lightly, turned in the direction of the skid. How come nothing worked?"

The patrolman shook his head: "Nothing you could do. All four of your tires were bald! A brand new Chevy, with bald tires! Figure that one out?" He paused. "But tell me. How did you remember to turn off the ignition? That was real presence of mind.'

I looked at the officer, shook my head, smiled and said: "No that's real presence of one's son." And he looked at me puzzled.

Post Script: I couldn't let go of the contradiction of a new car with four bald tires. So at my first opportunity, I put the question to Don, whose car it was after all. Sheepishly he explained that they were having trouble keeping up the payments for the car, so he sold the tires, replacing them with the baldies "temporarily," thus enabling him to keep up the car payments. However, the car was totaled, so in effect he lost the car anyway. And since the accident was a consequence of his negligence, he couldn't collect from his insurance. And so, for a long while I provided him with a ride to his job. I guess one could say, that just as, "Diligence is the mother of good fortune" (which is what was written about me in my college yearbook), so is "Expediency the mother of misfortune." And that bit about expediency I just now made up—because it sounds right.

THE END

XVII. ANTIGUAN IDYLL

Our meeting was unanticipated and unplanned. I was sitting on the balcony of our rented, second story unit of the Antiguan Motel watching the sun sink slowly into the Caribbean while my Sanyo cassette played Mendelssohn's "Hebrides", an appropriate musical accompaniment for the incoming tide. I was feeling sad to witness the passing of another day: three days of a ten-day vacation gone; my wife, Jean, asleep and here I sat alone sipping some rum concoction.

At least I thought I was alone. The breeze became a gusty wind rustling the broad palm leaves and my attention was called to some front fronds, which had been clipped short. Apparently, these fronds had dared to intrude onto the screenless porch and had affronted someone and had suffered the consequences. They must have been very attractive fronds and now they were just amputated limbs. I gulped my Cuba Libra, and shook my head sadly, bemoaning the crudity that destroyed such symmetry and grace.

My dejection deepened with the advancing night and commensurate with the emptying rum glass. And then my slightly spirituous eyes glimpsed a vaguely visible full-leafed frond in the purple shadows—a long, slender, elegant stem with a full complement of slim "finger-leaves." Its completeness was in sharp contrast to the stumpy amputated fronds.

Hastily, I refilled my rum concoction and peered into the

deep purple. A strong breeze blew the full frond closer to me; its finger leaves creating the illusion of a waving hand. Simultaneously, the rustling of the leaves of the nearby Seagrape tree harmonized with the gurgling incoming tide and the whistling wind so that I thought I heard a barely audible: "Hello, I'm Freddie...Freddie...Freddie."

I blinked, gasped and again drained my glass. I peered into the night and saw a full palm frond in all its moonlit magnificence waving wildly in the wind in perfect accompaniment with Mendelssohn's Hebrides music. As I watched, mesmerized, the wind subsided and the wild waving slowed to a methodical nodding. Yes—without a doubt, the frond was waving to ME, its finger-leaves gesturing a friendly "Hello." And again the rustling leaves, the rumbling tide and whistling wind all combined, connived and contrived to melodically murmur: "I'm Freddie . . . Freddie...Freddie."

I amazed myself by replying: "Hi, Freddie. You're certainly friendly. Yes, Freddie, the friendly frond." I chuckled at the alliteration as my despondency lightened.

And then the wind subsided and Freddie's movements slackened and he waved what only could have been a silhouetted "good night."

As I said at the start, our meeting was unanticipated and unplanned. Certainly it was unorthodox.

The next morning in the brightness and sobriety of the Caribbean sun, and to the accompaniment of Chopin, I looked for my newfound friendly frond. There were twelve or thirteen limbs close to the porch. As I noticed the night before the five or six closest had half or more of their stems lopped off. Freddie must therefore be of the next generation, grown tall, long and symmetrical, capable of darting in (like a playful puppy) but also able to soar above the punitive porch.

And then I saw him. "Hi, Freddie!" I called, recognizing him even without my Cuba Libra. You see, not all fronds are alike.

With the help of the Caribbean breeze, the friendly frond waved a timid 'how do you do' but would not come closer.

"What's the matter, fella? Are you more bashful in the daytime?" I teased, leaning over the railing to get closer.

"Who're you talking to?" my wife, Jean asked from inside the motel-apartment.

"Uh—to the birds in the palm trees. The yellow-bellied ones," I said. I didn't think she would understand a truthful response.

"Are they the birds you've been feeding crumbs to?" Jean asked.

"Yes," I replied, winking at Freddie who still kept his distance while some of the other fronds waved daringly over the porch. Some things are best kept to oneself, right? I mean we all have our Walter Mittey's, right? Our fantasies? Illusions? Right?

"By the way dear," Jean added, "please turn the music down a little."

I looked in the direction of her voice, and then at Freddie. "There she goes again. I tell you Freddie, that woman...!" But I complied and turned the volume down—very slightly.

That night in the presence of another full Caribbean moon and warm wind, and a Brahms background my friendship with Freddie flourished. Jean was again asleep. But I was not alone. I sipped my third rum and coke and spoke softly to my new companion who proved to be that rarity of rarities—a good listener.

"Well Freddie, my new-found friend, another one of those days of mis-communication, or at least misunderstanding. Sigh. Know what I mean?"

Freddie nodded up and down, up and down, encouraging me to continue.

"Yep...seems I play my cassette 'corder too loud for some people." I sipped my drink and looked to my buddy waiting for a reaction.

"How so? Freddie seemed to ask by venturing closer—closer than I had ever seen him. I feared for him, and took another sip. "Easy Freddie," I cautioned. "Better back off before somebody does a machete-job on you like they did on the others. Down fella."

He pulled back. And from the safer distance, wagged his finger-leaves in disapproval of any such fate. And then he quieted down and waited, rustling restlessly now and then.

I took another sip and continued the one-sided conversation. "Well Freddie, did you know that the hearing tolerance levels differ between men and women? Women have more tender and sensitive auditory senses. They like music played at much lower volume. Did you know that my friend?"

I peered expectantly into the evening. This time Freddie's nod was most emphatic and he danced in so close that several of his finger-leaves brushed my brow! Which gesture, of frond to forehead I found to be most supportive.

I paused and sipped my rum concoction: "But y'see Freddie, it's not just the difference between male and female decibel levels. It's also the ability to understand the function of different types of music."

Freddie was quiet, waiting patiently. "Yes?" he managed to convey.

"Some music," I continued, "is merely for background—strictly atmospheric or mood—hardly to be heard, or noticed, certainly not to interfere with other sounds. But—and I eyed him carefully—classical music is to be listened to for its own sake. Take List's Piano Concerto #1 that we're hearing right now, so low, so soft, so subdued. But y'know Freddie, it's too soft—too subdued, one can't fully appreciate the piece.

Freddie nodded up and down—up and down. And then it was up, and up, and up. What was he trying to tell me? If only he could really speak. But he was speaking. Suddenly I felt impelled to turn the volume up and sat back to enjoy the full impact of List's genius, warmed inside by rum and coke—cooled outside by the Caribbean breeze and waving palms.

The idyll, however, was too soon interrupted by an awakened Jean shouting from inside: "What's going on out there? Why is it so loud? My god, you'll wake all of Antigua."

Reluctantly I lowered the volume and replied: "Nothing dear. Go back to sleep." And then I grumbled: "Could stand some awakening."

Freddie hung in mid-note in mid-air and then he came in closer, fluttering his finger-leaves. He was seeking an answer for the sudden interruption of our concert.

"See what I mean, Freddie? Fronds are not the only ones to be lopped off; there are many ways to be cut off. Know what I mean?"

Freddie came in closer still, nodding emphatically. I reached to grasp the tip of his extended stem. But he retreated and managed to convey: "Don't touch! Please!"

I was initially puzzled, but then it dawned on me! Considering what the porch-people had inflicted upon his species, why should any frond (even a friendly one) trust any porch-person (even a friendly one)? Touching Freddie then became a goal to be achieved before the end of our stay.

We spent many enjoyable evenings together; me listening to my music and at the same time experimenting with the many rum concoctions: Freddie experimenting and perfecting new choreographies in concert with the winds and breezes and in harmony with the music. Yes, we were good for one another. Freddie's love of classical music gave us something else in common and my fondness for him increased measurably (certainly in direct proportion to my increasing appreciation for the limitless rum concoctions.) And I believed that his affection for me increased as well since I came across as a friendly fellow—just as I recognized him as a friendly frond. And he brushed my forehead ever more frequently.

And so on Friday, our last day on Antigua, I finally achieved two of my goals, proper volume and the touching of Freddie.

It was another bright, breezy day. I was sitting on the porch reading (all about palm trees), listening to Chopin's Polonaises and Waltzes and all the fronds were wafting and waving and dancing happily, including Freddie, while the yellow-bellied and red-breasted birds feasted on my crumbs. Freddie paused in his play to observe his feathered tenants, listening all the while to the melodic strains now pitched at my preferred decibel levels. He came in closer and managed to get my attention by some vigorous flitting of his finger-leaves: "Hey! Hey! Hey!"

"Well, good morning Freddie." I walked over and leaned against the white-painted wood railing, observing the blue Caribbean waters reflecting the billowy and cushiony clouds: "What? The music? Well, that's Chopin. Do you like it?"

Freddie hesitated. His gesture was difficult to interpret (without a rum concoction), but he seemed to ask: "How come it's at the decibel level you like?"

I smiled contentedly: "Oh well, Jean finally learned to enjoy Cuba Libras." I winked. He nodded knowingly, up and down, up and down.

And now I looked straight at my friend: "By the way Freddie, we're leaving in a little while. Time to go home."

Freddie reared up. I thought I heard whining—but it must have been the wind rustling the Sea-grape leaves.

Then Freddie darted in close, closer than ever before.

"Yes, Freddie. All good things must come to an end."

And with the next breeze Freddie almost enveloped me with his entire leafy arm.

"Whoa! Freddie, I like you too! Believe me, you're the only frond that I ever made friends with. In fact, you're my one and only frond!" I looked around to make sure we were alone—but I meant every word.

And with that, Freddie did envelop me with his total palm being and then he allowed me to gently, but firmly to grasp the tip of his frond stem. I selected five of his finger-leaves and we shook goodbye.

THE END

XVIII. SAN ANDRES SABBATH

> "Whither can I go from Your spirit? Whither can I flee from Your presence?"
> Psalm 139. In "Gates of Repentance"
> The New Union Prayer Book, 1978

We three couples wanted "an out-of-the-way-get-away—from-it-all place" for our next vacation.

We got more than we bargained for when the Hotel El Dorado on San Andres (a Caribbean island 125 miles off the coast of Nicaragua) denied ever having received our reservations, but deigned to assist us in obtaining quarters at the Caribbean Hotel at the opposite end of the island. It was after 1:00 A.M. when we booked into the primitive hotel. That first night was memorable for its out-of-the-wayness.

The next morning, after failing to obtain better quarters at the third remaining hotel, closer in, Lennie Kater asked: "So, want to swim home? It's only 2500 miles to Boston."

"Well, let's make the most of it. After all, we did want to get-away-from-it-all," I reminded our buddies and traveling companions.

"I didn't want to get away from EVERYTHING! Have you tried taking a shower at our, pardon the expression, 'hotel'? This morning I ran out of even cold water in the middle of soaping up," Jack Clayman complained.

"Some vacation," his wife, Ann, griped.

Rose Kater looked up from the travel guide and said: "Okay, okay. No sense standing around bellyaching. Let's do the town."

My wife, Shirley, nodded. "Makes sense. I'd like to do some shopping."

But there wasn't much of a town 'to do.' The streets were narrow and all cobblestones. And while there was merchandise in abundance, most of the stores were ramshackle affairs. The Mediterranean Shop was the exception. It was clean, well organized, with attractive display cases and counters. A four-blade fan, suspended from the ceiling, rotated lazily, giving the illusion of air-circulation.

Behind the front counter, stood a stocky, dark-complexioned man in his mid-thirties, who smiled beckoningly and in an unidentified accent asked: "May I help, please"

Lennie and Jack remained absorbed in the merchandise, but when I looked up, I saw a Hebrew ornament on a gold chain, nestling on a hairy chest, framed by an opened sport shirt.

"Excuse me. Is that a 'Chai' pendant you're wearing?" I asked.

On hearing 'Chai,' Jack and Lennie also looked up and peered at the neckpiece and its wearer.

"Sure is," Jack said.

Lennie smiled. "Definitely looks like one."

The proprietor's grin broadened: "Yes, it is. You must be Jewish people from the United States, yes?"

"Yep, we plead guilty on all counts," Jack said. "Although you really couldn't tell by me because I'm a redheaded Aryan. So, it must be these two guys who gave us away," he chuckled.

The proprietor called to his wife: "Chanah, please come here. Excuse her, ladies."

"Those ladies are our wives," I explained and invited them to join us.

Smiling, the proprietor said, "My name is Moshek. We so seldom see Norteamericanos—especially Jewish ones. We meet Jews from Honduras, Bogota, Guatemala, and Costa Rica. But from United States—almost never."

His wife nodded in agreement, and we noticed she was wearing a Star of David pendant.

"Are you people from San Andres?" Ann asked.

Moshek shook his head. "No, no! We are from Israel." He waited for the answer to sink in, anticipating, and enjoying our surprise.

"Israel " we all chorused. "How come you came to San Andres?"

Chanah's large, dark, pretty eyes roamed over the six of us and smiling, she turned to her husband and chattered something in Hebrew. He nodded emphatically, turned to us and, with his most engaging salesman's smile, said: "Chanah reminds me that today is Friday. You would honor us to come to Friday services, please."

I couldn't believe my ears: "Friday night services? Here? On San Andres?" I asked.

"I didn't think there'd be ten Jewish men here for a minyan," Lennie added.

"Tonight there's enough," Moshek smiled. "Most Friday nights there's also enough."

We were amazed. "Well, normally we're not Temple goers . . ." Shirley began.

"Who attends your services?" Ann interrupted.

Moshek smiled. "Well, we have four Jewish families on San Andres. The rest are Jewish touristas from San Jose, Managua, Panama City, Bogota and Cartagena—that is in Colombia, you know. Also, some from Caracas, Venezuela."

"And Israel," Jack said. "I still want to know how come you and your wife are here."

"Come to services tonight, and I'll tell you about it," Moshek teased.

Lennie smiled. "Okay, you got us. Now—where are the services conducted?"

"Upstairs—over Senor Mordelas store," Moshek stepped outside and pointed down the narrow street.

After dinner we made our way to Mr. Mordelas' store, but found it locked. We looked for another entrance, but saw only an unappetizing, narrow alleyway and surmised that this was the way in. We single-filed down the narrow passage and found the entry leading upstairs. The door at the top of the steps was ajar, issuing a beckoning beacon of yellow light. We stepped into a large kitchen, its linoleum floor covered with Spanish language newspapers. (A dim memory of a Jewish household in Brooklyn, circa 1930's flickered: the floor washed for the Shabbat and covered with Jewish newspapers. I blinked myself back to 1976).

The kitchen opened into a large dining room whose furniture had been pushed against the farthest wall leaving the cleared space filled with fifteen wooden folding chairs. The services undoubtedly would be held there. The kitchen table was also pushed to the wall leaving the middle of the kitchen cleared for milling around. On the kitchen table was a cloth-covered challah, a Shabbos Candelabra (with the candles burning brightly), a bottle of deep purple kosher wine, a Kiddush cup, and an ancient prayer book. The other side of the kitchen opened onto a tar-covered roof, accommodating another fifteen wooden folding chairs. For what, I wondered.

Standing next to the kitchen table was Moshek alongside another man. Moshek grinned at us and introduced Senor Mordelas.

"Good Shabbos. Moshek said you would come. I'm so glad," Senor Mordelas said grinning broadly. His ebullience seemed matched by the brilliance of the old-fashioned chandelier blazing in the dining room.

Their impatience unchecked, Jack and Lennie pulled Moshek aside: "So, what's the full story?" Jack demanded. "How come you came to San Andres, of all the out-of-the-way-places?"

"Later," Moshek replied with his perpetual grin. "I must help prepare for the services. Mix around and meet the people. I am sure you will find it interesting."

So we mingled. It was cooler on the roof, where another eighteen people (mostly women and some children) were milling about. The conversations were mostly in Spanish. But I detected some German and some Yiddish. I could hear Moshek shifting from Yiddish to Spanish, then to Hebrew and finally to English. How many languages does the man know? I wondered.

And then we became aware that we were the objects of curiosity and the centers of attention—in fact three clusters of discussion; Ann and Jack in the kitchen; Lennie and Rose in the dining room, and Shirley and I surrounded on the roof. Yet, the thrust of the conversations in each cluster ran roughly parallel, as we compared notes afterwards.

"You really come from United States of America?"

"Why did you come to San Andres? U.S. Virgin Islands has better buys."

"Where is Boston? Is it part of New York?"

"How can someone get into United States?"

"Can you help us? We have relatives in Chica—Chico—how you say?"

"Chicago," I assisted.

"Si, Si! Chicago."

We managed to answer most of the questions. And then it was our turn to do the asking of questions. And the answers provided us with a fair history of the Jews of Central America.

We learned, for example, that in all of the six countries of Central America, there were only 6000 Jews: Panama with over 2000, Costa Rica and Guatemala with about 1500, El Salvador with 350, Nicaragua, 200, and Honduras about 175.

We also learned that, although Nicaragua never had more than 200 Jews at any one time, those 200 produced a Delise Krauss as a General in the Army, Carlos Huek, a Finance Minister, Raczkiewsky who was a Mayor of Managua, and topping them all—Rene Schick Gutierrez who was President of Nicaragua from 1963 to 1966.

We learned that Colombia, South America usually has about 12,000 Jews, most living in Bogota or its suburbs and that while the Jews of Colombia were not allowed to officially conduct campaigns for Israel, the Colombian government looked the other way as substantial funds were indeed raised—and this, despite the fact that the contributions could not be claimed as deductions for tax purposes.

And finally we learned that in 1963, FEDECO (Federation of Jewish Communities of Central America and Panama) was established to serve and unify the six Jewish communities of Central America and to enlist their resources for Israel and other Jewish causes. Shirley and I were so engrossed that we were startled when Senor Mordelas came out to announce the start of services.

The men on the roof went inside while the women inside hurried out onto the roof, thus clearly establishing that this was to be an orthodox service.

I left Shirley, Ann and Rose on the parapet and took a seat next to Lennie, Jack and our host, Moshek in the dining room-converted to sanctuary. We opened our well-worn, dog-eared prayer books. One of the older San Andrésans served as cantor and conductor of the service. I thought it interesting that outside the United States the accepted format was still the Traditional, and that only in the United States (and

Germany where the Reform movement began), were there any major variations from the Orthodox.

Of course, I knew the differences went deeper than merely the way services were conducted. The Chazzan led the services and the congregants vied with one another in loud recitals of the particular portion. Even in the swaying of the bodies, there was energetic competition designed to call the Almighty's attention to each one's zealousness. There was no dignity to the proceedings, I thought.

But then, I felt ashamed of my criticalness as I realized that it had been a long time since I had attended services of any denomination. Who was I to judge? I relented and was caught up with the responsive reading: "Amen," I chorused. "Amen," again.

Even though the English was not before me I knew what the Hebrew words were saying: "It hath been told thee, oh man, what is good and what the Lord doth require of thee; Only to do justice, and to love mercy, and to walk humbly with thy God." Ah yes! I ruminated: What does the Lord require of me? Only to be a fair and just person, a merciful, compassionate and caring person, who maintains humility and humbleness. Does it matter whether this is conducted in an Orthodox, Reform, Conservative or even Reconstructionist mode?

My ruminations were jolted by the recitation of the Shema: "Shema Yisroel, Adonoy Alohaynu, Adonoy Echod: Hear Oh Israel, The Lord, Our God, The Lord Is One!' I became aware of warm, wet tears streaming down my cheeks and felt a choking sensation. I flushed, embarrassed, until I looked to my compatriots. I wasn't the only one with tear-stained cheeks.

Jack and Lennie were also in tears. I couldn't speak for them, but for me, it became quite clear: here, twenty-five hundred miles away from home, and more than thirty-five years away from Brooklyn and the Bronx, my heritage was catching up with me. Here on San Andres Island, an isolated and get-away-from-it-all island in the Caribbean (who had heard of it before this past February?) over thirty Jews managed to provide more than the necessary minyan to usher in the Sabbath!

Then I recalled Moshek saying; "Most Friday nights we have enough." To manage a minyan most Friday nights to conduct Shabbat services on San Andres was amazing! I marveled at the fact that Jews from Central and South American countries, from Israel, and even the United States, had assembled for the Shabbat! I thought of the languages spoken: Spanish, Portuguese, German, Yiddish, French, Hebrew and English. But despite the different tongues, there was no Babel: only one people! As the services ended there dawned for me an understanding of the staying power—and the "survival secret" of the Jews. I felt pride, kinship, and nostalgia, guilt, all mixed up as in a variegated quilt.

This time it was the Kaddish, the Mourners Prayer that disrupted my musings. And then I heard: "Shabbat Shalom" and everyone were shaking hands, partaking of challah and wine, and milling around. The services were over. But there remained Moshek's story to be heard.

As our three wives came in from the roof, we all surrounded Moshek and Chanah, and hustled them back onto the now deserted and quiet roof.

"Okay, chaver—how did you come to settle on San Andres?" Jack demanded.

Moshek slowly settled himself on a nearby chair and the rest of us did likewise, waiting with mounting impatience. He smiled. "All right. So, here is my story. Three years ago, Chanah and I were coming to visit some of our family in Bogota. And suddenly Aerovias Condor—the airline of Columbia, developed engine trouble..."

"So what else is new?" Lennie asked.

"Shush, don't interrupt," I said.

Moshek continued. "The plane made a forced landing here on San Andres. I have a bad heart. The anxiousness was too much. I had an attack and was put into the hospital here."

He paused as Senor Mordelas came out to inform us that all the other participants had gone. "Excusa, por favor. Moshek, please continue," he said.

Moshek did so: "The hospital here is small, but very good. The airplane people told Jacob Mordelas about me. He and Sarah took Chanah into their home. And this was good, because I was in the hospital for three weeks. Jacob and Sarah came every day with Chanah to visit. They also prayed every day together with the three other Jewish families. The others also came to visit. I think because of the Jewish people here on San Andres, I am today alive. That is why we stay."

Jacob and Sarah Mordelas sat quietly—embarrassed. Then Jacob Mordelas spoke, in his broken English. "God is good to us here. Is good to pray on San Andres. Si!" Sarah nodded her agreement.

It was time to leave. We bade "Shabbat Shalom" and "Buenas Noches," and "Adios" to our San Andresan cousins and left. We wondered about next Friday night, and the new tourists, either seeking a duty-free bargain or maybe also seeking to "get-away-from-it-all."

But, if they are Jewish tourists, they will discover (as we had) that, for a Jew, there is no getting away from one's heritage.

THE END

XIX. SILENT CRITIC

("Trust No One!" King Herod to Emperor Claudius in *I Claudius*)

Henry O. Zelman was a self-made man. His family in Lynn, Massachusetts owned and operated one of the last independent department stores not only in Massachusetts, New England but probably the nation. He was the oldest son and was expected to follow in his family's footsteps by working in the store and moving up to managerial positions and ultimately taking over the operation entirely.

But HOZ, as he liked to be called, had a mind of his own and was not keen on being a merchant and retail store operator. He loved sports, ever since he was a young child and became very proficient in all of them. In public school, then high school, and finally at college he excelled in baseball, tennis and swimming, but was most proficient in football making the varsity at Tufts University located in the Boston area. When he graduated from Tufts, he disappointed his family by refusing to come into the business, opting instead to try his hand at a variety of small enterprises, all related to sports in one way or another. These included selling refreshments, scorecards, trophies and banners at ball games. Being a very enterprising person, in time he built a business focused on printed material relating to sports contests, including programs and scorecards for football, baseball, tennis and swimming events. All of which he also tied in with the operation of the refreshment concessions.

Henry was practically raised at the Lynn YM-YWHA, playing all sports but was especially proud of being a member of its varsity basketball team. Following graduation from college he served as a member of the Y's Health & Physical Education Committee, moving on to become its chairman in a relatively short time—and ultimately he became ensconced as its perennial chairman. As a consequence he also became a member of the "Y"s board of directors, moving up through the various positions until finally becoming its president. Since the "Y" had a strict policy of no more than three years for any president, HOZ had to step down after his third year, but continued to serve as a life member of the board by virtue of being a Past-President.

While sports and physical education were his prime interests, he nevertheless supported all the other activities offered by the agency. But, because of his own background in sports and physical education he was an especially harsh critic of the agency's sport, athletic and physical education staff, being very demanding of excellence. This criticalness and demand of excellence then expanded to include all staff up to the supervisory and administrative levels. While his criticisms were meant for the agency to have the very best, it became increasingly difficult for it to retain any professional staff, especially executive directors, for any sustained period of time. In fact, the joke in the Jewish Community Center and "Y" field was that Lynn, Massachusetts had the fastest revolving door in the country. So, when the "Y" went out on a capital funds campaign, to raise a million or more dollars for a new building to be located in neighboring Marblehead, this problem of keeping professional staff again surfaced; the executive director who began the campaign was fired almost at its very beginning and few, if any, professionals were interested in replacing him.

Solomon David Wise was also developing a reputation—that of being the "JCC Doctor" because of his successes in several communities of either establishing new Jewish Community Centers or YM-YWHAs or of revitalizing or rehabilitating existing ones. His one "failure" in Jacksonville, Florida was more than offset by his successes in Houston, Texas, Chicago, Illinois and Dallas, Texas. And now the Boston North Shore was beckoning him. He had heard the stories of the "Revolving Door" at the Lynn YM-YWHA—now renamed the North Shore JCC, but after five years in Dallas, where he completed the move of the old Dallas Jewish Center from its former quarters in the southeast section of the city to a new building in the north/central location just off the Central Expressway, and expanded its membership and programs to a new high, he was ready for a new challenge. To attract Wise and complete the "shiddach" (marriage) HOZ agreed to "withhold his fire"—or at least to be a silent critic.

It was fortunate that almost immediately after Sol's arrival, in August 1966, at the very first board of director's meeting, the philosophies and strategies of the two men coincided with regards to whether the agency should purchase a 110 acre tract of land in Middleton, ten miles away from both Lynn and Marblehead (the current and future sites of the North Shore Jewish Community Center) to be used as a day camp facility as well a rural picnic and outing place for the membership. The site would, of course have to be developed to include a large, Olympic-size swimming pool along with bathhouses, locker rooms, ball fields, tennis courts, recreation hall and other facilities, which would, of necessity, increase the amount of money needed to be raised by the Capital Funds Campaign.

The debate at the board meeting raged back and forth, with conservatives urging fiscal restraint and responsibility and others, led by Zelman urging a "do it now" philosophy. At first Sol felt that, being so new he ought not to render an opinion although he did have one. His mind raced back to his "failed journey" to Jacksonville, where eager beavers there screwed up an opportunity by massive bulldozing of orange groves to make way for a new center site and in the process put the entire property in danger of sliding down into the St. Johns River. On the other hand, he believed that if you were going to build a new center, having the opportunity of obtaining and developing a day camp site should be part of the master plan. He remembered P.N Golman in Jacksonville telling him "Make no little plans." And suddenly he was pulled from his reveries when he heard Henry O. Zelman direct a question to him.

"I know Mr. Wise has just arrived and taken up his duties as executive director and he's not had a chance to familiarize himself with many details, but with all his experiences in other agencies and communities, I wonder if he would care to add anything to our very important discussion."

Sol felt all eyes on him as a sudden quiet fell on the scene. Barney Mazer, the leader of the conservatives-go-slow faction seemed to shake his head, while others seemed to want to hang on his every word. Prudence told him that he would be readily excused if he begged off by virtue of his newness. And yet if he did so, this wonderful opportunity of expanding on the plans for the new center might forever be lost. And so he threw caution to the winds and expressed his honest opinion that as long as they were engaged in a capital development program and a campaign to bring it to reality, it made sense to him to include the purchase and development of the Middleton property. Certainly from a program point of view, having a country day camp site was far superior to conducting one on the premises of the center proper—although many centers did just that. But he could honestly say, that any center executive who was presented with the opportunity of having the country day camp site would opt for that instantly.

And with their new executive director holding forth so eloquently, the proposal for the Middleton property passed with only two in opposition and one abstention. And following the end of the meeting Henry and his wife Hazel—who it so happened, was the chairman of the day camp committee—came up to him to thank him profusely and to again welcome him to Lynn and the North Shore. "I think we finally have ourselves an executive director!" Henry exclaimed.

Barney Mazer also came up to him, but he said that he thought it was a mistake for Sol to have involved himself so early in so contentious a matter, but he also admired a person who was forthright and had the courage of his convictions and—not being a vengeful guy, Sol could still expect his continued support.

Sol was pleased with his auspicious beginning, especially his having gotten off on the right foot with the notorious professional-staff-killer, Henry O. Zelman. And the next several years they worked relatively well together, raising the now $2,750,000 required for the new JCC building in Marblehead and the day camp site in Middleton. Nevertheless, Zelman made it clear that despite the successes, there was still a line between hired help and board members as far as he was concerned. And he kept his pledge of being a silent critic—but not an altogether dumb one—for Sol was yet to learn that there were three cardinal, unforgivable sins, harbored by Henry O. Zelman, which were yet to be committed by Solomon D. Wise.

THE HEALTH CLUB CONTROVERSY

The first one revolved around differing philosophies regarding Health Clubs in "Y"s and Jewish Centers. Over the years, many such agencies had installed in their buildings separate facilities featuring steam rooms, dry heat rooms, exercise equipment in special rooms and separate lounges for Health Club members paying substantially higher annual membership fees. It was a way of helping to support ever-escalating budgets while trying to maintain nominal fees so that everyone in the Jewish community could belong to the "community center."

But in time, as is so often the case, the people paying higher and special fees insisted on having not only their special Health Club privileges and services but having a larger voice in the running of the agency and determining its policies and procedures; a sort of–one-dollar-one-vote philosophy—and there thus evolved a two-level (if not caste) membership system. The Lynn YM-YWHA, in its long history, had developed into precisely such an entity with much of the general membership feeling that the Health Club tail was always wagging the YMHA dog.

In the many communities that Sol had worked efforts were made to eliminate such a two- tiered membership system, allowing Health Club facilities to be used by the entire membership. And as the North Shore JCC Health & Physical Education Task Force mulled over the building plans and policies and procedures for the new building to be erected in Marblehead Sol attempted to focus their attention on the newer-emerging philosophies concerning the use of Health Club facilities. Even the National Association of JCCs was now espousing the more democratic philosophy of all members having use of the so-called Health Club facilities—even to getting away from the use of the term Health Club in favor of "exercise and fitness facilities."

Following one of the H&PE Task Force meetings, HOZ "invited" Sol to his office in downtown Lynn. "Okay Sol, strike one! I've kept pretty quiet for the past few years about some of the things about you that I didn't like, but last night you pushed my button. I'm for democracy and all that but how the hell do you think we've been able to maintain the stability of the 'Y' and be able to take in as members everybody that wanted to be a member. This crap about some people paying higher membership fees without getting any additional services just wont fly. It doesn't make any sense. Very few, if any, people will give good money and not expect something extra in return."

Sol attempted to point out that in places like Chicago that very concept had proven to be successful only to be rebuffed with the retort that Lynn/Marblehead was hardly comparable with a city like Chicago, followed by the warning that the Health Club would remain as a separate and special facility requiring additional fees. Sol then expressed his regrets that they could not always be on the same wavelengths, as was the case with the Middleton day camp site. And while many newer members were sympathetic with Sol's position and the newer philosophies, Henry Zelman and his Old Guard held sway and the separate Health Club was incorporated into the plans for the new building in Marblehead. Having won that battle, HOZ resumed his role of silent critic, realizing that Solomon D. Wise was still vital to the success of the project.

PORTENT OF THINGS TO COME

In the fall of 1971, five years after Sol's arrival and just after Ross Silversmith took over as president, succeeding Kenneth Goldman, Sol and his board of directors found it necessary to move into the only-half-finished building in Marblehead because the Lynn Redevelopment Authority-which had purchased the "Y" building some years before as part of the City of Lynn's Urban Redevelopment Program and leasing it back to the agency on an annual basis—could no longer postpone the building's demolition. So without missing a day of activities, Sol and his staff began operating on the lower level of the uncompleted building while construction continued on the second floor. In fact, while the wrecking ball was demolishing the old "Y" building, records and files were still being moved from the old building to the new. Ken Goldman, who had been appointed as chairman of the Dispositions Committee (selling off the furniture and fixtures of the old building) valiantly fought off resounding headaches as he tried to get the best possible price for library shelving and even the bronze railing of the main staircase while the wrecking ball swirled and smashed overhead!

Despite such a portentous beginning, 16 months later, on November 26, 1972—with the second floor 60% completed, including the Health Club and its facilities—the new building in Marblehead was dedicated! It was the only JCC facility in the country overlooking a body of water, such as the Atlantic Ocean! While there were still parts of the second floor to be completed—such as the game rooms and youth and older adult lounges and arts and crafts studios (the construction of which would continue as additional monies were raised)—the new North Shore Jewish Community Center was officially open for business. The Capital Funds Campaign had begun with a million dollar goal. The project, including the Middleton site would finally total $2,750,000 and have taken slightly over six years to accomplish—with an additional five years for the final completion!

The Dedication Banquet was a black tie affair with Barney Mazer as its Chairman and, of course, Henry O. Zelman a prominent member of the committee. Sol made the mistake of not paying too much attention to the committee's planning, feeling that he had his hands full with the programming and final completion of yet necessary facilities. And he remembered Barney's earlier assurance of support and felt that Ross Silversmith and Ken Goldman could be trusted to do what was right.

The affair was an elegant one, with speaker after speaker extolling the virtues of all the lay leadership and past presidents and a dramatic presentation of the "Y"s history in a "This Is Your Life" format. Sol, sitting on the second tier, lower dais, thought to himself that thus far the entire proceedings were a mutual admiration society and wondered if it wouldn't have been a lot easier for Barney Mazer to have asked everybody in the gymnasium-converted-to-banquet hall to stand and then pat his nearest neighbor on the back! He waited to hear some mention of the staff role in bringing about the current reality, but the accolades to the lay leaders' accomplishments rolled on. And then he heard Chairman Barney make a perfunctory mention of staff as having done "a good job" and didn't even invite Sol to stand and take a bow as representative of the staff. Sol was seething inside as his wife Shirley squeezed his hand.

The next morning Henry Zelman came by and sat across Sol's desk commenting on what a great affair it was and Sol wasn't sure whether the man was gloating and "sticking it to him" or genuinely unaware of the great slight done to Sol and his staff. So Sol straightforwardly focused on that fact.

Henry pondered Sol's complaint and then responded: "Well Sol, see, again you fail to understand the respective roles of staff and lay leadership. I distinctly heard Barney compliment staff on a job well done. And considering the fact that staff is paid and expected to do a good job—well what more can you have a right to expect?"

Memories of an earlier experience in Essex, New Jersey—where that exact dichotomy between staff and lay leadership was spelled out by one of his committee chairman—suddenly flooded in upon Sol. Nevertheless, he attempted to focus on the now-expanding view of "lay/staff partnership" espoused by the NAJCC and particularly as he experienced it in other communities—notably Chicago—only to again have Zelman reject any comparisons of the North Shore with Chicago, Illinois.

As he left Sol's office, Zelman smiled and said he would, however, convey Sol's feelings to Barney and the other members of the Dedication Committee. And Sol found himself wondering what the hell THAT meant and whether he could; in fact, trust any of the members of that committee.

LEAP FROG (The Second Cardinal Sin)

Jack Quicker was a young lawyer aspiring to even greater things. He was a second vice president, after Murray Goldwitz, and purported to represent the younger leadership seeking to counter the influence of the long-time "Old Guard." Now that the move from Lynn to the new building in Marblehead had been completed, and with Ross Silversmith's three year term about to expire, Jack aspired to become the next president. But ordinarily he would have to wait for Goldwitz, the first vice president who was slated to succeed Ross after he completed his three-year term. But Jack Quicker's needs dictated that he could not or would not wait that long. After all, the North Shore JCC, although still not completely finished, was obviously a success and a young, ambitious attorney could derive much benefit from being identified as its president. So he announced his intention of succeeding Ross Silversmith, thus leap-frogging over Goldwitz, an action unprecedented in the agency's long history.

Sol attempted to persuade Jack to wait his turn, but Jack would not hear of it and let it be known that if the nominating committee did not put his name in nomination for the presidency, he would conduct a campaign on his own—although he vowed that if elected he would limit his term to merely two years.

Murray Goldwitz, a very patient man with a highly successful law practice and seeking harmony for the agency, smilingly agreed to allow Jack to become the next president with the comment: "He seems to need it more than me at this time. I think we can survive his ambitions."

But Henry O. Zelman—a recognized client, friend and mentor of Goldwitz cried "Foul!" and "Strike two!" against Sol again in his downtown Lynn office, despite Sol's disclaimer that he had no veto power, or any power, over the Nominating Committee.

Still the building was not yet completely finished and Murray Goldwitz prevailed upon his mentor and client, HOZ to bite his tongue and bide his time and the man agreed to do so and returned to his role of silent critic, at least publicly. Fortunately, Jack Quicker's two-year term passed quickly if relatively uneventfully and Murray Goldwitz assumed the top lay position.

THE THIRD CARDINAL SIN

President Murray Goldwitz worked well with Sol for the next three years, insuring the continuing raising of Capital Funds necessary for the final completion of the building. And at the end of each year of their "partnership" (for Murray at least paid the concept some lip-service) issued a very positive evaluation of the professional—as had all his predecessors.

At a national NAJCC conference held in New York in September 1978, the North Shore JCC sent a good-sized delegation, including Sol, Henry, now-immediate Past President Murray Goldwitz, and the recently installed president Irving Black, among others, to celebrate finally the total completion of the new building in Marblehead after having moved into it seven years before! All were basking in the many compliments being voiced by lay and professional people at the conference, and Sol, after 12 years on the job, was beginning to feel a degree of security.

At one point, Sol found himself alone at the table with Henry and having imbibed one too many martinis was feeling free and reckless. In his mind's eye he reviewed the twelve years of continuous fundraising, the over-seven years of construction in starts and stops and the many hurdles overcome. But the building was now, finally a fully completed reality. "A toast to a job well done" he said, raising his glass to Henry O. Zelman.

Henry eyed him coldly. "Hmph! That's the difference between us, Wise. Building a JCC isn't just a job. It's an ongoing, never-ending labor of love."

"Well okay, I was referring to the physical completion of the building. You have to admit that's an accomplishment and it wouldn't have been done without our working together."

Henry shifted uneasily in his chair. "Maybe. I guess I could agree that your contribution was adequate if not brilliant."

Sol was taken aback for a moment and then retorted: "HOZ, don't you think that's a contradiction of terms if not an outright oxymoron?"

Now it was Zelman's turn to be taken aback. "Well Mr. Hired Hand, just remember that as far as this 'moron' is concerned you're still on probation."

Sol couldn't be sure if Henry was pulling his leg, or really didn't understand the term 'oxymoron'—a figure of speech in which opposite or contradictory ideas or terms are combined— and so he hastened to clarify that he had not called him a 'moron' concluding with: "And after 12 years you still regard me as being on probation? Well, don't worry Henry, I always remember who is the oiler of the revolving doors." At which point others rejoined them and the conversation drifted to other things.

Sol and Irving Black, the newly installed president succeeding Murray Goldwitz, were off to a good start. Irving had called Zelman's attention a few year's before about the lack of tennis courts in the Capital Development program and HOZ, in his inimitable way of involving people, charged him with determining how two courts could be squeezed into the very limited acreage and if he could do that, to then undertake the campaign to raise the necessary monies for them. And Irving Black had more than met the challenge, with the tennis courts being the last of the outdoor facilities to be constructed. Naturally Irving had been elected to the board and very quickly moved up the ranks to third vice president. And when the two vice presidents before him, each with compelling personal reasons declined to follow Murray Goldwitz, Irving Black filled the void.

At first, Sol and Irving liked and respected each other, Irving extolling Sol's diligence, perseverance and his having provided stability to the executive director's position after it's revolving door history; and Sol admiring Irving's creativity and diligence in making the tennis courts a reality. But very soon their mutual admiration would dissipate as a consequence of Sol's having committed the third cardinal sin against Henry O Zelman at the recent conference—insulting HOZ; or at least Zelman's having perceived it as such.

HOZ BLOWS HIS WHISTLE

It was ten a.m. on a Sunday morning when the phone rang at Sol's home. Most Sunday mornings Sol was at the center, meeting people in his office, making rounds, spending time up in the Health Club schmoozing with its members. But this morning he had decided to sleep late, read the paper and go to the center in the afternoon.

Shirley answered the phone and handed it to Sol with a terse: "It's Henry Zelman, and he sounds upset about something."

Sol's "Hello" was cut short with a blast that even Shirley could hear across the kitchen.

"Why the hell aren't you here at the Center? Vandals have spray-painted the entire outside of the building! You better get your ass over here in a hurry!"

"Take it easy Mr. Z. There's no need for obscenities. I'll be over in half an hour."

Sol lived a half-hour away by car from the center and he managed to shave, shower, dress and still arrive within that time frame. As he entered his office he encountered a livid Henry Zelman sitting at his desk in his chair and found himself thinking what a clever ploy—and immediately plopped himself in a chair across from his adversary in front of his own desk. Zelman demanded to know what took him so long in getting to the center and Sol, struggling to remain cool, calm and collected (his favorite three "C"s which he continually doodled when he had paper in front of him), looked Henry straight in the eyes and replied that he owned a car and not a helicopter and would Henry show him the wholesale defacement that he was complaining about.

"Don't get smart with me!" the angry man snarled, rose from behind the desk and strode out of the office at a brisk pace, followed by Sol and joined by several other Health Club members who had been waiting outside the office. They walked to a lower level of the terraced building site, around to the back of the building on which was sprayed in black paint some obscenities and anti-Semitic remarks.

While the defacement was unsightly, disconcerting and annoying, still Sol wondered how something so small and so easily correctible by the use of another can of white spray paint could cause the near-hysterical reaction of a man such as Henry O. Zelman. But he humored the man by not expressing such thoughts, shaking his head to express his own dismay and assuring HOZ that he would make certain the

Maintenance Department would correct the defacement the first thing on Monday.

October was traditionally the time for the evaluation and assessment of the executive director by the president in consultation with the personnel and executive committees and the year 1978 was no exception. In Sol's discussions with his new president, Irving Black, the tone was positive and, as with all previous evaluations, a favorable recommendation forthcoming. And this also appeared to be the case at the combined committee meeting so when Irving suggested to Sol that he excuse himself so that the group could go into closed session to finalize its discussions and arrive at a recommended salary increment—and that there was no need for Sol to wait at the center but should go home instead and he, Irving, would contact him the next morning—Sol thought nothing of it and did, in fact go home.

Sol went home and, responding to Shirley's question, indicated that everything was going as expected and Irving would share with him the recommended salary figure in the morning. He then settled himself comfortably in his favorite chair, with a beer in hand, and began reading the Boston Globe.

At around 10 p.m. the doorbell rang unexpectedly and Sol and Shirley exchanged curious glances. Sol opened the door and encountered a visibly disturbed Irving Black standing in the doorway apologizing for bothering them at this time but stressing that he felt that what he needed to share with Sol couldn't—or shouldn't wait until morning.

Sol invited him in and Irving slumped into a side chair, muttering; "Negative, negative, all negative. I don't understand it, all negative!"

"What's negative?" Sol interjected.

"Your assessment and evaluation. I had no idea. I didn't expect anything like this."

Sol offered, and Irving accepted a cup of coffee, which Shirley promptly supplied. And Sol then suggested that Irving start at the beginning, which—after a few sips of coffee, he did.

Irving described how, after Sol had left the meeting, immediate-past-president Murray Goldwitz raised a few points, including the recent defacement of the building and Sol's absence from the center when it was discovered. Not that that was such a terrible thing, Murray insisted, but it seemed to be a part of a pattern of many small things lately, like Henry Zelman being insulted at the recent conference, and Sol's failure to spend more time up in the Health Club. And then others began remembering other small things, not that any of them were of major significance, but maybe there was a pattern developing after all.

And now Sol began to see the hand of Henry O. Zelman at work, but he did not verbalize his suspicions. Instead he asked about the "bottom line" to the meeting and Irving replied that that was the problem; with each anecdote prompting another recollection it became an almost "can you top this" contest. So much so that he, Irving, suggested that since it was getting late any final recommendations should be postponed to another meeting—to which all the past presidents who had worked with Sol over the years, would be invited. And Irving added, that since all the past presidents had in the past given positive evaluations he thought this would be helpful to "them"—by which Irving meant Sol and himself.

Sol acknowledged Irving's round-a-bout expression of support but asked if he, Sol, would also be invited to participate in that new meeting and Irving grimaced and said that since it was an extension of the "closed session" he would not be invited to participate. Sol then suggested that for that meeting to have any appearance of fairness the center should at least invite a professional staff member of the Personnel Bureau of the NAJCC and Irving agreed with him. As he left, around 11 pm Irving said that he felt better having discussed the matter with Sol and he felt optimistic that it would all work out well in the end. And Sol wondered about how Irving had turned the thing around so that Irving felt like he was the victim rather than Sol and that Sol needed to be the one to try to cheer Irving. Weird, he thought.

The next morning Sol called the NAJCC to inform them of the latest developments and was told by Martin Fader of the Personnel Bureau that Irving had already called and invited him to attend the next meeting. Fader however assured Sol that in light of Sol's record and reputation that he tended to agree with Irving Black that it would all work out well in the end. In any event, he would meet with Sol prior to the meeting and following it.

Fader kept his word, and met with Sol briefly before attending the special Personnel/Executive Committee meeting attended also by all the past presidents who had served with Sol. And then he also kept his word by coming to Sol's home after the meeting to talk with him about what had transpired. Sol was astounded to hear the man struggle with giving a coherent description of events; instead he listened to him expound, "on the one hand this" and "on the other hand that" until Sol urged him to come to the bottom line.

"Well, the 'bottom line' as you call it is that there seemed to be a lot of people that were unhappy with your performance and are thinking of replacing you. Yet, there was this vice president, Morris Gordon, who was quite vociferous in his opposition to any such action, and so there was no final decision or action taken. At least not yet." And Martin Fader wiped his brow.

"And what was your role as a representative of the Personnel Bureau of the NAJCC in all this?" Sol asked directly.

"Well I explained that they, of course had a responsibility to you which had to be properly discharged and NAJCC would insist upon that. Irving Black can fill you in with the other details of the meeting.

"That's rather vague and I will get the details from Irving Black. But frankly Martin I'm afraid that what you've succeeded in doing just now is confirm for me what I, and many professionals in field have long suspected; that when push comes to shove, the NAJCC comes down on the side of the agency in any dispute involving the professional and his agency. We professionals realize that, since the NAJCC depends upon the affiliation fees paid by each agency and the allocations granted by each community for its survival, the NAJCC actually has a conflict of interest in such disputes, which manifests itself in a bias in favor of agencies."

Fader shifted uncomfortably in his chair, smiled weakly and replied: "Y'know Sol, just between the two of us, and unofficially, I agree with you. I had the same feelings when I was in the field. Actually the National Association of Center Workers, the NAJCW, should really exercise the Personnel function. And I've suggested that the Personnel Bureau be transferred to the center workers' organization. And believe it or not, it is receiving serious consideration."

"Happy to hear that, but in the meantime, in my conflict with my agency, I'm not really getting the support I should from the agency I'm supposed to look to."

"Well, let's see what happens" Fader meekly suggested.

Realizing that there was nothing more he could expect from Martin Fader Sol bid him goodnight, muttering, "Yeah, let's see what happens."

But the next morning, when Irving Black failed to call him by 10 am, Sol called him and was told that Irving preferred to postpone their conference because he had to have some more discussions with Murray Goldwitz, Fader and Zelman and some others. And hearing Zelman's name mentioned again Sol concluded that the clouds were indeed gathering. So he called Morris Gordon—who invited him over to his office immediately.

MORRIE GORDON

Morris "Morrie" Gordon was a perpetual vice president of the center who preferred to work on the program committee level rather than aspire to the top job. He was a successful attorney who had also been active in the old "Y" (and now the center) and involved in most of the program committees, serving as chairman of each of them at one time or another. And then he was elevated to a vice presidency with his major assignment being chairman of the personnel committee. It wasn't that he was gun-shy about succeeding to the top post, just that he felt he could be more effective on the program and personnel committee level. He and Sol had worked on a number of successful programs together and grew to admire and respect each other. When the "shit hit the fan" as Morrie described it, he called Sol and assured him of his continuing support. And here Sol was sitting in his office.

"Sol, after 25 years as an attorney I learned that one could build a case for or against anybody or anything. But in all my years I've never seen anything like I witnessed last night. I mean if it wasn't so despicable it could almost be a comedy. Watching Henry Zelman twist and distort was like watching a magician on stage making things appear or disappear. He used his old technique of asking each of the past presidents—who initially were prone to be positive—'in what way could it have been better?' Well, you know, things could always be better and so in that way he made the perfect the enemy of the good. And Sol, you know as well as I, once one gets a particular train rolling—or to mix my metaphors—start lining up a row of dominos, all that's then needed is a little push from a little finger. For example, Zelman took the fact of seven years for the raising of funds and the completion of the building as being a negative rather than the miracle it actually was. As I said, that's the same technique he used to get rid of the other professionals and executives. And for years I wondered why he had to do such a thing and I finally came to the conclusion that the man must love the "Y" and the center so much that he really believes that no one could really do the job that he could, but since he has a business to run, well you have to hire other people."

Sol smiled through his discomfort with what Morrie was describing and said: "Wow Morrie, you're a psychologist as well as a lawyer! You're probably right about his unconscious motivations, but maybe a little too kind."

"You better believe it that a lawyer also has to be a psychologist to see through people's distortions and contortions. And yes, I guess I am being too kind."

Sol then asked what was the role of the NAJCC man, Milton Fader, and Morrie described the man as being completely surprised and unprepared for what was unfolding. "As the train rolled on, Fader finally asked what the gathering was proposing and Zelman jumped in with: 'isn't it obvious? We want to replace Sol Wise and for your agency to start sending profiles of candidates.' And at that point I jumped in and said: 'hold on there! I'm still chairman of the personnel committee, a member of the executive committee and the board of directors and I don't recall any one of those entities arriving at that conclusion or any such recommendation. And I for one would not concur in any such recommendation. And the meeting ended without any definite conclusions."

"But Morrie, what's to stop Henry Zelman from doing the same thing he's done at the committee meetings when the matter comes up at the board meeting?"

Morrie sat up in his chair and said: "If and when it comes up at a board meeting! It still has to go through the personnel committee, and even if they try to bypass that committee,

I'm also a member of the board. And there are a few others on the committee and the board with integrity and sense of fairness who also remember Henry's shenanigans from the old days."

Although encouraged by his session with Morrie Gordon Sol anxiously awaited his weekly conference with Irving Black. And at that meeting, although not altogether unexpected, his worst fears were realized.

"Sol, after two meetings of the expanded personnel committee and conversations with many key leaders of the center, and for the sake of the center and the community, it's been decided that I should ask for your reservation."

"I believe you mean my resignation, don't you Irving? Well, I know how uncomfortable you must feel, but I'm sorry to have to tell you that I don't believe there are any grounds for me to submit my resignation. Besides, I understand that the personnel committee has not officially made any recommendations to that effect, and if it did, it would still have to come to the board for final action. And I truly believe that the agency and the community is best served with my continuing on as executive director."

Irving was visibly flustered and confused. "Sol, let's not make this any more difficult than it already is. I mean, let's not prolong this any longer than we have to. Many people still do like and respect you and prolonging this thing would only turn such people against you. Even Henry Zelman said that he was ready and willing to use his good offices to help you get a teaching job at Tufts University."

Sol smiled at what he regarded as a bribe, but he avoided labeling it as such. Instead he replied: "I have no desire to prolong a situation which I did not initiate or instigate. But if there are grounds for my dismissal then the agency must do what it must do. And I have to do what I have to do, but that does not include my submitting my resignation."

"Well then Sol, I guess I'll have to make a list of the grounds and send them on to you."

"And I am entitled to rebut any such lists, according to our Code of Personnel Practices."

HIGH NOON

When Sol left Irving Black's office he found himself beginning to feel like Marshal Will Kane (played by Gary Cooper) in the 1952 movie *High Noon* as he prepared to meet the released killer and gunfighter, Frank Miller and his three cronies seeking revenge for the Marshal's sending Miller to prison. At first most of the town was behind Marshal Kane, but slowly, person by person, this support eroded with one excuse or rationalization after another being offered by Kane's erstwhile friends leaving the Marshal to face the four gunmen alone.

Sol was very impressed when he saw the movie a good few years back because he felt the story was an acute exploration of human nature, the baser elements triumphing over the nobler inclinations. As one character says it: "People have to talk themselves into supporting Law and Order." He could just as well have said: "Support right over wrong." After some exciting chases and gunfights, the Marshal, after killing the four gunmen, triumphs and as he stands alone with his newly-wed wife, the townspeople gather around him and he throws his tin star to the ground in disgust. Henrik Ibsen, the Norwegian playwright, if he were in America at the time, would have pointed to him and exclaimed: "He is strongest who stands alone!" So Sol thought.

Henry Zelman was right about the North Shore not being comparable to big cities like Chicago and even Boston, especially about the small town aversion to privacy. And certainly the un-folding battle between Zelman and his cohorts and

Sol Wise, the executive director of the North Shore Jewish Community Center for the past twelve years, was grist for the gossip mill. For despite Sol Wise's tenure of twelve years—that was small comparison to the lifelong residency of Zelman and his backers. Shades of Lenny White and Essex, New Jersey, Sol remembered! So Sol and Shirley found their circle of "friends" shrinking as the issue dragged on—and the weeks developed into months. Even their close circle consisting of Anne and Jack Clayman and Rose and Lennie Kater—who had joined them for their four vacations in the Caribbean, were not uninfected. In fact, the gossip/grape vine had Anne Clayman talking around that she was not surprised that "this" had occurred because, "well Sol and Shirley had not **really made an effort** to really become part of the community."

It was Anne and Jack Clayman's turn to host the monthly cycle of Saturday gatherings of the six vacationers in their home in Marblehead. At first the conversation was lively, focused on every conceivable topic other than that which was of most concern to Sol and Shirley, namely the battle that Zelman had instigated and initiated. But when they had exhausted all discussions about the New England Patriots and the Boston Celtics, and the latest events in the Middle East and Israel, the conversation dried up and an uncomfortable silence assailed them.

Finally Shirley and Sol rose from their chairs, announced that they had to leave and before Anne, Jack, Rose or her husband Lenny could respond, they left.

The next morning Rose Kater called Shirley bright and early to ask why they had departed so suddenly while the evening was still so young. And Shirley let her have a broadside complaining about their four friends insensitivity and lack of at least verbal support in their trying times.

Following an uncomfortable pause, Rose agreed with Shirley and apologized profusely. She admitted that before their Saturday gathering, she had confronted Anne about "her loose mouth" and that perhaps contributed to the total silence about Sol's battle to keep his job.

And when Shirley told Sol about her conversation with Rose, his only comment was: "It's another variation of the church scene in *High Noon.*"

Sol and Shirley had also become very friendly with Martha and Harold Fischer, or Hal, as he preferred to be called. They had come to the North Shore a few years after Sol and Shirley, arriving from Minneapolis where they were active in the Jewish Center and Federation there. Martha was a CPA and Hal a Judge in the Social Security Administration with offices in Boston. Although Hal expressed his disdain for the hypocrisies that they had encountered in the communal services of Minneapolis, he and Sol nevertheless hit it off, as did Shirley and Martha. Thus they attended concerts, plays, and dined out together frequently as well as visiting each other in their respective homes. And this particular Saturday evening the Wises were the guests of the Fischers in their condo at Crowne Pointe in Swampscott.

Sol brought them up-to-date with the developments at the center and Hal commended Sol for the stand he had taken but then he suggested a broader two-stage strategy; that if the board accepted a recommendation from the personnel committee to replace Sol, for Sol to challenge, resist and fight it every step of the way.

Sol interrupted: "But Hal, as I've described, I've already begun to do just that. And the personnel committee has not yet made any formal or official recommendations to the board. Still, how can an employee fight to keep a job if and when a board decides it doesn't want him?"

"Well that's the second stage that you interrupted me from telling. If keeping the job is no longer feasible then you fight for the most liberal discharge conditions, and that includes maximum severance pay and benefits. You told us that you've been on the job now twelve years. Responsible employers provide one month for each year of service so you should be entitled to at least a year's severance pay plus existing benefits—if it finally comes to that."

"I don't think our Personnel Code provides for that much, although the NAJCC recommended code does" Sol said.

"Well that's why I said you have to fight for the most liberal, not the most restrictive. Most agencies have very timid provisions. And my guess is that's why Black asked for your resignation because when a person resigns severance pay doesn't kick in. And besides, from what you told us, there has not yet been any official action by either the personnel committee or the board, right? And my other guess is if they can get you to resign, there doesn't have to be any actions on their part. Sol, they know that you have a lot of support out in the community and that's why they're moving so cautiously."

Sol said he was happy to hear about all the support out in the community, but added that Marshal Kane in *High Noon* also started out with a lot of support in the community and he was beginning to feel like Marshal Kane on the one hand, and Dr. Stockman in Ibsen's play *Enemy of the People* on the other.

"I thought Arthur Miller wrote that. It was on Broadway a few years ago and Martha and I wanted to see it but never got around to it." Hal said.

"Well actually Arthur Miller adapted it from Henrik Ibsen's original play. But I can't recall the plot and theme" said Martha. "Sol do you remember some of the details?" she added.

"Hey, don't encourage him doll" Hal said, using his favorite term of endearment.

"Well if you insist," said Sol, taking a long sip from his extra-dry martini and a long, deep breath. "Remember, you asked for it."

"AN ENEMY OF THE PEOPLE"

Sol began: "It was supposed to be a comedy/satire written by Henrik Ibsen in 1882, if I remember my European literature courses. In it he expresses his belief that even amongst the best people there exists a mixture of wisdom and folly and that self-interest is one of the greatest and most powerful of motivations. His protagonist, Dr. Thomas Stockman proclaims that 'the minority is always right and the majority always wrong' and that 'the strongest man in the world is he who stands most alone'—usually paraphrased as; 'he is strongest who stands alone.'"

Sol paused to take another sip of his drink and continued: "Dr. Stockman is the Medical Officer of the recently completed Municipal Baths. His older brother is the mayor of the town and Chairman of the Baths. When Dr. Stockman discovers that the water being used for the Baths, as well as for drinking, is polluted by microscopic bacteria (and hence a threat to the health of the entire community) he is pleased that he can call attention to the problem so that action could be taken to resolve it. In this he is both idealistic and naïve.

"He enlists the assistance of the local paper whose editor sees himself as a progressive crusader but whose secret agenda is the doing away with the upper classes. Likewise with the local printer and others, each with their own hidden agendas and self-interests. But when Mayor Peter Stockman expresses opposition to his brother's discovery—because of the enormous costs to remedy the situation—he at first tries to dissuade Thomas from publishing his report and when the Doctor insists on doing so, resorts to all his bureaucratic powers to stop him. Anyway the report never gets published because the printer turns against the doctor who finds himself increasingly isolated and alone and finally branded 'An Enemy of the People.' One by one people desert him, because each person has been threatened or intimidated or otherwise having his personal interests affected. And the battle of Might versus Right is joined. And you get one guess as to which one wins." Sol paused again in his summary to take another sip.

"Now, now Sol, let's not get too cynical" Hal commented.

Sol smiled and continued: "Well, by the end of the play we find Dr. Stockman and his family, isolated, ostracized, vilified, attacked by stones thrown through all their windows, but determined and unbowed."

"That's better" Hal said.

"That he and his family are isolated, ostracized, vilified and stoned?" Sol sneered.

"No, that they remain determined and unbowed." Hal sneered back.

"Great synopsis" said Martha and don't let Hal get your goat. He really admires and respects you," she added.

"Yes, great job of story telling, Sol. But don't over-identify with either the Marshal or the Doctor. You're idealistic and naïve, that's true; but I credit you with more intelligence. Have you and Shirley been watching the TV series *I Claudius*? Well, if you have, a better character for you to identify with is the Emperor Claudius, played by Derek Jacobi. Man, he's great! Especially the scene where King Herod—his boyhood friend and now King of Judea with the permission of the Romans—is visiting Claudius, right after he was proclaimed Emperor and Herod advises Claudius: 'Trust no one!' Now that's whom you should be identifying with. I mean, he finally learned how to fight dirty—which is something I've been trying to teach you. but you keep resisting."

"Hal, back in Jacksonville, Florida there was this NAJCC field secretary who also wanted me to get into the gutter to deal with the local obstructionists trying to prevent the Jewish Community Alliance from succeeding. I wouldn't do it then and I'm not about to do it now." Sol announced haughtily.

"Yes but I remember you telling me that in the end you had to leave that place." Hal retorted. "No matter; from what you've been telling us Sol, you're doing just great. Just hang in there." Hal concluded.

"Great? Yeah? Well now you remind me of the boxer in the ring who is getting beat up pretty badly by his opponent, but at the end of each round, when he goes back to his corner, his manager keeps telling him how well he's doing and he finally explodes and says: 'Is that so? Then somebody better keep an eye on the referee because somebody in there is beating the shit out of me!'"

STALEMATE

It was now nearly four months since HOZ blew his whistle over the defacement of the building episode and precipitated the current series of events and now Sol waited to receive the detailed outline of "charges" that Irving Black, at their last conference over two weeks ago, said he would send. When Sol discussed this with Hal Fischer over the phone, Hal thought that was a very good sign, because it meant that they were having difficulty in coming up with charges that could be made to stick and he offered to discuss the matter further with Sol once he received the material from Black.

Finally, on a Saturday morning, the packet arrived by Certified Mail and Sol put it on his desk without even opening it.

"Aren't you going to open it?" Shirley asked him incredulously.

"Nope! It's Saturday, my one day off and a day of rest. It took Black all this time to get the damned thing to me, so I'm sure it can wait until Monday. Look, I'm as anxious as you to know what the hell's in there, but it can wait. I'm certain I can rebut each and every one of the so-called charges. Besides, I think time is on my side. They still have not actually fired me, and I haven't resigned. And the NAJCC Bureau of

Personnel can't send them any profiles until the position is officially vacant by one means or another. So, as they say in chess, it's a stalemate."

On Monday Sol took the material to his office, secluded himself and asked for his calls to be messaged as he poured over the ten typed, double-spaced pages rebutting each and every charge. He referred frequently to his files of past president's positive evaluations and excerpted quotes from them to be applied to the appropriate charge cited in Black's papers, concluding with the statement that since, in his opinion there existed no valid cause for his dismissal or resignation as documented by his rebuttal, he would not submit his resignation and he would have to contest any action leading to his dismissal. He made copies of Irving Black's material and his response to it and sent them to Martin Fader at the NAJCC, Morris Gordon as chairman of the personnel committee and his friend and putative lawyer, Hal Fischer. And then he sent the original to Irving Black by Registered Mail.

Although Irving received the material the next day, it took him a week before he called Sol and invited him for a conference. Again it was obvious that the man was in distress, as he leafed through the material, shaking his head sadly so that Sol actually felt sorry for him and the morass that he had walked into unwittingly. "Sheesh Sol. What a mess! If we start slugging each other with all this written garbage, no one is going to come out clean and happy! Look, I've been a businessman a long time and I know that when an employer wants to get rid of an employee, he gets rid of him! None of this back and forth. Even Henry is getting impatient, but he repeated his offer of helping you get a teaching job. In fact, he's ready to help you get a job at any university or college you're interested in and not just Tufts."

Sol eyed Irving sympathetically before responding. "So, HOZ has doubled his offer has he?" Well Irving, you—and probably most of the other lay people—don't know that over the past twelve years I've turned down over a half dozen academic offers from a variety of schools because I felt I had a commitment to the agency and the community. I'm pretty sure that if I wanted a job in academia, I would have no difficulty getting one on my own. And I believe that I ought to tell you that over the past month I've been meeting one-on-one with most every member of the board of directors presenting my side of the case. After all, you excluded me from the series of meetings that precipitated this impasse."

"Yes, I know that you've been doing that, and I didn't want to stop you even though Henry and some of the other guys thought I should do so. But, (he sighed) it's a free country and for a guy like me, coming from Austria, to try to suppress speech would be like resurrecting Hitler and the Nazis." Irving paused and then resumed. "Have you met with Carl Sloane yet in your marathon of meetings? Y'know I was the one who proposed him for the board."

Sol replied that he had not yet met with Carl...that he was scheduled to do so the coming week, and yes he knew that Irving was the one responsible for bringing Carl onto the board.

Carl Sloane was a business consultant to major Boston businesses and corporations. He had come onto the board after being proposed by Irving Black and thus was, in a sense, part of Irv's incoming administration. In the same way that Sol conferred with Hal Fischer, so Irving had consulted with Carl unofficially, of course, when the imbroglio ensued.

At their meeting, in Carl's downtown Boston office, Carl was visibly impressed with Sol's presentation of his side of the issue saying: "Well there's no doubt, Sol, that you've done your homework and your presentation is very persuasive. However, I'm sure you also know that any business organization has the right and authority to request its executive's resignation. It's done all the time in the business world."

"Except Carl, the Jewish Community Center is not a 'business' although many lay people would love to have it considered as such. Many are always saying that 'the Center has to be run like a business' when what they really mean is that it must be run efficiently. I'm sure you'll agree that not all businesses are run efficiently, else how account for the large number of bankruptcies every year. Centers, and other communal services, are eleemosynary—not for profit—institutions. Certainly businesses are not deliberately 'not for profit'—or at least try not to operate as such. And there's good reason for the 'not for profit' philosophy governing such communal institutions and why their personnel practices codes strive to provide some greater protection for its employees. Professional communal workers receive only a fraction of the salary that their counterparts receive in the business world. Certainly communal service agencies do not provide—or are they capable of providing—the Golden Parachutes that are awarded to fired or dismissed corporate executives."

"You make a powerful case Sol. I never thought of the differences in quite those terms. You're absolutely right about the need for greater protection of employees in non-profit agencies and it's something I should talk with Irving about—although I'm sure you must have already told him the same things you just told me," said Carl.

It took several more weeks before Irving decided to call another joint meeting of the personnel/executive committees. Apparently that time was needed to hold some more back-room discussions among center leaders. Sol was satisfied that Carl Sloane was invited to participate as well as Martin Fader of the NAJCC. Conspicuously absent was Henry O. Zelman.

Irving asked Carl Sloane to address the group, knowing that Carl's reputation as a nationally recognized consultant and advisor to businesses and corporations would command attention.

Carl rose and looked around the room into the eyes of each attendee. "It's been a very difficult six months for everyone" he began. "And each side can make a very compelling case for its views. But our challenge is to come up with a 'win/win' situation and not one where one side wins and another loses. One can make the case that in the business world the employer can ask for the resignation of an executive with or without cause. But Sol has helped me realize that a Jewish Community Center, or any other communal agency, ought not be viewed strictly in terms of a business. In the business world, when a corporation asks for the resignation of its executive the corporation generally provides what has come to be called 'A Golden Parachute.'"

"And while a communal agency can hardly afford 'Golden Parachutes' it nevertheless has the responsibility of treating the departing employee as generously and flexibly as possible. It is not for me to determine what those conditions should be, but for the agency to work them through with the affected employee and his agents, in this case the NAJCC—which I understand does have a model code of personnel practices."

Martin Fader rose, thanked Carl for his remarks and said he wanted to add some of his own. He acknowledged receiving the material from Sol, and his reading of that material supported Sol's position that there were no real causes for his dismissal or for his resignation. But he was sure, from his long experience in the field that professionals eventually decided that it was not wise for them to try to continue on a job where they felt they were no longer wanted. But there was another factor that the North Shore

JCC had to consider in this specific case, and that was the factor of Sol's age of 57 going on 58. In any event, the Personnel Bureau could not consider sending profiles of other candidates until the executive director's position was officially vacant or soon to be vacant."

Then Morris Gordon spoke. He said that he personally still supported Sol, but while what had been presented at this meeting was helpful he didn't think that a group as large as was present that evening could work out any specifics. His suggestions was for the personnel committee alone to meet with Sol and Carl Sloane and Irving, and any other persons that Sol wanted to invite to help represent him, to see if anything constructive could be worked out. And Morrie looked to Sol, who nodded his agreement.

Sol met with Hal the next evening and asked if would agree to sit in at that proposed meeting and Hal declined on the basis that he tended to be a hothead and could too easily lose his self control. He felt he could be best helpful in the way they were now doing things, namely review with Sol the benefits and provisions that Hal felt should be included in any agreement, if Sol felt he was ready to go with such an agreement.

The personnel committee, meeting alone without the executive committee but with Sol, Irving and Carl present, met a few weeks later and hammered out an agreement that included twelve months severance pay with benefits, allowing Sol to remain on until he could find another position, either in academia or the center field (if his age could be overlooked) or a family counseling agency. For his part, Sol, once he was prepared to announce his retirement and thus submit his resignation agreed to give two to three months notice so that the agency was not left pilot-less for too long a period.

The Agreement was presented to the next board of directors meeting for ratification and was accepted and ratified with just one vote short of unanimity. That dissenting vote was that of Henry O. Zelman!

The NAJCC Bureau of Personnel had Sol update his profile and began sending it out to various communities in need of an executive director. While several communities expressed interest in him they declined to invite Sol for an interview because of his "advanced age." And Sol and Shirley began to share their mutual concerns with each other and with the Fischers. Sol explored the prospects of academia and while there were some offers, accepting any of them would required the Wises to accept a drastic reduction of their living standards.

But six weeks later Sol received an invitation to come to Rincon, Arizona for an interview. The Jewish Community Center there was in need of "The JCC Doctor" because the agency needed to move from its old building in the University area (because of the relocation of the Jewish population) and the need to build a new facility in a new location still to be determined. It was something Sol had done before in many communities—and right up his alley.

The interview went very well, but afterwards, when the president of the Rincon JCC followed up some of Sol's references, including the one from Morrie Gordon, the age factor came in for questioning. Morrie later told Sol about it.

"Dr. Oldman called me and said they were all very impressed with you and your credentials and they felt sure that you were the man for them. But then he asked about the age factor—you know you're being 57 going on 58. And I asked him how long he felt it would take to get their new building and he said about five or six years. So I asked him what was the problem since in five or six years you would still be only 63 or 64 and Dr. Oldman laughed and agreed with me. My guess is you've got that job if you want it."

Sol and Shirley wanted it. They had lived in the southwest two times before, once when Sol worked in Houston, Texas and again when he had the job in Dallas, Texas. They liked the leisurely life style of the southwest and even though this time they would be moving there without any of the children, both Louis and Linda having flown the nest, they looked forward to it—should he get the job.

And after a month, Rincon called offering him the position.

Sol submitted his resignation to Irving Black and gave two months notice and although the center was not able to hire a replacement within that time frame, it agreed to his departure at the end of September 1979 because Sol was to report for duty in Rincon by the first of October.

At the farewell party tended the Wises by their shrunken circle of stalwart and loyal friends, Hal Fischer, as spokesman, toasted them and then roasted Sol with the presentation of a special gift—which he insisted Sol open right then and there.

Sol opened the thin package and took out a tee shirt, which Hal insisted he put on right then and there. Sol removed his jacket and shirt and pulled on the tee shirt and walked around the room for all to read. It had imprinted on it: "TRUST NO ONE!"

At the board meeting, a month after Sol's departure, Morris Gordon proposed a resolution that; "The Board of Directors of the North Shore Jewish Community Center hereby acknowledges with sincere appreciation the unique, profound and lasting contributions to the North Shore Jewish Community Center made by Soloman David Wise during his thirteen years as Executive Director, from 1966 to 1979."

Again there was only one vote in opposition—that of Henry O. Zelman.

THE END

XX. SWISS ARMY KNIFE

What a unique gadget! Three sizes of knife blades, two types of can openers, a Philips screwdriver, a pair of scissors, set of tweezers and a tooth pick, all ensconced into a compact three and a half inch body faced on two sides with a hard, red plastic, one side blazoning the Swiss Cross. Yep, I always wanted a knife contraption like that! And my ever lovin' wife Shirley got it for me for my 64th birthday. Selwyn Arons, sixty-four years old, imagine that!

I really like this fifteen-year-old kid. His name is Jason Black. And I use him to help me clean my kidney-shaped pool (along with other odds and ends around the yard). Actually I didn't really need him—even though Shirley opined otherwise—but he and his mom (Lynn), dad (Neal), and kid sister (Sally) were our back yard neighbors for about five years until Neal and Lynn split. He went to L.A. and she and the kids stayed on in the house in Tucson until the bank finally forced her and the kids out after months and months of Neal's non-payment of the mortgage. She and the kids finally had to move into one of the many garden/pool apartment complexes springing up all over Tucson like mushrooms after a heavy monsoon. And since we liked Lynn and the kids—well I figured this was a way of giving Jason the chance to earn a few bucks and take some of the pressure off Lynn regarding her inability to give him an allowance.

So I asked Jason one day—before they moved out of their house into the complex—"Say Jason, how'd you like to make yourself some money?"

His handsome, angelic face lit up like a Chinese lantern; "Hey man, awesome! Heavy metal!" he said.

"Does that mean you're interested?"

"Yeah, of course. It's outrageous!" I interpreted his response to be positive.

"Well, you'd better ask your mom if it's O.K."

"It's O.K. I tell you. It's rad really."

It was hard to believe that this kid was born in England of English parents and English (well Welsh anyway) grandparents, "Well, ask your mom and let her tell me its O.K."

He grimaced, hesitated and then dashed inside his house and within—I swear—seconds came back out dragging diminutive Lynn after him: "Tell him it's O.K.! Tell him I can! Tell him Mom!"

Lynn tore herself free from her tall, thin zealous son, smoothed her blouse over her petite chest, brushed away strands of brown hair from her attractive, childlike face and approached the fence. "Selwyn, Jason tells me you'd like him to help you to clean your pool. Do you really want him to work with you? I mean, he's so irresponsible, so unreliable."

Jason scowled and muttered: "Thanks Mom. That's helping a lot!"

I couldn't help but chuckle. I was two generations linguistically removed from the boy. But I rallied and replied: "Yes, I'd like him to help me, if it's alright with you. I could use the help, he could use the money and I'm sure you could use the time away from him."

So that's how it all started, Jason helping me with the pool, and moving on from there to other chores around the yard. Oh he was O.K. with the pool cleaning since he enjoyed jumping into the water and vacuuming the pool "from the inside"—as he described it. But weed pulling and other yard work—well he described it as: "Man it sucks." He just didn't like it and his not so little con-boy brain worked overtime figuring how to stretch the breaks and minimize the work. This personable, lovable, always smiling con-boy was like his dad, Neal, in so many ways, relying more on his personality, charm and gift of gab than on a job well done. His breaks became longer as he began to feel more and more at home—at my home.

"Sel, can I use your bathroom?"

"Of course."

And after what I thought was more than enough time to do all conceivable toilet chores I'd go after him, knock on the bathroom door and bellow; "Hey Jase, you OK in there?"

"Yeah, sure. Comin' right out."

Coincidentally, around the same time that I was given my Swiss knife, Jason also got one from someone—for his birthday, I think—and we compared instruments. They were like two peas in a pod, although Jason insisted his was bigger, sharper and redder. It really wasn't any of these, but who was I to argue with an opinionated, obstinate, but very charming fifteen-year-old con-boy?

Devilish experimenter that he was, Jason succeeded in carving up the bulk of their Camino Seco apartment with his Swiss and Lynn had to finally take the damned thing away from him and stash it away somewhere. But Jason found it and compulsively continued his carvings.

The third time around Lynn finally hid it so well that even she, for the life of her, couldn't remember where she hid it.

My one and a half year old granddaughter, Sara, visited us every Sunday and her mother, Sonia, insisted on making our domicile as "child-proof" as theirs was. And my ever'lovin' Shirley agreed with her. So everything loose, compact, sharp, blunt, toxic or enticing in any way was to be removed or nailed shut for the duration. I didn't mind too much at first until the crusade enveloped my small writer's corner consisting simply of a very comfortable contour chair and a Danish end table in which was stored my writer's tools and the Swiss Army knife. Without my prior knowledge this unique gadget—my 64th birthday present—was removed and "safely stored"—banished really—to a safer repository, the exact location my dear Shirley could not, for the life of her, remember.

"Shirley! Where the hell's my Swiss?"

"We put it away out of Sara's reach, remember?"

"No I don't remember. Do you remember where you put it?"

"Hm, let me see now. I think I put it in one of your chest drawers in the bedroom. Let's look."

And that's when we ransacked our place looking for the damned, unique, seldom-used gadget.

"It'll turn up when you least expect it," Shirley prophesized.

"I need it now!"

Well, we never found it in our periodic searchings and I wondered where the hell Shirley had put it.

"I hate to say this," Shirley said one day, "but you know you've been allowing Jason too much free rein. He's taking advantage of you. He's too familiar. You allow him too much leeway all over the place."

"What the hell's that got to do with your remembering where you stashed my Swiss Army knife?" And suddenly I caught her meaning. "Oh c'mon now! What are you suggesting? The kid's got to go to the bathroom now and then. Am I supposed to say to him: 'sorry kid, you can't go into my holy house. Piss or shit in the yard.' The huskies do enough of that!" I was, of course, referring to the two adorable Siberian huskies my daughter and her family brought with them whenever they visited us—which was frequently, considering that they lived only a few blocks from us in Tucson.

"Well, I don't know what else to think." Shirley concluded.

So, I was out my Swiss and Sonny Boy Jason was out his—both for the same reasons—our respective women (my wife and his mother) couldn't, for the life of themselves, remember where the hell they stashed them!

One day I was over at Lynn Black's Camino Seco apartment sipping coffee and I heard Jason's Toshiba portable blasting from his bedroom. "Is Jason still home? I thought he had to be at Sahuaro High School at 8 a.m.?"

"Oh no. He's at school. At least I hope he's at school. He always leaves his radio on high, blasting. I keep telling you he's so irresponsible. I refuse to even go into his pig-sty room." She left no doubt about her annoyance with her rambunctious son.

"Do you mind if I turn it off? 1 can't hear my slurping of the coffee?"

"Be my guest, but don't sue me if one of his booby traps goes off."

So I entered his room, choosing my steps very carefully, as if traversing a minefield of sneakers, socks, bits of clothing and what not. I reached the Toshiba on a little stand at the head of his bed and clicked off the radio. A bright red object on the stand next to the radio caught my eye. It was a Swiss Army knife! I gawked at it and then picked it up. It was just like mine. But I remembered that Jason's and mine were like two peas in a pod. Hm, I opened the large knife blade. So, it was a large knife blade. I opened the straight blade and discovered that it was a straight blade. But then I open the small blade and...blood rushed to my temple! The small blade had a small nick at the tip just like my Swiss—in fact, exactly like that! I had planned to sharpen it out on my Carburundum one of these days but still hadn't gotten to it.

The little bastard! But wait. Hold on. Am I sure? Was this really mine? Maybe Jason's also nicked on the same blade. Could be. Don't jump to conclusions. Then I recalled Shirley saying: "You give him too much leeway. He's got the run of the house." Yeah, but you can't just go accusing without really hard evidence. I like the kid. He's not the world's hardest worker but he's fun, a joy to be with—as long as I'm not his parent. But face it—he's a con-boy, like his dad.

This is your knife man! So, prove it! So, like Fagin sang in *OLIVER* "I think I better think it out again."

I walked back into the kitchen to rejoin Lynn, flipping the Swiss Army knife in my right hand. "Lookee what I found on Jason's table."

Her face grew beet-red, reflecting both her surprise and her consternation. "Oh dear. He found the hiding place again—and I still don't remember which hiding place it was."

"Lynn, remember I told you about our not being able to find my Swiss—which Shirley stashed away so expertly? Well—I'm not saying this is it or not—although it has the same nick on the small blade as mine has. But if you could remember where you last hid Jason's, and if Jason's is still there, then we could be sure whether Sonny Boy has added expropriation to his other talents. But if Jason's knife is not where you hid it—then I will publicly apologize to him and you as well."

"Oh dear. I wish I could remember,"

"Take your time. And remember, in America one is innocent until proven guilty—even sons and daughters."

"I'm sure he's guilty. He's so irresponsible and so unreliable."

"He's adolescent, and he's your son."

But the seed was planted and only a few days passed when Lynn called. "Sel, I've been turning our place upside down and I found Jason's knife where I last hid it. I'm so embarrassed and mad-fit-to-spit. I confronted Jason with it and—well if you could come over—he has some-thing to say to you."

So I hastened over to Camino Seco and confronted the Black family.

"So Jason, what have you to say to Selwyn? Speak up!" Lynn demanded of her son.

Jason stepped forward slowly, sheepishly, sorrowfully his eyes focused on the carpet. "Sel, I'm sorry, very sorry I took your knife. It was wrong. I know. I guess I was so mad at my mom for taking mine away. Anyway, I remembered yours—and I saw Shirley putting it away in your chest—and then one day when you said I could use your bathroom, as I passed through your bedroom—I don't know what, but something made me go to your chest. It was wrong, I know, but when I opened the top drawer and saw my—'scuse me—your Swiss Army knife—I just had to have it. I'm sorry. Very sorry. Really. Forgive me, please."

His soulful brown eyes set in such an angelic, sweet face melted my anger. No, not really anger but deep disappointment. After all I had begun to feel grandfatherly towards this wild and rambunctious testing, challenging adolescent.

"Please forgive me. Please!"

I wanted to do so on the spot. But something inside me-intuitively—held me back. Would I really be doing this kid a service by so easily forgiving his thievery? "Well, I don't know Jason. Let me think on it. After all, you did steal something, which was not yours. And you violated a trust, a confidence. You know what I'm talking about?"

"Yeah. Yes. I think so." He smiled wanly, pleadingly.

"O.K. Jason. I'll let you know."

Well, I went through some soul-searching for a few days trying to figure out what was the right thing—and the best thing to do—since I think you'll agree that not always is the right thing the best thing especially as it affects a fifteen year old boy. I was heavily inclined to simply forgive him and say something trite like "Don't do anything like it again." You know, give him a second chance, and all that. But the more I thought on it, and the more I thought on what my wife Shirley was pointing out, the more I realized that I could better help this kid by not excusing or indulging his shortcomings and limitations.

So I fired him! Not because of the theft of the Swiss Army knife, but because he was a lousy worker. I wrote a note (previewed by Lynn) forgiving him for the theft of the Swiss Army knife but then detailing eight reasons why I no longer required his services and signed it "Fondly, Selwyn"

Of course he didn't take kindly to what he called "the nasty note" and he didn't speak to me, or acknowledge my existence in any form at any time in any place for a good few weeks.

At Christmas I gave Jason a present of a Swiss Army knife, the smallest blade of which had a nick in it. And my ever-lovin Shirley gave me a Swiss Army knife for my sixty-fifth birthday. Selwyn Arons, sixty-five years old, imagine that!

THE END

XXI. COLLECT CALL

The jangling of the phone jarred me out of my preoccupation with my latest guardianship report to the Superior Court. "I have to remember to soften this damned bell," I muttered to myself as I reached for the receiver. "Hello"

"Mr. Selwyn Arons? Will you accept a collect call?"

"What?"

"This is the operator. Will you accept a collect call from Jason Black?"

"A collect call from Jason?" I repeated. From where was he calling, I wondered? Jason and his family had been our back yard neighbors for over five years until his mom and dad divorced and his dad, Neal moved out of Tucson to L.A. and Lynn, Jason and his younger sister Sally moved into a garden apartment on Camino Seco, not far from our respective houses. But despite their move, Jason continued helping me with the cleaning of my pool and yard work. I knew the fifteen-year-old boy was having problems at school and was "on ice" this week for cutting classes. "On Ice" meant that he had to attend from 12 noon to 4 p.m. whereas the regular schedule was from 8 a.m. to 2:30 p.m. and here it was only 9:20 a.m. Did he run away and from where was he calling? And why?

"Will you accept the collect call, sir?" the operator repeated with a touch of impatience.

"What? Oh yes, of course, put him through operator."

"Selwyn?"... A broken voice asked.

"Jason? What's the matter? And where are you calling from?"

"A ph...phone booth. I didn't have 25 cents. Sel...could you come to the apartment—please? The tremulous, adolescent voice pleaded.

"What happened Jase?"

"Please come to my place...I'll be waiting out front. Please come!"

"Jason, what happened?"

There was a long pause and then: "My mom threw me out of our apartment last night. I slept over at Mike's. I can't get into our place. The building office won't give me a key and I broke a window trying to get into my room to get my clothes for school. It was an accident, I swear. We didn't mean to do it—and now I don't know what to do, or where to go. Sel, please come. Please... " The plea trailed off into sobs.

"Hold on Jason, I'm coming right over. Hang on son." I could hear a weak "Thanks!" as I hung up the phone. Within seconds I was into the car and on my way to the Camino Seco apartments, a mere five minutes by car.

Things had been deteriorating for Lynn, Jason and Sally Black since the divorce. Lynn found it increasingly difficult to cope with the "sturm und drang" of Jason's adolescence. Jason tied in with four or five boys—all from single parent, fatherless homes—the boys tottering on the brink of juvenile delinquency. Ditching classes was the least of their testing and experimentations with Jason, at one point, being caught in the vicinity of where pot had recently been smoked. After what he claimed to be a very superficial test, he was pronounced "under the influence of pot" and again "put on ice." His relationship with his mother was dominated by a series of tumultuous verbal explosions. I was therefore not altogether surprised to hear that Lynn had at last locked—if not thrown—him out.

As I turned into the Camino Seco complex I spotted Jason sitting on the grass, a lonely, forlorn figure. When he saw me he jumped, as if grasping for the proverbial straw and entered the front passenger seat. The expression on his normally handsome, angelic face was a mixture of pain, gratitude and uncertainty and his lips twitched.

"Thanks for coming" he said.

"Have you had breakfast?" I asked

"I'm not hungry. And I got a lousy headache. Thanks for coming. I didn't know who else to call, or what else to do." He looked at me plaintively, his eyes puffed and red.

"It's O.K. I'm glad I was at home. C'mon, we'll go to my place and feed you some aspirin if not some breakfast."

He was quiet on the five-minute ride to my house, but I sensed his anxiety and agitation. When we entered my place, going straight into the kitchen, he blurted out: "Damn! I hate my mother! It's not fair. Just not fair. I want to go live with my dad—or even my grandparents!" He sat on one of the kitchen bar stools and held his long, brown-haired head in his slim-fingered hands, shaking the head to and fro as in bereavement, sobs bubbling up from the deep pit of his stomach.

"Yeah, Jase, let loose. Have a good cry. It can't hurt."

He looked up at me, a little lost puppy. "My head hurts somethin' awful."

I hurried to give him some aspirin and as he was swallowing I said: "Of course you know Jason that going to live with your dad in L.A., or your grandparents in England is not practical."

"I know."

"So, we have to think about what's practical, right?"

"Yeah, I guess you're right."

"So tell me what happened last night. But first, do you want something to eat, like corn-flakes or some eggs?

He was calming down. My deliberate slow enunciation of the available foods seemed to activate his salivary glands. His tongue caressed his lips. "Yeah. Can I have some cornflakes and eggs?"

"Of course. What about toast?"

"Yeah"

"Yeah what?"

"Oh, yes please." He smiled sheepishly.

"So, what happened last night?"

"We had another argument. She wanted to ground me—again—for nuthin—so I wouldn't let her."

"In what way didn't you let her?" I shoved the cereal box, bowel and milk towards him.

"She said if I went out, I didn't have to come back because she'd lock me out."

"But you went out anyway, and she did lock you out, right?"

He looked at me uncertainly. "Yeah! I went over to some of the guys and after awhile I cooled off and came home. Must've been about ten thirty and she wouldn't let me in. I knocked quiet-like at first, but then when she yelled at me through the door to go away, I really banged on that door for her to let me in. I yelled; "Hey it's my home too! I live here! Dad sends you money for me to live here! Open this damned door! But she wouldn't open the lousy door. I must've banged for about a half hour. I sat down against the door. It was getting cold, real cold and then I figured she wasn't going to let me in. Damned! She threw me out! And I really got scared. So, about almost 12 midnight, I think, I went over to Mike's. His folks wanted to call my Mom, but I guess they thought it was too late. Anyway, they let me sleep on the couch."

He was finishing the cornflakes so I pushed the plate of scrambled eggs to him. "You didn't say how you wanted the eggs. And here's the toast. You can't complain about the service in this cafe, can you?"

He flashed a weak smile. "No complaints—yet," he said. "O.K. So come morning, what happened?"

"Well you know my mom has to be at the baby-sitting job by 8 am and I figured she might be over her mad at me after the night. So I called her about 7:15 from Mike's. And you know what? She didn't want to even talk to me! Well, she said she didn't have time to talk to me—and she hung up! I was mad—at first—but then I got scared more than mad." He swallowed the last of the egg. He was looking better and I asked him how he felt.

His headache was just about gone. And he felt better, but still at a loss as to what his next moves ought to be. I encouraged him to continue his story.

"So I went over to the office to get the key to my apartment and Chris wouldn't give it to me. She said my mom told her not to give me the key. To my own place! Can ya dig that? So I went back to Mike's. He didn't have to be in school until about one. And the two of us went over to my place to see if I could climb into my room to change into my school clothes. And Mike was trying to lift the window sash out and it broke, and we both got scared and beat it out of there, and then we didn't know what else to do. So that's when I called you." He heaved a heavy sigh and looked at me as if to indicate the ball was now in my court.

"And I came and I got you. But Jase, what if I hadn't been at home working on my court reports? What then?"

He squirmed uncomfortably, frowned and replied: "I dunno."

"Son, you have to begin to know. You're fifteen and a half."

"But Selwyn, it's not fair! She's not fair! My dad sends her money for child support. She's gotta take care of Sally and me. We're the children!"

I looked at this handsome but befuddled and unhappy adolescent caught in the web of one of the 20th century's most distressing problems: the 50% divorce rate and the subsequent sundering of the involved families. What did HE do to cause the problem? Why should HE be expected to pay a major price for it? There was no real answer. But I felt I had to give him some answers.

"Yes Jase. You're the children. And the children always pay the price for their parent's mistakes. But Jason, that's the way it is. It sucks! But the fact remains that it is an adult world. Your mom is your mom, and she's the adult, and the rules are her rules—whether you like it or not. This entire experience should teach you one thing if it teaches you anything. That it is an adult world, run by adults, with rules made by adults. So, Sonny Boy, if you're going to get on in this life, you have to learn to accept the hard realities. Don't screw around with what's fair or not fair. Your mom rules her roost. It's her home. You either live by her rules or you get the hell out! You dig me?"

He sat listening, his mouth and eyes wide open. "No one ever told it to me that way before" he complained in a half-whisper.

"So now you know."

After a significant pause—which I hoped indicated that some of my admonishments had penetrated his thick, adolescent preconceptions—Jason bestirred himself. "Should I rinse these dishes?"

"Is that the most important thing to do right now?" I asked.

He looked at me momentarily puzzled and then replied: "I guess not. Do you have my mom's phone number at work?"

"No, but I believe we could look it up"

I handed him the phone book and he searched and found the number and after several nervous mis-dialings reached his mother. "Mom, I'm at Sel's. Mom, I'm very sorry about what happened. What? No, Sel picked me up after I called him. I didn't know what else to do. Mom! It's not fair. You're not being fair. Oh god, mom I said I'm sorry. Yeah. Look, we broke the window to my room. But it was an accident! I swear! No, we didn't do it on purposes Mom! Mom!"

He turned to me his face ashen, wrenched with agony. "She hung up on me! She said she's pissed because we broke the window. Selwyn, I swear, we didn't break the window on purpose! Oh Sel, I hate her! What am I goin' to do, Sol?"

I held him awkwardly in my arms and then the grandfather in me threw caution to the winds and I embraced this distraught, this sobbing, frightened, unhappy fifteen year old child.

"O.K. son, O.K. Let's take it one step at a time. Have a good cry, god knows you've earned it." And I fought back my own tears in remembrance of the frightened orphan that I was many, many years ago.

"Selwyn, what should I do?" he sniffed between sobs.

"Well maybe it would be a good idea to get ready for school. You've got to be there by 11:50, right? Well its 10:45 already."

"I haven't got my school clothes and I haven't had a chance to get cleaned."

"You can shower here—and you'll have to go to school with the clothes you have on. They're passable. You can try calling your mother again before going to school."

He seemed relieved to hear that there were things he could do. "Yeah, that's a good idea." But first he collected the dishes, went to the sink and rinsed them and—at my instructions—left them in the sink for future placement in the dishwasher.

"Just like you always do at home, right Jase?"

He turned from the sink, a puzzled expression on his face. "What? Oh, I get ya. Yeah, I mean, no, I never do any of that at home. I get ya. You mean I should be more helpful around the apartment, right?"

"What do you think?"

"Yeah, I guess I should. Sometimes I take out the garbage. But a lot of times I forget. And then that causes arguments. Yeah I see what you're getting at! He smiled, seeking my approval.

I nodded and smiled.

"Yeah. Well, O.K. I guess I better take the shower—if it's OK by you."

I nodded again with another smile.

He took a long time showering and I did not disturb him. I knew how calming and cleansing a long, hot shower could be. When he emerged, his frown was gone and he seemed to glisten. "Ah yeah, I feel better already. I think my mom will talk better with me now too." This pleasant anticipation spurred him to dress quickly, blow-dry his hair and sit himself down on a kitchen barstool next to the phone. He looked at me anxiously, accepting my encouraging nod, and nervously dialed the appropriate numbers. "Sheesh, I'm nervous," he said.

"It's understandable," I said.

He drummed his fingers on the countertop as he waited for the phone to be picked up at the other end. "Mom, its me again. Please don't hang up on me until I've finished. Yeah, I'm still at Sel's. I had breakfast. I'm getting ready to go to school. Yes mom. Look, I'm very sorry. I really am. I promise I'll try to do better from now on. No, I swear the window breaking was an accident." He listened awhile and then responded: "But you told Chris not to give me the key and all I wanted was to get into my room to change to my school clothes. And I wasn't even the one who broke it. Mike did."

He listened again. "Yeah, you're right—it's still my fault. I'll try to earn some money to help pay for it. Yeah. Sel will drop me off at school. We're leaving as soon as I finish talking with you." He fidgeted in his chair as he listened to some additional admonitions from the other end. And then, his fingers drumming even more nervously on the counter top, he asked the all-important question: "Mom, can I come home after school—please?"

"Thanks mom. Thanks. I'll be good! I promise! I love you." He hung up, beaming. "Let's go to school," he said.

I drove him to Sahuaro High School. He thanked me profusely and got out of the car. I watched him walk to the entrance. As he disappeared into the building I wondered what the future had in store for him.

THE END

XXII. TAZ'S TATOO

At first glance the red lettering on the youth's lower left shoulder appeared merely scratched on with a red ballpoint pen. "Tasmanian Devil?" Selwyn Arons sounded it out slowly to make sure he was reading it correctly. "Tasmanian Devil, eh?"

Charles Cordell eyed him suspiciously. "Yeah! Tasmanian Devil! It's something like a badger—a vicious flesh-eater! Nothing messes with it. It's my tattoo."

Sel nodded, yet wondered about the fellow's bellicosity. He seemed so easily provoked.

"As soon as I get an extra forty bucks I'm gonna have this tattoo finished with a picture of the devil—all in color," the young, hired hand said.

Before Selwyn could catch himself he heard himself ask: "Yes, but why would you want to further desecrate your body, Charlie?"

Charlie's stony stare confirmed for Sel his error. The last thing this nearly eighteen-year old, blonde, blue-eyed, belligerent fellow needed was sermonizing.

"Sorry. Forget I asked." Selwyn apologized.

Apparently appeased, Charles mumbled "O.K." and resumed applying redwood stain to the slats on Sel's back porch overhang. After several minutes of silence the young adult explained: "It identifies me. In fact, it's my nickname, T-A-Z for short." He spelled it out, substituting a 'z' for the 's.' "People who really know me call me Taz."

"Ahuh," Selwyn grunted not sure how else to respond. Did this attractive but apparently volatile young adult want Sel to address him as Taz? Or was he saying: "Hey man, you don't know me yet, so back off; I'll let you know if and when I want you to call me Taz?" Sel wasn't sure and as a graduate-trained social worker (now retired) he knew he needed to know more before responding.

Selwyn had begun using Charles as a part-time helper after the guy had lost his shipping clerk job. The tall, muscular youth had helped Sel spread crushed marble around the pool and now was helping him replace and stain the slats. Charles had provided Sel with only a sketchy biography: problems with his parents and involvement with juvenile authorities in Denver resulting in his coming to Tucson to live with an aunt and uncle only a few years older than himself. "So what do you want me to call you?" Selwyn Arons finally asked.

"Like I said; people who really know me call me Taz."

He was sly all right. "Well, since I really don't know you that well I guess I'll still have to call you Charles, or Charlie, right?"

The youth shrugged and continued his staining in silence. Convinced that Sel was not going to question him further, Charlie suddenly let loose a torrent of biography. His childhood in Denver had been turbulent, involving alcoholic parents and an abusing father in particular. Between the ages of ten and thirteen he was frequently removed from his home and placed with foster families or in group homes, but after a brief period, each time he was returned to his own, unchanged home environment. When he was fourteen the bad situation became unbearable. His father, in one of his drunken states, beat him to the floor, sat on him, and spat in his face. "You know what you are? You're nothin' but shit! Ya hear me? Shit!" When the parents were asleep Charlie ransacked the house, gathered together nearly $500 in cash, and boarded a Greyhound bus going to San Antonio.

"Why San Antonio?" Selwyn asked.

Charlie looked at him incredulously. "That's where the bus was going!"

"Of course. How stupid of me. So?"

Well, he met a man at the back of the bus and the man shared his bottle of Jack Daniels with him, and—boy! All he remembered was the bus driver shaking him violently, telling him they were in San Antonio—and did he want the driver to contact anyone? Or should he better turn him over to the cops? No! No! Not the cops! He would call his aunt and uncle and they would pick him up. Of course he had no aunt or uncle or any relatives in San Antonio. That's where the first bus he grabbed was going.

Selwyn remembered him telling him that. "So?"

So he staggered out of the bus with his duffel bag and walked across the street to a Texaco station—where he remembered to look in his wallet and he was shocked to discover that all his money was gone! And for one of the very few times in his life, he cried, as he suddenly felt frightened, lost and alone!

"I know that feeling," Arons said empathetically.

Charlie barely heard him as he continued his saga. An older guy—who was maybe in his forties, noticed him and asked if anything was wrong, and Charlie quickly concocted a tale about how he was supposed to go on to Houston, and he lost all his money and he couldn't make his connections, and it was so late at night—or really early morning—about 3 a.m. So this guy called his wife and got her consent to bring him home. He stayed with this couple for 4½ months, cleaning house and doing yard work to earn his keep and during all this time he refused to call home.

Charlie expressed surprise when Sel opined that it seemed strange to him that intelligent people would accept a strange fellow into their home without informing any social agency, or even the police, or further inquiring about his Houston destination or about his parents. But Charlie ignored Sel's probing and continued telling his story. After 4½ months with this couple he accepted the invitation of a woman (whom he frequently met at the supermarket) to come stay with her—again in exchange for housework and yard work. Charlie was even more vague about this relationship, except to stress that, after about a month and a half, the woman finally convinced him to call his parents on the Run-Away-Hot-Line. And after doing so, he agreed to return home—after an absence of six months!

"That's some story," Selwyn said. "You were very lucky. Many runaways have problems with shelter, hunger, sexual exploitation, get caught up in drugs and don't survive too long."

"Yeah. I guess I was lucky to meet up with nice people. I mean, except for the bastard who got me drunk on the bus and took all my money." Charlie searched Sel's face for further reaction to his story.

Selwyn George Aron's social work training and experience had taught him that almost all stories had at least a germ of truth and this history—presented in such a sudden, cathartic torrent not only interested, but challenged him. Apparently Charlie had succeeded, thus far, in surviving in a very hostile and punitive environment by wile, guile, cunning and manipulation. But Sel realized that he needed to be careful that Charlie's skills not be allowed to envelope their developing relationship. And right now, Charlie was waiting for some further reaction on Selwyn's part.

"So we agree that you were very lucky that time. But that was over four years ago. What happened after you returned home?"

"Like I told you: my dad and I don't get along and we fight all the time—especially when he's drunk—which is almost all the time. And so this friend of my dad rapes my fifteen year-old girl friend and they let him get away with it. I was so mad I nearly burned the bastard's house down. I was put on parole. Can ya dig that? The rapist get off and I get put on parole until I make restitution for burning his house—about $1800 I hafta pay." He scowled, scratched his tattooed shoulder and continued: "Shit! Paying that thing off is gonna take forever. It's been two years and I only paid off half of it."

"How come they let you leave Denver?" Selwyn asked, applying more stain to the slats.

"That's a good question. Well, like I keep telling you, my dad and I don't get along. And my aunt in Tucson offered to let me come and stay with her and my uncle. It took about six months for Denver to finally approve it. I have to report to a Bill Ringer, the local parole guy with the Arizona Department of Corrections, Juvenile Services, once a week." Charlie breathed deeply and continued: "Well everything is going along pretty good with me working and sending money back for the restitution and then—shit—my place folds and I'm outta work! That's the way it's always been with me; things seem to be going good and then everything blows up in my face! As if, somehow it's my fault. I dunno, maybe I'm jinxed." He lowered his head and his brush and heaved a heavy sigh.

"You're not the first guy to lose a job." Arons said.

Charlie resumed staining, slowly and methodically. "It's not just the job. Now my aunt and uncle are fighting a lot—about money and his screwin' around."

"Oh?" Sel paused in his staining to listen more attentively to Charlie's description of the deteriorating relationship between his aunt and his uncle.

"... and it's hard for me to avoid the fighting because y'see I don't have my own room. I sleep on the couch in the living room. So I have to walk out of the apartment to get away from it"

"Well you know Charlie, there are marriage counseling agencies that..."

"Shit! Don't tell me about counseling agencies! I know all about those bullshit outfits! I been through them all—counselors, social workers, parole officer, cops—and none of 'em ever did me any good!"

"I was talking about your aunt and uncle going for marital counseling." Sel said softly.

Again Charlie stopped staining and stared sheepishly at Sel. "Oh? Well—I'm sorry. It's just that—well I get so mad when I think about what I've been through. And I didn't mean to insult you. You're a social worker, aren't you, an MW or somethin' right? I saw the diploma on your wall inside the house. And somehow you seem different from all the others."

Sel peered at Charlie on the other ladder. "Yes, I'm an MSW. It means Master of Science in Social Work. And if I appear to be different, it's probably because I'm the first MSW you've ever met." Still, Selwyn Arons considered to himself the possibility that the young man was just pitching him.

There was a long silence as Charlie digested Sel's observation, then he nodded and said: "Hm, now that you mention it, you're probably right. I shoulda known. Yeah, your style is different! I like it. Yeah. All the other dudes and dames that tried to work on me—shit man, I knew I could do a better job than any of them—be a better parole officer or counselor or social worker than them. But you—and believe me man, I'm not conning you—you're different! And if it's the MSW that makes the difference, hey that's for me!"

Selwyn Arons eyed him suspiciously. "What do you mean, 'that's for you?'"

"I mean that's what I want to be—an MSW social worker."

Sel sighed and smiled. "Just like that, eh? You don't seem to realize that MSW represents four years undergraduate and two years graduate schooling. And right now you don't even have a job much less the proper prerequisites such as a high school diploma—I'm guessing. Am I right?"

"Right on the first but wrong on the second, or at least partly wrong. Y'see I already passed my GED—the equivalent of a high school diploma—before coming down to Tucson. And as for the job—well I got applications in all over town. It's only a matter of time before I land one." He smiled as if triumphant. "Well, we can at least talk about it, can't we?" he added.

Having completed staining the slats, and generally satisfied with Charlie's quality of work, Selwyn Arons continued using him as they moved on to the painting of the exterior of the house. Sel listened patiently as Charlie complained about his lot in life and the lousy cards he was dealt and how the deck was stacked against him—the latest evidence being the impending break-up of his aunt and uncle's marriage, the suggestion of marital counseling having fallen on deaf ears.

"Well Charlie, it does appear that you've been the victim in all these situations and that you've had more than your share of life's unfairness. But you know Charlie..."

"Why don't you call me Taz?" the young man interrupted.

"Because that's a fantasy world you've created and trying to live in. I prefer not to be part of that fantasy."

"What d'ya mean?" Charlie snarled, feeling the rejection.

"I think it's clear enough. And as for your being a victim in all those situations—well, one can go two ways with that: you can continue to bellyache about it and use it as an excuse for not getting anywhere's; or two, as the Chinese proverb tells it: 'a thousand mile journey begins with one step.'"

Charlie scowled. "Yeah, it's easy for you to talk, man! Look at all you got, man!" And his arm waved indicating the house, the pool, and the grounds.

Now Sel's dander was up! He glared at the invidious youth. "Hey guy! You really think I was born with all this, or that I inherited it from wealthy parents? Well, for your information, buddy, I lost both my parents at age six. And knowing about your parents, I guess I was lucky at that. I was raised in an orphanage where they beat the hell out of you for the slightest infraction. At eighteen I was turned loose with a cardboard suitcase and a lousy job as a cutter's apprentice in a New York dress factory. But, Buddy-boy, I learned one thing…"

Selwyn Arons' sharp retort startled Charlie who, now somewhat subdued, interrupted: "Yeah, what was that?"

"To use my one big asset Buddy-boy. Sel paused for effect, then continued. "My brains Buddy-boy, my brains. In the orphanage we learned that you couldn't beat the system head-on—that you had to be patient and use your brains."

"You mean jump through all the hoops!" Charlie sneered.

"If the thousand mile journey wound through hoops, then we jumped through hoops. My thousand-mile journey involved aspirations for going to college. I was told that an orphan should not expect to go to college. He should be practical—learn a trade, like being a dress cutter. And that's what they set me up for when they kicked me out of the place."

"Obviously you got to go to college anyway because you're an MSW social worker, right? How didya do it?"

"The hard way, Buddy-boy, the long, hard way. You see, I also learned early on that there really are no short cuts, like you're still looking for."

Charlie bristled: "Hey man, I know I'm crazy in many ways, but I'm not stupid!"

Selwyn stared him down. "You're not stupid. Not by a

long shot. You probably have an eight cylinder brain—but so far operating on only four."

Charlie struggled to control his temper. "Very funny. That's what you think, huh? Eight cylinders, eh? Only four, huh? Well...I dunno, maybe you're right and then again maybe not." There was a long pause as Charlie fidgeted with his paint roller, dripping paint on the driveway and hastening to clean it up with rag. He looked at Arons, shrugged his shoulders and continued: "So, tell me how you got your college education, Mr. Hiker of a thousand miles."

Sol put his brush down and weighed his answer carefully. He didn't want it to sound like the grandfatherly tales of hardship on the frontier. But there was no other way to tell it. "Like I said, Charlie, the long, hard way. City College of New York had provisions for people who lacked either the subject requirements or grade point average, or both. So, after establishing my city residence, I started night school as a Special-Conditional student. And seven years later I graduated with my BSS. Then two more years at Columbia University for my Master in Social Work, the MSW."

Charlie was listening intently. "But that's nine years man! Nine years! One year short of a decade!"

Sel smiled, "Well, I see that you're good in arithmetic. Yes, for me it took nine years, but for someone else—maybe you—possibly less. But Charlie, the years will pass whether you do anything constructive with them or not. Of that you can be sure."

Again there was a very long silence as Charlie rolled the paint onto the side of the house with the long-handled roller that he had convinced Sel to buy. Then he stopped and turned to Sel. "Yeah, I see what you mean. Yeah the years pass anyway. They sure do. Hey! I almost forgot to tell you! Sel, I got that Management-Trainee job at Pizza Hut. It pays minimum and has crazy hours, and I wont be able to give you as much time."

Now it was Sel who put his brush down and approached the young man, his right hand extended. "That's great Chuck! Congratulations! And don't worry about the time with me. We can work around your Pizza Hut schedule—that's if you still want to work with me."

Selwyn grasped Sol's extended hand. "Thanks!" Then suddenly it hit him: "Hey, did you just call me 'Chuck?' I haven't been called 'Chuck' since I was ten or eleven. I like it."

Selwyn smiled. "It just slipped out. Seemed so natural."

"Yeah, I always liked it. And of course I want to continue working with you. But... er Sel, there's one thing about the Pizza Hut job. There's a kinda catch. I don't know if I should ask you. I just dunno."

"What is it? Spit it out."

"Well y'see Pizza Hut provides you with the red vest, but you have to provide the black pants. And I don't have a pair of black pants and I don't have the twenty-five bucks they cost... not right now anyway." Charlie smiled entreatingly.

Aha, here it comes, Sel thought. The bite! But he caught himself and further reasoned: it is a reasonable request. Hear him out. "So you'd like me to lend you the money, right?" Sel asked.

Charlie kicked at the gravel. "I'd pay you back out of my first pay check—in about two weeks."

Sel pondered the situation: they were at the crossroads, one road leading to the difficult thousand-mile journey, the other merely a repetition of numerous scams and manipulations. Was he, Selwyn, prepared to take a chance on this young man? He could say: "Sorry Charlie, but I don't believe it's a good idea to become so personally involved with..." with what? A client? This was no client. Yet—for all practical purposes, he had been "social-working" the kid pretty good. This was a very bright young man, with tremendous untapped, unrealized potential... Hell, twenty-five dollars!

"What d'ya say, Mr. A.?" Charlie, bit his lips.

"Huh? Oh, well, OK Charlie. I'll lend you the twenty five dollars."

A broad smile split the young man's handsome face. "Thanks Sel. Thanks. But Sel, please call me 'Chuck.' I like that."

"Better than Taz?"

Chuck's smile lingered, but the furrowed brow indicated cognitive processes in excess of four cylinders at work. "I think so. Yes, better than Taz."

A week later, as they completed the painting of the outside of Sel's house, Chuck replied to Sol's question: "Oh Pizza Hut's OK. The Management Training program is really a gimmick as far as I'm concerned. But it provides me with the money to eat and pay the rent. Talking about paying rent—did I tell you my aunt and uncle split and I had to find a furnished room. Hell, again I'm in the middle getting screwed even though I did nuthin' to cause the mess. Believe me, I'm not complainin'—just telling you what happened. I'm trying to think with all eight cylinders, and I do want to talk some more about college. Hey man, we don't have a CCNY in Tucson."

"No we don't. But we do have a Pima Community College, don't we?"

Chuck's face brightened. "Hey yeah, we do, don't we. I'll have to check into their next semester's program. And Sel, before I forget, here's your twenty-five dollars. And thanks a lot." He lowered his long-handled paint roller, placed it carefully in the pan, took two tens and a five from his wallet and brought them to Sel on his ladder.

"There's really no rush on this Chuck. You sure you can spare it now?"

"Yeah, take it before I piss it away on sumthin' else—like finishing the tattoo of the Devil." He paused. "Sel, what d'ya think? I've got the money now to have the Devil finished, color and all. But I'm not sure anymore. I mean, since we've been working together—and talking—and all—I'm mixed up. What d'ya think?"

Selwyn smiled. "C'mon Chuck. You know my feelings on that subject."

Chuck smiled back. "Yeah, I know."

In the fall Selwyn drove Chuck to the south side campus of Pima Community College. As Chuck left the car to walk to the main entrance, and thus begin his thousand-mile journey, he turned to ask: "Sel, how much d'ya think it would cost to have my tattoo removed?"

Sel grinned. "Chuck, I really wouldn't know. But why pay anything to have it removed? Why not keep it as a reminder of where you've come from?"

Charlie nodded, reflected further and then said: "Yeah, and y'know, I suddenly realized that it's not what's on the surface of the skin, but what's underneath it that really counts. Right?" And without waiting for a reply, he wheeled and walked to the Main Entrance, turned, smiled and raised his hand, fingers forming the "V" for victory sign.

THE END

XXIII. ARIZONA JOURNEY

("No Good Deed Goes Unpunished." Anonymous)

The Rincon Jewish Community Center in Arizona was suffering survival problems. When it was first located in the University/Broadway/Speedway/Plumer neighborhood of the City of Rincon in southern Arizona in 1948, it was because the small Jewish population of about 4500 people tended to concentrate there. But as the city grew, the Jewish population growing along with it, tended to move out from that concentration, first to the northeast side of the expanding city, and then in an ever-increasing volume to the northwest side.

Seeking to offset the loss of its Jewish membership, the JCC took in an ever-larger number of non-Jews—to the point that, when in June 1979, it contacted Solomon David Wise, the "JCC Doctor" (then still with the North Shore Jewish Community Center in Marblehead, Massachusetts)—non-Jews made up more than 55% of the Rincon JCC membership! This further upset Jewish members particularly those families concerned about the weekly dances and other social programs and their impact upon their teenage children.

Sol Wise had established a reputation serving as the executive director of JCCs requiring rejuvenation, rehabilitation, relocation or even beginning them from scratch in various parts of the country—which was why he was dubbed the "JCC Doctor." In July '79 he was invited to Rincon for an interview, along with four other prospects, and awarded the job in August '79. After giving the North Shore JCC two months notice, Sol, Shirley and their dog Patches arrived in Rincon on October 4, 1979, Shirley's 53rd birthday—with Sol to observe his 58th just 15 days later.

Sol called the center from a restaurant phone booth and was told that their real estate agent was trying to reach them to tell them that their furniture had arrived a few hours before and was being unloaded at their town house—which Sol had purchased before leaving Rincon at the end of his interview a few months ago, having felt confident that he would be offered the job. They drove over to their new home and supervised the remainder of the unloading and were thus able to spend their first night in their own home rather than another motel—of which they had tired after their six-day motor trip from the Boston North Shore.

INITIAL SURPRISES

At the JCC on Monday, Sol's first day on the new job, he was greeted warmly by the staff but as he entered his office and sat down at his desk, his secretary and office manager, Phyllis, followed him in, smiled and told him not to get too comfortable since the center was to move out of its 102 N. Plumer Street location of over 25 years at the end of the month.

"When was all this decided? And why?" Sol asked.

"Well, actually all within the last few days. I tried calling you, but you had already left the North Shore and were on the road, and I didn't know where to reach you." Phyllis explained. "And as to the 'why', you better talk with the president, Ted Oldman" she added.

Sol had lunch with Dr. Theodore Oldman that very day and asked about, what to him seemed like sudden and precipitous actions. Conventional wisdom dictated that one does not throw out the old water before one has the new and that included not moving from current quarters before having the new. When he was in for his interview Sol was told about the ten acres of land in the northeast part of the city donated by four community leaders to be used as the site of the new JCC. While he had some questions about its location because he believed there was need for a population survey and demographic study before finalizing the location, he made no comments at the time—other than to express admiration for the donors. But this news about moving out of the 43,691 square foot Plumer Street facility into....what?...was a surprise, to say the least.

"And what did Phyllis mean when she said that even my desk in my office was not center property but rather the property of the 'Senior Adult Generation' or 'SAG' as she called it?" Sol concluded.

Ted smiled nervously and replied: "Well let me first respond to the SAG piece—which most of us call 'SAD' over the loss of the Senior Adult Department. It started as a typical Golden Age club for people over 65, but when Grace Govdul took over the Senior Adult Department she really expanded the program into her little empire. She's a very aggressive, diligent and creative worker with a remarkable capacity to get federal grant monies for older adult projects and she was able to build not just the senior adult programs, but before anybody realized it—make of it an autonomous entity. Some critics say it's become the tail that's wagging the dog." Ted paused and then continued: "No, let me finish; I can see you're eager with some questions if not some comments. You see, when the center's budget could not afford the purchase, or replacement of furniture and/or equipment, Grace's SAG was able to do so. That's why, over time, much of the center's furniture and equipment became, technically, the property of the SAG." Ted finished and resumed eating his salad.

After a long pause, indicating deep thought, Sol responded. "Well, once we have a new building to move into, we'll need new furniture and equipment anyway, so I guess that's no big tragedy" he said. "But about the sudden move from Plumer...and to where?" he added.

"Now that—in a way—is a consequence of your interview, when you responded so fully to questions regarding your experiences with the 'Center Without Walls'. You know, when you told us about your work in Chicago and the Niles Township suburbs, with your administrative offices located in a storefront and where you rented facilities in synagogues, temples, churches and schools. Believe me—that impressed everybody a lot! Anyway, we've rented a 1500 square foot storefront at 5410 E. Pima Street to be used as administrative headquarters and we'll rent other program quarters as necessary, just as you did in Chicago/Niles Township."

"I see. So you're saying it's my fault, Sol joked. "But that still doesn't answer the question, why now?" he pressed.

Ted wiped his mouth with his napkin and replied: The Rincon Jewish Federation was able to get a grant from HUD, you know, the federal Housing and Urban Development agency to build low income housing for the elderly and the center's outdoor facilities, including the pool and ball fields were tagged as the ideal location. And the SAG has been tagged to provide the recreational, nutritional and social services for the residents of Council House—that's what they plan to call the low-income housing—and in order for SAG to do that it will need the center's current group service facilities. The center, of course, will be reimbursed for the facilities taken over by SAG to service the residents of Council House. So that's the reason for having us move out now."

Sol continued to digest all that his president Dr. Theodore Oldman had just shared with him. And after another few moments said: "So, after more than 25 years of being a full-service center, the Rincon JCC will find itself in a storefront facility, running its programs out of rented quarters, having to carry-out a Center Planning Task Force, a population and demographic study, re-educate a much-expanded, widely-dispersed and seemingly disinterested community and raise millions of dollars for a new building. Is that about it, Ted?"

Ted answered: "Yep, that's about it. But we figured you're the guy that can do it."

"Thanks. But I have to be honest. I have some concern about the ethics involved here. I mean, expecting the center to make the necessary, immediate sacrifices in order to benefit another segment of the Jewish community. On the other hand, I can see some positives in these developments. It allows us the opportunity to distance what will be the new center from that of the old. By being forced to move from its 43,691 square foot facility on 6.4 acres into a 1500 square foot storefront on 5410 East Pima Street, the JCC becomes both 'homeless' as well as a 'Center Without Walls'. We could use that sympathy factor."

Ted smiled. "See, already you've come up with some additional angles."

Still, when it came time for the move out from the Plumer Street building into the storefront at 5410 E. Pima Street at the end of October, 1979 Sol was flabbergasted to find that one small moving van was sufficient to move what remained as center property. Which only proved to him that this was more than the proverbial tail wagging the dog; that actually in this case the tail devoured the dog! Still, Sol rationalized that it was just as well, since the storefront could only accommodate what the van delivered and thus the center would save considerable monies in storage fees for old, dilapidated furniture and equipment. Which was another reason for Sol to feel that the moving out of the center from its Plumer Street address was a blessing in disguise.

But he wasn't so sure that going ahead with the "Consecration" of the ten acres on Grant Road in the northeast part of the city was also a blessing. He was fearful that it might be interpreted as a "ground-breaking"—for which they were hardly ready! That program too had been planned during the interim between Sol's interview and his leaving the North Shore to head for Rincon. And he wondered what other surprises lay in store for him. Again he lunched with his president, Ted to share with him his reservations—and to pump from him any other tidbits that might have been inadvertently withheld from him.

And Ted profusely apologized, assuring him that there was no conspiracy to withhold any information, just that things had moved so quickly that most of them had been caught unawares. It was the feeling of the four donors—which included David Silvers, Morris Menchen, Sam Nibot and Jacob Rivers—that since the center was seen as moving out of Plumer, it would help to calm concerns by showcasing the new site as a commitment that the community did intend to go ahead with the building of a new center. As an aside, he added that, of course, it didn't hurt the four donors with their tax write-offs for the donation to be claimed before the end of the year.

And then he further explained that originally the property consisted of thirty acres and even after deducting the ten acres for the donation of the new site for the center, a nice profit was realized from the sale of the remaining twenty acres. So, it was a win-win situation all around, Ted concluded.

"Maybe yes, and maybe no," Sol countered. And then he laid out his professional opinion that before going ahead with the construction of a new building, the community had better be sure that they were building it in the right place. With the current fluidity of the Jewish population the only way to determine "the right place" was to have a demographic study—a population survey—which would also lay out the trends and hence the future concentrations. "It's like shooting a rocket to the moon. You don't aim the rocket at the spot the moon is currently located, but rather at the spot you scientifically determine the moon will be when the rocket arrives. And equally important, I have to wonder about community reaction when, and if, it turns out that we don't go ahead with the Grant Road site—which I hope is the case."

Ted was visibly impressed, but also disturbed. ""Hey, I didn't realize you were a rocket and space scientist in addition to being 'Doctor JCC'. And now that we're analyzing it so thoroughly, I have some other concerns; how do you 'look a gift horse in the mouth', so to speak. How do you say to the wealthy big shots; 'say guys, that's very nice of you, but hey, the ten acres you've donated to us—almost four acres more than we had on Plumer—is not good enough'?"

Sol acknowledged that could be tricky but added that he felt big-business types like the four donors could be convinced of his concerns and arguments and a way found to move ahead with the project, but on sounder grounds—"pardon the pun." He felt that there were ways to go ahead with the Consecration program without making any more verbal commitments about the finality of that particular site.

And Ted agreed that what Sol had focused on made sense and that he would support Sol in finding a way out of the dilemma. He suggested their involving Al Reese, his immediate predecessor as president and who, in fact "roped me in to succeed him. Al, as a developer himself probably would respond favorably to the suggestion of—what did you call the population survey?

"Oh yes, some demographic studies, because he's always telling me how he does that in planning his developments. And besides, he's chairman of the Consecration Committee."

Al Reese concurred with Sol's assessment and with his help, others involved in the Consecration program were cued-in to avoid verbal commitments to the Grant Road site in their remarks but to stick to generalities about the assurance of the center's future. On a bright, beautiful Sunday morning in late November, the ten-acre site on Grant Road was "consecrated" as representing the future of a new Rincon Jewish Community Center.

Yet there remained one other surprise for Sol; not of the magnitude of the Grant Road site, but indicative of how far they would have to go in realizing a new center building. He made it a practice, as part of his orientation to a new community and "spreading the gospel" to meet one-on-one with as many leaders of the community as possible, either for lunch, or at the person's office or whatever the person's convenience. And this particularly included religious leaders, the rabbis of the existing congregations. His luncheon with the rabbi of the orthodox and later the conservative congregations were of no particular significance, but his luncheon with Rabbi Joe Westheimer of Temple Emanu-El provided him with another surprise.

"So why did you come to Rincon?" he pointedly asked Sol. "Actually we don't need a Jewish Center. We have the three congregations serving the orthodox, the conservative and the reform."

"And who serves the 50% of the Jewish community that is unaffiliated?" Sol asked also pointedly. "Although I don't mean to suggest that centers are only for people who choose not to affiliate with congregations. As a matter of fact, most members of congregations are also members of Jewish Community Centers. And many people and families first join centers prior to linking up with a congregation," he added with a wry smile.

Rabbi Westheimer did not expect such a rapid and complete response. He smiled back and said: "Maybe I came on too strong. All I meant was that with three congregations, having to compete with a Jewish Community Center would only weaken all our positions."

"It doesn't have to. My experiences throughout the country are that we can complement each other. Certainly centers—and I don't mean congregations that call themselves 'Jewish Centers' so prevalent in the east—do not involve themselves in religious activities but recognize that as the province of the congregations. And yet many JCCs assist congregations with their youth groups, or other group and social activities. You have to admit that, congregations, by their very nature, compete for membership and as such tend to be divisive in the community, whereas JCCs, by its all-inclusiveness, tends to unite communities. Which is why, increasingly, Jewish Community Centers are viewed as 'The Center of the Community'."

"Well, I can see that you've been through this experience before," Rabbi Westheimer said.

"Yes, I have, Joe. Many times before!" Sol replied. Nevertheless, Sol was reminded that he had his work cut out for him.

CENTER PLANNING TASK FORCE

Following the Consecration program, president Ted Oldman appointed his immediate predecessor, Al Reese to chair the Center Planning Task Force, which would conduct the Self Study. And from December, 1979 through October 1980 hundreds of volunteers devoted countless hours as members of six major study groups, surveying, questioning, debating and hammering out a Final Report and Recommendations relating to the facilities required and desired; in short, a blueprint for the programs of the new Jewish Community Center.

Simultaneously, Sol involved the University of Arizona to help with the demographic study and population survey. This included, among other things, the pinpointing of every Jewish household on a huge wall map to provide the immediate, visual impact necessary to command attention. But mostly it sought to project the movement of the population and thus predict the future areas of concentration.

All this study activity was all very well, but it was essential that there be continuing programming for all age groups and interests. As he had done in so many other communities, but especially Niles Township in the Chicago area, Sol and his staff operated programs in rented quarters in Jewish congregations, Christian churches, park facilities, school gyms and even some limited classes in the storefront facility itself. Since only temporary partitions divided the 1500 square foot area, the clerical staff was continually competing handling incoming telephone calls with the music for a dance class in the large multipurpose room!

In November 1980 the center celebrated its 25th anniversary with a Gala Dinner Dance in a downtown hotel with its theme "As Ye Sow, So Shall Ye Reap"—which Sol borrowed from *Ethics of our Fathers*. This was followed a few months later with another social affair with a distinct western theme and flavor—"The Hay-moishe Hoedown" featuring square dancing and country/western music. And a few months following that, still another social/cultural affair with a "Cabaret" theme. The success of all of which, Sol correctly predicted, would strike new sparks and stimulate renewed interest in the Jewish Community Center and pave the way for the Capital Funds Drive further down the road.

And all of which led Ted Oldman to comment to Shirley, Sol's wife, at a shared table at the "Cabaret" affair while Sol was table-hopping: "He's really a workaholic, isn't he?"

Shirley smiled. "Some people say that, but from his point of view, he puts in whatever time is necessary to get the job done. For him, it's not just a 'job' but also a challenge and a labor of love. Maybe it's because of his orphanage experience—being denied so much."

"Sol was raised in an orphanage? Back in New York? I didn't know that."

"Yes, in the Hebrew National Orphan Home in Yonkers. And so was I; in the Pride of Judea Children's Home in Brooklyn. We met when he came to work at the Pride after he was out of the HNOH a few years. I was one of the older girls—monitor of younger kids."

By December 1980 the Center Planning Task Force produced its final Self Study Report and Recommendations, which exhilarated some and astounded others. Initially the assumptions were that, since the old center was a total of almost 46,000 square feet on six acres of land, it could be replaced with 65,000 square feet on ten acres. Imagine the surprise—and consternation in some quarters—when the recommendations called for at least 100,000 square feet on at least 30 acres. The recommendations were backed up with detailed reports and statistics, and particularly stressed the fact that the new center would have to serve a rapidly growing population over the next thirty years! And it made frequent references to the analogy of shooting rockets to the moon and the necessity of planning ahead for the anticipated population growth.

The population survey and demographic study projected a continual, geometric rate of growth to an anticipated Jewish population of 30,000 to 40,000 within the thirty-year span. And it also indicated that there were developing two concentrations of that population, one in the northeast and a newly developing one in the northwest. Therefore, it recommended that the new center be built midway between those two concentrations, predicting that the area between those two concentrations would rapidly fill with Jewish families because of the JCC—"where it would be equally inaccessible for everybody," one board member skeptic stated.

There were, of course, additional skeptics who challenged the study, its findings, its conclusions and its recommendations—especially about the need for thirty acres. But that part of the argument was quickly and easily overcome with reminders of the constant, chronic parking problems at the old Plumer Street building and with the formula provided by the Building Bureau of the National Association of JCCs.

More important was the climaxing of the dilemma of the ten acres on Grant Road, which, according to the Report and Recommendations was insufficient both in size and location. And Sol and Ted and the center leadership realized they could no longer avoid discussing this with the four donors. Sol suggested that they invite Murray Rosenberg of the NAJCC Building Bureau (who had been advising Sol all along) to help them make the presentation and with the discussions. At first Sol met some resistance by some members of the executive committee.

"I mean, you're supposed to be the 'JCC Doctor' aren't you Sol?" Rose Kanter, first vice president said. "Why do we need to spend extra money flying down another expert?"

Sol smiled knowingly. "Well, it's been my experience that once the 'expert' becomes just another resident of the community he's working in and for, he ceases to be the 'expert'. Murray is the expert/consultant of all issues relating to new center buildings. He's an expert on space requirements, both in land acreage and square footage for each activity room. We'll be using him when we get around to hiring an architect to make plans for the building itself. But now we need him to sell the bigwigs on the size and location of the building."

With Murray Rosenberg present, Sol and the center leaders, including Al Reese in his capacity of Chairman of the

Planning Task Force, made their presentation to Dave Silvers, Morris Menchen, Jacob Rivers and Sam Nibot. When they finished, there was an uncomfortable silence as everyone scanned everybody else. Finally Sam Nibot voiced his concern about the project appearing to be getting out of control. He was one of the skeptics about the need for so much land and so much building, not to mention the anticipated size of the Jewish community. Jacob Rivers, for his part, could accept the extrapolations about the population, and was willing to hear more about space and acreage budgeting; while Morris Menchen thought it all very interesting and was a proponent of looking ahead, like shooting the rocket to the moon.

Only Dave Silvers, who was the acknowledged leader of the four, a developer and one of the wealthiest men in the community, listened carefully but said nothing. And as all heads and eyes turned towards him he smiled shifted in his chair and said: "Well, I'm fascinated by the presentation, especially by Murray and Sol. Actually you guys (indicating his partners) know damned well that, in our businesses, we do exactly what these people are talking about, although we may use different business terms, like 'market research.' I don't think we'd have any problem selling the ten acres, at a profit no less, and apply the proceeds from that sale to the purchase of thirty acres of land in the midpoint of the two concentrations. What do you guys think?"

And all the other three nodded their head vigorously as Dave turned to Murray Rosenberg and said: "You should be a salesman." And Murray responded: "I was, a very successful one. But I like what I'm doing now much more."

Dave then turned to Sol and said: "Very well done Sol; very impressive preparation and presentation. If there's anything else we can do to help, just let us know."

"We'll need help in raising many millions of dollars" Al Reese chimed in. "You'd make a great General Chairman for the Capital Funds Campaign, Dave," he added.

DODGE AND RIVER ROAD SITE

Ted Oldman's term came to an end when Rose Kanter, the first woman president in the history of the JCC, succeeded him in January 1981. At his farewell luncheon, Ted thanked everyone for their support during some very difficult times and concluded by saying: "And if I'm remembered for nothing else, I want to be known as the guy who brought Sol Wise to Rincon."

"Ted, we'll be giving you many opportunities to be remembered for other things as well" Rose replied and immediately appointed him Chairman of the Architect Search Committee as well as the Space Budget Committee while Alex Reese was appointed to begin structuring the Capital Funds Campaign Committees.

From his arrival in Rincon, Sol recognized that his lay leadership lacked sufficient knowledge about what was required for a modern, up-to-date JCC. And yet he had to be quite diplomatic about this lack. He had been "educating" the lay leadership via a "learn-by-doing" system as they tackled each problem as it arose and making certain every board member was assigned to at least one of the six study groups comprising the Self Study aspect of the Center's Planning Task Force. For example, upon his arrival, Sol inherited a Bingo Program operated by the center designed to bring in much needed revenue. The core of the volunteer corps needed to operate the program were members of the board of directors, who (as a condition of serving on the board) committed to attending the bingo games at least twice a month in one of several capacities. Most board members disliked the chore and griped incessantly. And Sol voiced his disapproval of the activity on the grounds that it sanctioned gambling as an official program of the center. Yet, no one had proposed an alternative that could bring in the $10,000 for the year that the program netted.

Sol urged, and Rose Kanter appointed a small study committee to consider this additional dilemma. Participating in the committee's deliberations, the center's program director, Morris Rothberg—who had worked for the Phoenix center before coming to Rincon—suggested a Community Directory. This was essentially an ad-book, which, according to Morris, yielded the Phoenix center from $15,000 to $20,000 per year! The committee very quickly determined the bingo games to be a very inefficient money-producing activity. Considering all the money-prizes that had to be awarded at each game and throughout the evening, the yearly net was only 10% of the gross! The strategy that emerged was to recommend each board member to be responsible for procuring at least $500 worth of ads. With 40 board members, that would produce a minimum of $20,000 gross, with printing and other costs resulting in a net of $15,000. And the beauty of it was that the board members had almost the entire year to procure the ads.

It didn't take too much persuasion at the next board meeting to accept the committee's recommendation and the Bingo Program became a part of the Plumer Center history.

In October 1981 Rose appointed Gary Simons, one of the JCCs vice presidents, to head the Facilities Investigation Team. Gary was a builder specializing in multiple units, such as apartments and duplexes and flew his own six-passenger plane. Sol seized on that and arranged for Gary to fly Rose and himself, the Jewish Federation executive director, Sam Nibot (one of the land donors) and Jack DeBartolo, a principal partner of the architectural firm Anderson, DeBartolo & Pan—or ADP for short—to Dallas, Texas to visit the recently enlarged JCC there and talk with Harry Rosen, the executive director and his staff. Sol had worked in Dallas from 1961 to '66 completing the construction of a new center after its move from its old site near downtown Dallas to a new location in north-central Dallas adjacent to the Central Expressway. It was a situation not unlike that which faced the Rincon community.

ADP, a Rincon-based firm, had been selected as the architect for the new Rincon JCC building following a process developed by the Architect Selection Committee chaired by past president Dr. Ted Oldman. Over fifteen architect firms and individuals—some from as far away as San Francisco—presented their qualifications and bids and after nine months (a full gestation period) the choice was made.

The trip to Dallas was Sol's idea and inspired by his desire to "educate" the Jewish lay leadership of Rincon—both center and federation—as to what an up-to-date Jewish Community Center contained in the way of physical facilities and consequently, what programs it offered. While some of the lay people, Gary and Sam Nibot included, came away from Dallas still skeptical about Rincon's ability to cope with such major facilities and their costs, Sol and Rose regarded the trip as a great success, if for nothing else, all who participated now had a better idea of what facilities were essential and what they could cost. And it made it easier for the board to approve visits to other centers around the country.

Which was precisely what a sub-committee, consisting of Sol, Gary, Sam Nibot and Jack DeBartolo did, traveling to three JCCs in the northeast and three in the northwest over the next six months between November 1981 and April 1982. In fact, on their trip to the JCC of Essex County, New Jersey they encountered Dave Silvers and his wife attending a wedding at the JCC.

Dave stared unbelievingly as he spotted the four wandering through the corridors. "What the hell are you guys doing here?" he bellowed.

"Hey, I'm sure I told you about the Facilities Investigation Team—you know the team that goes around visiting other centers" Sam Nibot responded.

"Well, you said something about that, but I never dreamed you'd be coming this far to look at another center" Dave retorted. "But hey, I'm glad we're going about this in the right way especially since they asked me to be the General Chairman of the Capital Funds Campaign."

"So, are you going to do it?' Sam Nibot asked.

"I don't know yet. I'm pretty bogged down with a lot of other things. I told them I'd have to let them know."

Also in October 1981 the Grant Road site was sold and a new 44-acre site at Dodge Blvd. and River Road was purchased. The new site was located midway between the two concentrations of Jewish population, just as the Self Study had recommended, and a giant step taken on the proverbial thousand-mile journey that begins with one step!

HEART ATTACK

The year 1982 was a very busy one with January witnessing the publication of the first Jewish Community Directory finally allowing the center to discontinue its Bingo Program while February saw the establishment of the Site Planning and Development Committee which would include a Building Subcommittee working closely with the selected architects Anderson, Bartolo and Pan. May featured the First Annual Maccabiah games on the new site with more than 1,000 people in attendance watching over 300 athletes of all ages and sizes involved in a wide variety of athletic and sports competitions. Through the first six months, the Facility Investigation team visited the three JCCs in the northeast and then three JCCs in the northwest, and following each visit the participants came back more emboldened regarding what Rincon could do.

"Hell, if Portland and Seattle can put up, and operate, centers like they're doing, so can we!" was the increasing consensus. Which gave rise to a new slogan for the project, quoting Theodore Herzl, the founder of Zionism: **"If you will it, it is no dream."**

And in early July the tempo caught up with Sol. At home one Saturday, while unpacking some shelving for assembly, Sol felt some sharp pains in his left shoulder and a experienced a shortness of breath. As he sat to catch his breath, Shirley and his son Louis noted how white he had turned and asked if he was allright.

"I think so. Probably strained my left shoulder getting this damned shelving out of the carton. I'll just sit here for awhile to catch my breath."

But as he sat there, gasping for air and turning white, Shirley and Louis became more concerned and suggested that he go to the HMO's emergency room. He resisted the suggestion at first, but as he found himself not feeling any better he agreed to go with Louis in his car to the emergency room accompanied by Shirley.

Describing the symptoms he was quickly examined by an attending physician who determined that he was indeed suffering a "myocardial infarction".

"Which means what?" Sol demanded.

"Which means angina, a coronary—at least a mild heart attack. We should get you to the hospital, preferably by ambulance."

"Ambulance? You mean sirens and flashing lights? No, no ambulance." Sol declared.

So they compromised and agreed to have the ambulance not use any sirens or flashing lights. And Louis and his mother Shirley followed the ambulance to St. Joseph's Hospital where they waited patiently before being allowed to visit Sol in his room.

The hospital confirmed the diagnosis of the physician at the HMO emergency and together with Sol's primary care physician, Dr. Melvin Weinberg, decreed that Sol remain in the hospital at least for four days and then stay home from work for at least four weeks, with medications and plenty of rest.

   Phyllis, his office manager and secretary visited him at home daily, bringing him the most vital issues for his attention; likewise, Morris, his Program Director. Rose Kanter, his president visited him twice a week, reviewing areas of concern. Sol was deluged with cards from center board members, as well as the general membership, but he was most impressed to receive one from Dave Silvers calling upon him to make a rapid recovery since they were all eagerly awaiting his return to full, active duty. Yet, despite, Sol's condition, from his "home office" he was able to oversee the installation of an interim baseball field and some temporary tennis courts, allowing for some limited, continuous, ongoing athletic activities on the new site.

   But even after his return to full, active duty, the administrative headquarters continued to operate out of the storefront on Pima and the bulk of group services activities continued in rented facilities throughout the city in a continuation of the "Center Without Walls" concept. In fact, because this concept was proving to be so successful—at least in the minds of some of the federation leaders—new arguments arose about the need for an expensive new building. Fortunately, all the studies, planning and task force operations now proved their worth with overwhelming votes by both boards of the federation and center to "stay the course" and proceed with the planning of the new center. And in December 1982 the architects, ADP presented their eagerly awaited Long Range Plan and preliminary sketches of the site plan—which included not just a building for a new center, but land and space allocation for the Jewish Federation, the Jewish Post, Rincon Hebrew Academy and the Jewish Family Service, assuming their interest in being located on the new Jewish Community Campus!

"GETTING ON SITE"

In April 1983 the tempo of planning and implementation increased. Only the western third of the new 44-acre site fronted on River Road, the remainder cut off by three private estates; the Quirk, Gallo and Clark properties. Sol and Murray Rosenberg (the consultant from the NAJCC Building Bureau) had been stressing that "you can never have too much land" and Sol added to that, the importance of "Getting On Site" administratively as well as programmatically. He kept referring to it as "the ingathering of the center refugee programs" still scattered throughout the city. Thus, when the Gallo House, comprising 6,000 square feet located on 3.7 acres abutting the center property on the north and fronting on River Road, east of the Quirk property, went on sale, it was immediately purchased and renovated allowing the center to finally vacate its Pima Street storefront and move onto site, its new address becoming 3822 E. River Road. The house itself was renovated to allow for administrative offices and some program space; some garage facilities in back were to be renovated to accommodate four preschool classes; a detached bungalow would house the new Infant/Toddler program; and that summer Camp Shalom, the JCCs day camp was conducted on center property for the first time in many years!

The bungalow housing the new Infant/Toddler program—taking in infants as young as six weeks—had a special, personal meaning for Sol. His first grandchild, Sara Michelle, was enrolled and Sol spent whatever free time he could muster to be with the two-month-old child. The joke at the center was that Sol had installed a special extension phone so that he could be in the bungalow. Which was not altogether true, but it was a revelation for Sol that now he was building not only for "the community" but for personal reasons as well. Sara would spend many hours at the "J" throughout her seventeen years in a wide variety of programs and activities, including pre-school, day camp, arts and crafts, swimming, social activities, basketball and even having her Bat Mitzvah party there! "As ye sow, so shall ye reap" truly applied in this situation.

In December 1983 the center's Annual Meeting was held on the new site and Will Reiner was elected to succeed Rose Kanter as president. Through the first few months of 1984 ADP carried through its surveying process consisting of meeting with clusters of center members and the community at large determining interests and using Murray Rosenberg to determine a space budget from which emerged the total square footage required and its estimated costs. And at a special joint meeting of the federation and center boards of directors in April 1984 the figures for size and cost and recommendations were presented.

THE PAST WE INHERIT; THE FUTURE WE CREATE

The architects ADP made a very impressive presentation with colorful charts of the site development and architectural renditions of buildings. The title of their presentation, researched by Sol and taken from the Talmud, was: "THE PAST WE INHERIT: THE FUTURE WE CREATE." The presentation was impressive and recommendations—SHOCKING!

ADP presented as its objective—A FULL SERVICE CENTER FOR MANY YEARS SERVICE. Total square footage would be 110,000 on the now 47-acre site at a cost of at least $10,000,000! ADP acknowledged that the objective would probably need to be achieved in several stages. And a full debate erupted ranging from the opinion that it was all totally ridiculous to quoting Theodore

Herzl's slogan **"If you will it; it is no dream."** And the debate rolled on, with those saying there simply was not that kind of money in the Rincon Jewish community, and others demurring saying they were not sure that was the case.

Finally Dave Silvers rose and spoke. He said that a few years ago, he and many of his colleagues believed that ten acres of land at Grant Avenue was sufficient to construct a 60,000 square foot facility to replace the 45,000 building on Plumer Street. "Then along came Solomon Wise who convinced us that that was not the right thing to do. Sol reminded us in the business world that when dealing with the community business we must do that which we do in our business world all the time—namely market research! Well, the market research on this project has produced some unexpected results—challenging results!" Dave went on to say that he wasn't sure whether that kind of money could be raised for such a project. He happened to believe that the money was probably there, but could not be sure it could be raised for this specific project!

Dave paused, as he looked around the room at the anxious faces. And then he continued that there was only one way to find out, and he for one was willing to try to find out. He had deferred giving an answer to whether he would accept the position of General Chairman of the Capital Funds Campaign. He was now ready to give his answer. He would accept the position!

And he would expect his friends and colleagues to join him in this noble experiment!

Silence greeted Dave's remarks, then one, and then another began applauding. "The die is cast!" shouted one board member. "We've crossed the Rubicon," cried another. "Yeah, all we need now is to raise ten million dollars! Good luck to us!" said a third.

It didn't require too much arm-twisting on Sol's part to convince Dave and the other lay leaders of the wisdom of hiring a professional fundraising firm. And in May 1984 the Milton Hood Ward firm from New York was hired to provide that service. Milton Hood Ward himself came for the interview that resulted in his being awarded the contract, but he had made it known that he himself did not provide the daily field service. People recruited and supervised by the MHW Company did this, usually retired Jewish federation or United Jewish Appeal professionals. And it was the practice of the MHW Company to allow the local community to interview and accept or reject the person designated for the field supervisor job.

In the case of Rincon, Dave Silvers "suggested" that he interview the designee first and if he approved, then he would be presented to the overall Capital Funds Campaign committee. The first one designated was Albert Goldstein, the retired executive director of the Jewish Federation of Houston, Texas. Al was an experienced and extremely knowledgeable, strong professional who could easily hold his own with any lay leader. Sol knew him from when he had worked in Houston back in 1953 to '56 and thought he would be an excellent professional to guide the local fund-raising effort.

But following his meeting with Dave Silvers, Al lunched with Sol and reported that he doubted that he would be the field man for Rincon and when Sol asked why he said this, Al elaborated, stating: "I'm too strong and independent for him. It's just something that I feel; the kind of feeling I used to get from some of my lay people back in Houston. Oh, he was careful not to say anything directly about not wanting me, but I could feel it. This guy is very strong-willed and likes to have things his way."

"You're right about that, Al. But I've found him ultimately responsive. I mean he came around on the Grant Road site and in accepting the General Chairmanship of the Campaign."

"From what I've heard, the Grant Road site deal was a 'no-brainer.' I mean everybody came out a winner. And it took him quite a while to finally accept the chairmanship, didn't he? Look, I don't know what his agenda is, but he's got one, believe me, and it could spell trouble. Milton (referring to his boss Milton Hood Ward) told me that at his presentation prior to being awarded the contract, Silvers was full of challenging questions, indicating that he was not totally accepting of the basic concepts governing the raising of capital funds."

"I remember that presentation, and yes I remember Dave's challenging questions. But that's Dave. I hope you're wrong about both your assumptions; that you won't be assigned as the field man and that Dave is not accepting of the concepts of capital fund raising—which you have to admit—take some getting used to."

"Sol, you can't argue with success. The Milton Hood Ward Company has been selected for over 70% of the capital funds campaigns, not only for centers, but Jewish hospitals and other communal institutions and reached the goal in over 85% of the projects."

Unfortunately Al Goldstein was right; he was not approved to be the field man for the Rincon project; Harold Benowitz, a retired executive director of the Corpus Christi Federation/JCC, was selected. Sol also knew Hal from his various positions in JCCs around the country but specifically when Sol worked in Dallas Texas 1961-66 and Hal worked as the executive director of the Corpus Christi agency. Thus they knew each other well, liked each other and would work well together on the task of raising ten million dollars.

Even though the announcement of the plans for ten million dollar building served to spur an increase in the center's membership and programs and the summer of 1984 witnessed the most successful day camp in the center's history, Sol was still disturbed by the nixing of Al Goldstein and his mind wandered back to the meeting where Milton Hood Ward made his pitch for his company to be selected for the fund raising job.

SECRETS OF CAPITAL FUNDS CAMPAIGNS

Milton Hood Ward was masterful in making the pitch for the selection of the MHW Company to be the guiding light of the very challenging fund-raising campaign facing, not only the Jewish Community Center, but the entire Jewish community. Never before had the Rincon Jewish community faced such a daunting challenge. But then again, as Milton Ward put it, never before had it faced such a rewarding promise: not only a new Jewish Community Center, but also a Jewish Community Campus with all the non-religious institutions clustered on one site providing for cohesion, convenience, and efficiency.

And then he leaned forward, as if ready to share some secrets with his listeners. He pointed out that in a major campaign, such as this one, 70% to 75% of the goal had to come from 10% to 15% of the community. Thus 10% of the community had to come up with $7,500,000! He waited a moment for the shock to subside and continued that for that to be attainable one did not ask for "donations" but rather sought to **sell** "Honorials and Memorials" and then he chalked on a blackboard listings of such Honorials and Memorials, beginning with the most expensive-such as the naming of the building, physical education complex, group services, preschool, tennis courts, camp grounds and running on down to even such things as drinking fountains! The prices for each, he continued, depended on how much money needed to be raised, and he then elaborated on his formula in arriving at the respective prices. He stressed that the crucial and determining factor was in correctly pricing each unit from the top on down. If one "low-balled" the first top facilities then everything that followed would be proportionately "under-valued" and it would be all the more difficult to reach the goal. And the final "strategy" was in allowing the pledges to be paid over a 3-5-10 year period depending upon its size. It all appeared to make sense—certainly tailored for the business tycoons and wealthy people who were targeted to carry the major responsibility.

Dave Silvers complimented Milton Ward on his "creative and original concepts and strategies" but had some reservations about underplaying the "donation" factor and especially about how high the "prices" would be set. Also, he felt that "the little man" had to be able to participate and feel part of the project.

Ward assured him that the final decision on prices would be made by the Capital Campaign Committee and agreed heartily that everyone in the community would have an opportunity to participate in the campaign. He clarified that his Honorials and Memorials were reserved for the two top divisions, namely the Advanced Gifts and Special Gifts. And following some additional questions and answers the vote to assign the contract to the Milton Hood Ward Company was unanimous. And in September, Sol proceeded to make arrangements for Harold Benowitz to come and live in the community, in a small one-bedroom apartment courtesy of Gary Simons. And also in September 1984 the renovations of the multiple garage facilities in the back of the Gallo House were completed allowing the Jewish Community Center Preschool to be reestablished after a lapse of five years!

While Hal Benowitz and Sol worked with the lay leaders in setting up the structure of the Capital Funds Campaign, debating the "price structure" for the Honorials and Memorials with Dave Silvers and others, the opportunity arose, in January 1985, to buy the Clark property just east of the Gallo House also fronting on River Road. Operating under the now accepted philosophy that you can "never have too much land" the 4500 square foot property was purchased expanding the total site size to over 50 acres! Designated the "JCC Annex" the new addition housed the Physical Education offices and following some renovation to the outside pool the aquatics department was re-established in May, after a lapse of more than six years.

Now only the Quirk property, fronting on River Road, remained in private hands and an approach was made to the dentist, Dr. Quirk, inquiring about his interest in selling. He was interested, but asked the ridiculous sum of over one million dollars and the JCC leaders decided that the property was not essential for their purposes after all. Thus the Quirk property remained surrounded by the Jewish Community Campus on three sides and the JCC went about its business of raising the necessary ten million dollars for the construction of its new center.

The squabbling over the "price structure" for the Honorials and Memorials went on for several months, delaying the actual beginning of the campaign. Hal and Sol were holding out for the pricing recommended by Milton Hood Ward, which was beginning with the naming of the building for two million and everything that followed priced proportionately. This was strongly opposed by Dave Silvers and others who proposed starting with a one million price tag and going down from there. An attempt to compromise at 1½ million was also resisted and Dave Silvers had his way with the naming of the building listed at one million and all the rest proportionately reduced accordingly.

A beautiful, multi-colored, glossy brochure showing an artist's rendition of the site plan and the 100,000 square foot, ranch-style building was produced with the caption across the top:

"THE PAST WE INHERIT; THE FUTURE WE CREATE: The Talmud." Inside the four page brochure were floor plans of the facility and graphics showing usage of those facilities with titles and descriptions. And accompanying the brochure was a separate black and white "price list" for the various Honorials and Memorials, beginning with the naming of the building at one million dollars and continuing on down to numerous drinking fountains. The campaign was finally ready to be launched!

"And then there's always the unexpected" is a famous line from the movie *"The Bridge on the River Kwai"* uttered by the British Colonel Hawkins. The County, in which the JCC site was located, outside the city limits of the city of Rincon, suddenly announced plans for the River Road/Alvernon Way Parkway requiring the realignment and connections of River Road and Alvernon Way. The county was considering three alternative routes ALL ACROSS THE JCC PROPERTY on its southern portion fronting on the Rillito River—dry most of the year except during the monsoon seasons. Each of the proposed routes would have significant impact upon the proposed site plan and outdoor facilities.

Anticipating months of prolonged negotiations with the county, the campaign was nevertheless launched and had significant initial success. In addition to the Advanced Gifts and Special Gifts Divisions approaching large "buyers" on a one-by-one basis, "selling" the various Honorial and Memorials, the General Campaign "pitched" the project to small donors via hundreds of parlor meetings in private homes. So, the end of 1985 had reached half of the goal! This despite the fact that Milton Hood Ward's warning, re-emphasized by Hal Benowitz with support from Sol, seemed to be realized, i.e. the "undervaluing" of all the facilities seemed to slow the reaching of the total goal of ten million.

Although these disagreements took place behind closed doors, between the principals, Dave Silvers was nevertheless displeased and conveyed this displeasure to the company head, Milton Hood Ward requesting that Hal be replaced. Ward resisted by alleging that he had no one immediately available to replace the field man, adding that it was not good policy, strategy or psychology to do so anyway. So, between the ongoing negotiations with the County and the slowing down of the campaign it was decided to put the campaign on hold.

In September 1985, at one of his weekly meetings with Will Reiner, Sol was surprised to hear his president ask: "So Sol, what are your plans when you turn 65 next October?"

"Will, that's almost a year away. And why suddenly such a question?"

Will shifted uncomfortably in his chair at the side of Sol's desk and wiped his mouth with his handkerchief. He was a decent man, a builder of single-family homes, who had worked up the JCC ladder in a variety of chairmanships, several years as vice president and finally succeeding Rose Kanter. He was part of the "new-young-guard" brought in by Al Reese who had also convinced Dr. Ted Oldman to take over the presidency seven years earlier. Finally he responded. "Well, Sol, one of the things we've learned from you is that one must make long-range plans. We will raise the necessary money and will construct our new center, but it also makes sense to begin to look beyond Sol Wise. It's been suggested that it would be wise—no pun intended—to start looking for the man who will succeed you and to bring that man aboard during the very early stages of the new building."

Sol pondered his president's remarks. On the face of it there was much sense to what he was saying. Yet, now-a-days reaching 65 did not constitute old age, despite the fact that the social security program provided for full benefits to begin at that age. And he voiced those thoughts, adding: "Will, when I take on a job I try to see it to its desired conclusion. That includes completing the campaign, constructing the building and getting the programs going. And that is my answer to the question you first asked me."

Will Reiner's discomfort was becoming more evident. "Yes, of course, Sol. What I meant was that we begin the nationwide search for a successor, have him come aboard, as your assistant, be involved in the construction and equipping and furnishing the building, handle much of the programming, and be prepared to step in when you finally decide to rest on your laurels."

Although Sol still had some misgivings and suspicions about the entire strategy, he felt it difficult to argue with the logic being presented. Certainly, he realized, he could not stop the agency from pursuing such a course if it had a mind to and so he concurred with the stated intentions.

But soon after, some other developments intensified Sol's misgivings. Dave Silvers insisted that Hal Benowitz be removed immediately and when Mr. Ward failed to act quickly enough the contract with the Milton Hood War Company was cancelled. The campaign was now stalled indefinitely—which was not necessarily all negative, considering that the negotiations with the County on its wanting to take, via its right of Eminent Domain, some 20 acres on the southern rim of the property for the new Parkway were continuing. And now the wisdom of the policy of "you can never have too much land" became evident, because even if and when the county took (and paid for) the 20 acres, the center would still be left with at least 30—the original minimum.

"READY OR NOT HERE YOU GO"

In January 1986 Peter Braun was recruited by Dave Silvers to succeed Will Reiner as president. Peter was a real estate consultant and property manager who had not been previously involved in the center, or any aspect of Jewish communal service. But he had a reputation of getting things done and represented a segment of the community not yet fully involved. And the first thing Peter did was to activate the search for Sol's successor. Except, Peter's understanding from Silvers was that the new man was to take over the executive director reins as soon as he could come aboard and Sol was to be retired—even if that was before his 65th birthday on October 19th!

And now the full shape of unfolding events seemed clear to Sol. This was Dave Silver's "payback" for Sol's having aligned himself too closely with Milton Hood Ward's position. No one was going to tell Dave Silvers, and others like him, how much money he would *contribute* for any cause. So he got rid of Benowitz, then the entire Milton Hood Ward Company and now it was time to get rid of Soloman D. Wise. But Sol had to admit, at least to himself, that this was a lot slicker than the battles fought many years earlier with Henry O. Zelman back in the North Shore of Boston involving the North Shore Jewish Community Center. Back then; HOZ was at least up front and open in his machinations.

Still Sol talked with the people he had been working with including all his ex-presidents and Al Rease. All were sympathetic and assured Sol they would do the right thing by him. But Shirley, his wife, cautioned him against repeating the experience at the North Shore. She argued that he had been involved in the creation or resurrection of numerous centers. He had been through it all. There was no particular glory in having to go through the construction of another building. It was okay, she thought, for him to accept retirement at age 65. Also, she stressed, that since they were planning on remaining in the community following his retirement from the center job, it was important that there not be too much controversy that could plague them after.

Al Schneider, a good friend of the Wises and a retired lawyer, agreed with Shirley. He pointed out, as had Carl

Sloane, the corporation consultant back in Marblehead eight years ago, that an organization could terminate any employee for any reason as long as it was done responsibly and with due consideration for the welfare of the employee. He continued that Sol did not have any legal case trying to hold the agency to the verbal promises made by Will Reiner, the immediate past president. But he could make a case for the center's moral responsibility to a loyal and dedicated employee who had made such important contributions to the survival and revival of the Jewish Community Center. And Al concluded by saying that he was personally ready to legally assist Sol in making certain that Sol be paid his full salary and benefits until at least his 65th birthday on October 19, 1986.

Sol thought about what Al was saying, then sadly shook his head. "Thanks Al, I know I can count on you. But you know, I'm beginning to feel like Moses, who after leading the Israelites out of Egypt and wandering in the desert for forty years, was not allowed to enter the Promised Land. He was allowed to look at it from some mountain top, but not allowed to enter."

Al smiled and said; "Hey, c'mon Sol! You've done a great job resurrecting and giving the center a future—for which you'll be remembered, I assure you. But Moses, c'mon."

And then Sol smiled sheepishly. "You know what I mean, not being allowed to break the ground, oversee the construction, introduce the new programs in the new building."

"But you've done all that many times before" Shirley repeated.

The personnel committee, after a nation-wide search, selected Richard Schwartz to succeed Sol Wise in March of that year. But it had not yet resolved the dilemma of what to do with Sol who still had seven months before his 65th birthday. And even though Dave Silvers had no official, elected position on the JCC board of directors, he nevertheless designated his colleague Sam Nibot (also without any official position with the JCC) to try to persuade Sol to step down upon the arrival of Schwartz.

Nibot invited Sol to lunch and at first tried wile and guile to achieve his goal—the voluntary retirement of Sol in March. But Sol would not be swayed and insisted upon receiving his salary and benefits through October.

Exasperated Nibot exploded: "If you were an employee of mine, we wouldn't even be having this conversation!"

"Well then, thank goodness I'm not one of your employees. And that I have a lawyer," Sol responded, rose and left.

Sol reported the luncheon incident to Dr. Larry Haussig, chairman of the center Personnel Committee, who presented the matter to the committee. He stressed that in the first place, he was incensed over having an "outsider" (albeit major contributor) interfering in what was essentially a JCC matter and secondly incensed with the insensitive and irresponsible manner in which it was handled.

"I won't be a party to this underhanded and demeaning and unfair treatment of a staff member who contributed so much to the success of our Center" he concluded.

The committee agreed with him, bristling at the arrogance manifested in the mishandling of the entire affair. And then it readily accepted it's chairman's recommendation that Sol be paid his full salary and benefits through October. However, it also clearly stated that Schwartz would assume the primary responsibilities of executive director with Sol being prepared to offer him whatever assistance he would need to insure a smooth transition.

On Rick Schwartz's arrival in March, Sol had several hours of conference with him, giving him a detailed update of where matters stood, regarding the stalled campaign, the negotiations with the county, the status of the various programs, and finally addressing the issue of a retiring executive director of an agency continuing to live in the community.

"Rick, I know from my own experiences around the country that sometimes that can be a bitch. I want you to know that once I'm outta here, I will take a very back seat and very low profile and busy myself with other matters. But I will be at your disposal. If there's anything that you need from me, either information, suggestions, or even an assignment or two, just pick up the phone."

Rick thanked Sol profusely, adding that he had heard some gossip about the "dealings" that Sol encountered and he wanted to express his personal regret. Yes, he would like to call upon Sol from time to time, including having some regular luncheons for them to go over any items requiring clarification. The two men were honest and direct with each other; they liked each other and both were convinced there would be a minimum of friction between them.

At the end of March Peter Brawn, the new president, hosted a lavish retirement party for Sol and his wife Shirley attended by JCC board members, federation and other community leaders. Speaker after speaker lavished praise on Sol and his seven years efforts on behalf of the Rincon Jewish Community Center. But the new center was yet to be built and some wags were asking whether after the seven fat years, came the seven lean ones.

EVERTHING TAKES LONGER THAN EXPECTED

In May 1986 the Fifth Annual Maccabiah on the new site gave testimony to the fact that while the Capital Funds Campaign was still on hold, programming continued at a hectic pace, both on the site and at the rented facilities still constituting the Center Without Walls. Still the delay in the completion of the campaign was causing consternation in the Jewish community with some openly expressing doubts about a new center building ever becoming a reality.

But these clouds however, also proved to have a silver lining. As part of the agreement finally reached with the county over its taking (for a reasonable price) the approximately 20 acres across the southwest portion of the property for the River Road/Alvernon Parkway, the county would reinforce the banks of the Rillito River with concrete thus guaranteeing protection against the fifty and hundred year flood threats. So while the center ended up with a smaller site of a little over 30 acres, it was a much improved and secured one. In addition, the county's taking of 20 acres forced the revision of the site plan resulting in a much improved, integrated one. And it also necessitated the revision of the building plans. With less acreage to spread out on, the new plans now provided for a two-story affair of 90,000 square feet.

With the county/parkway issue resolved the center was now free to turn full attention to the completion of the campaign. In December 1986 it hired a new Capital Funds Raiser and Development Consultants to resume and complete the Capital Funds Campaign. It took all of 1987 to come close to raising the full ten million dollars. And now the question was, even though the full goal had not yet been realized, whether to proceed with a groundbreaking and construction and plan to leave certain facilities merely "framed" or "shelled-in" (to be completed at later dates as the final monies were raised); or to wait until the full ten million had been pledged. Harry Rosen, who had succeeded Murray Rosenberg as the building consultant with the NAJCC, strongly urged that they move in that direction because the entire project had stretched out too long already. A Ground Breaking was planned for early '88.

For his part, following his retirement in March 1986 Solomon D. Wise—who was paid his full salary and benefits through October—played the role of the retiree for one month, two days and three hours. After which he picked himself up and went to see his colleague Marian Lupu, the director of the Council on Aging to see what volunteer opportunities she had to offer. And indeed she had a very challenging one "just up your alley" she said.

That first "alley" was the Armory Park Senior Center, where Sol set about to establish a social service department. He arranged for Armory Park Senior Center to be accredited as a field work placement for social work students attending the Rincon branch of the Arizona State University (home-based in Tempe, Arizona) School of Social Work and spent the year accomplishing that task. Before leaving, he had one of his graduated students take over as the paid Social Work director of the senior center.

Sol next accepted an assignment in early 1988 to help reform the Superior Court's Guardianship and Court Visitor's program. While that program was not devoted exclusively to aging or elderly clients, the Superior Court looked to Marian Lupu of the Council on Aging for assistance in achieving that goal. And Marian again told Sol that she had a challenge that was again "right up your alley."

And Sol smilingly asked: "Marian, when is it not up my alley?"

And she smilingly replied: "When it's a blind alley."

The Court Visitors project turned out not to be a blind alley, but on the contrary, a very rewarding one. Sol recruited two-dozen semi-retired "seniors"—many from his Armory Park involvement—trained them and succeeded in having the court agree to reasonable payments for the participant's time. And this kept him occupied through all of that year.

In April of that year he was invited to participate in the official Ground Breaking ceremony for the new center building—now reduced to 95,000 square feet. And following that ceremony Rick Schwartz invited him to his office.

"Sol, I appreciate you're being available for the luncheons we've been having, and so patient with the phone calls. But remember, when you said you'd be available for any special assignments? I know you write very well and have an affinity for history. Well, we'd like you to write an historical summary of the center to be used as an insert in next year's 1989-90 Jewish Community Directory as well as a stand-alone glossy promotional piece."

Sol eagerly accepted Rick's assignment, saying as he left: "Now **that's** up my alley!"

On Sunday, May 7, 1989 the new Rincon Jewish Community Center building was dedicated. And the special historical summary, titled **"IN THE BEGINNING"**, that Sol had written and which was distributed at the dedication concluded: "It had taken almost ten years (after vacating the building on Plumer in November 1979) and undoubtedly some children, teens adults and families were deprived the benefits of a full-service JCC during that decade. But the magnificent new Jewish Community Center offers the opportunity to again become the center of the Jewish community."

Prophetic words! Once the center moved from the Gallo House into its new quarters, the Jewish Federation purchased it, renovated it for its usage and moved in. The Jewish Post took over the bungalow that housed the Infant/Toddler program. The Clark House and property was bought by the Rincon Hebrew Academy, which demolished the old house and proceeded to construct a two-story yeshiva and full range school. The Jewish Family and Children's Services declined to become part of the Jewish Community Campus, citing confidentiality for its clients as its very valid reason.

And as for Sol, Marian Lupu of the Council on Aging finally found a project that was truly up Sol's alley for the long-term. And this one a paying job! The State Ombudsman for Long-Term Care (nursing homes and assisted living units) contracted with the Council to administer the Long Term Care Ombudsman Program (LTCOP) in the County. Sol, as the Coordinator would recruit, train and supervise a corps of volunteers assigned to monitor the care that ill and vulnerable adults received in long term care facilities. In September 1989 Sol began his new duties and with it a second career.

Epilogue: Soon after the opening of the new center, Sol Wise received an embossed and laminated Lifetime membership card with the number 15. And in September 1999, Sol was invited to participate in a 50th Anniversary Video celebrating the agency's golden jubilee. On September 17, 1999 he received a letter from the executive director commending him for his "sterling performance" and for being "an integral part of the video." And at the October 30th event he was duly recognized as an integral part of the JCCs history and survival, both in the video as well as "in the flesh".

THE END